The Upper Room
Disciplines
1999

The Upper Room
Disciplines
1999

UPPER
ROOM BOOKS
NASHVILLE

Contents

CONTENTS

CONTENTS

CONTENTS

CONTENTS

Foreword

In 1959 the staff of The Upper Room initiated a new publication that first was called *The Upper Room Companion* and later renamed *The Upper Room Disciplines*. For forty years, this annual devotional book has reached a large reading audience in the United States, Brazil, the Philippines, the United Kingdom, and beyond. Clearly *The Upper Room Disciplines* has been a helpful resource for many people who are genuinely seeking to grow in their faith.

This fortieth-anniversary edition continues the primary emphasis that characterized the first edition; namely, *The Upper Room Disciplines* is designed to help readers establish a regular pattern of reading scripture, meditating on scripture, and praying. The title word *Disciplines* refers to the concept of a spiritual discipline or a daily practice that helps us open our minds and hearts to the living Christ.

The Christian journey is one marked by change and maturation. God continually speaks to us, guiding us in paths of service and faithfulness. As we read the words of scripture and the reflections of other Christians, we have the opportunity to silence the clamoring noises and be attentive to God's presence in our lives. A resource like *The Upper Room Disciplines* helps us hear the freshness of the Bible message for our lives and for our faith. By reading the words of scripture expectantly, we see ourselves more clearly and find help for the decisions and challenges we face.

John Wesley felt that commitment to prayer and daily scripture reading was essential for a disciple of Jesus Christ. He wrote, "Serious and earnest prayer should be constantly used before we consult the oracles of God; seeing 'Scripture can only be understood through the same Spirit whereby it was given.' Our reading should likewise be closed with prayer, that what we read may be written on our hearts."

As you begin this annual cycle of prayer and scripture reflection, I invite you to think again about what it means to listen to God through the words of scripture and the words of your brothers and sisters in Christ. Take seriously Wesley's words of counsel that you pray before you read scripture for openness to hear and that you pray afterward that what you read may be written on your heart. Ask yourself each day, "What is God's word of life for me today?" And approach each day with the confidence that if we open ourselves to receive the bread of life, God is always faithful to give us what will nurture and sustain us.

May God bless you and guide you through this coming year, and may you experience the depth of Christ's love and grace for the living of these days.

JANICE T. GRANA
Former World Editor and Publisher
The Upper Room

All That Glitters May Not Be Gold

January 1–3, 1999 • *George Hovaness Donigian**

FRIDAY, JANUARY 1 • Read Psalm 72:10-14

One image of a kingly coronation brings to mind special costumes, ceremonious speeches, and rituals filled with pomp and nonsense. The coronation in Psalm 72 offers less familiar images. It focuses on justice and wisdom, on lifting up those who are oppressed: "From oppression and violence [the Lord] redeems their life." These images seem far removed from the commercial aspects of the New Year party season.

Yet the images for justice burn into my spiritual journey as I work with children in an urban setting. Each day I learn something new about their experience of childhood. I realize that these children are victims of the sins of omission as well as commission. I recognize that their lives are scarred as their parents' lives were scarred and their parents' parents' parents' lives. Caught in different prisons of poverty, some are able to leave, but most simply find an escape. Even so, I continue in ministry with others in the community of faith. We find joy in some very ordinary events and deeds.

Christmas and New Year celebrations may sweep me up in the blend of the ordinary and the extraordinary. I may find renewal in the study of scripture. I may feel myself drawn more deeply into the mystery of God's incarnation in Jesus Christ. I may find myself drawn into the awe surrounding Jesus. But I also know that the study and the piety goad me on to action just as much as the actions of ministry compel and propel me back to piety and study.

PRAYER: **God, the images of gold hang before me. Keep me from worshiping golden calves of power. Encourage me to remain open to the gold of your Spirit. Amen.**

---

*Writer, editor, and children's teacher; ordained in The United Methodist Church; living in Nashville, Tennessee.

SATURDAY, JANUARY 2 • Read Isaiah 60:4-6

Isaiah 60:1-3 offers a word of hope to fallen Israel. In verse 4 Isaiah's focus shifts from offering hope to the fallen to envisioning the time of restoration: Restoration takes place; Israel welcomes its scattered young. Isaiah 60:4-6 provides two rich images, both of an incorruptible gold.

The first image is that of hospitality. The now restored nation extends hospitality to its children and to visitors from afar. Having experienced the sorrow and desolation of exile, the nation now extends itself so others will not feel that pain.

You and I have experienced exile also. We have felt loss and loneliness, grief and separation, hostility and isolation. We also have experienced restoration and the renewing power of God's love. Having undergone alienating conditions, we can extend our hospitality in imitation of God's graciousness.

A joy radiant with love is the second image. The restored Israel beams with joyful effervescence as those who have been lost now return. This national joy of homecoming reminds me of the scene in Luke 15 on the younger son's return home. Here is a mature joy, a joy seasoned with the salt of alienation, a joy that now comes forth as a spring bubbling in a city park.

We easily skip to the references to camels and offerings of gold and frankincense in verse 6. Gold always attracts our attention, though the thrill of material goods never lasts. Material wealth is not as rich as the relationships that we have with one another in community or with God. This genuine gold cannot be taken from us: the gold of hospitality and the mature radiance of joy.

SUGGESTION FOR MEDITATION: **Where will I find this spiritual gold today?**

Early on in my pastoral education, a supervisor warned me, "When you go back to that local congregation, somebody is going to say to you, 'Preacher, this [program, agenda, business venture—you fill in the blank] is gold. This is genuine.' Not everything people in the church offer or promote will be gold. Use your nose. Some of it will stink like garbage." Herod beseeched the magi to search for the king. "Oh yes," said Herod, "when you find him, let me know so that I can offer him my gifts." As I play out this scene in my mind's eye, I envision Herod's adding, "Great will be your reward."

Maybe the magi believe Herod until they hear the Herodian chortle, "Yes, great will be your reward. That's gold!" When the magi sniff the air, they realize that Herod's gold stinks. Perhaps their study and devotion lead them to this conclusion. Perhaps their openness to God's leading awakens them to Herod's evil.

A new year fills us with hope and a sense of the new. Piety and devotion call us to rekindle our true love. We study. We act. Then we bump into the offer of disingenuous gold. Perhaps that offer derails us or causes a detour. Perhaps when the gold dust comes our way, we need to remember the discernment of the magi. They walk away from the court of the king and remember their commitment, their mission.

Our own mission comes in hearing, reading, studying the texts for this week and recognizing their call to us. Like the king in Psalm 72, we are called to have "pity on the weak and the poor." Like those who first heard Isaiah's prophecy, we are called to show hospitality and to radiate joy because we know of our own restoration. We follow the example of many biblical people and seek to discern the paths in which God leads us.

PRAYER: God, as you led the magi to discern the voice of truth, so help me discern your call in the midst of today's tumult. Have mercy upon me for the sake of Jesus Christ. Amen.

Baptized for Ministry

January 4–10, 1999 • Joseph P. Russell*

MONDAY, JANUARY 4 • Read Matthew 3:13-17

Next Sunday the church celebrates the baptism of the Lord. As we remember Jesus' baptism, we are to remember our own. The biblical word we read is never just history. This week we seek to understand the nature of our baptism as we prepare for Sunday's celebration.

The voice of God speaks through the heavens as God's Spirit descends like a dove: "This is my Son, the Beloved, with whom I am well pleased." Can we hear those words as they apply to us? Every baptized person from just-born infant to octogenarian and beyond is truly a child of God. "This is my daughter,...this is my son, the beloved, with whom I am well pleased." What a presumptuous statement! Yet at baptism, we affirm that Christ enters into our lives; Christ abides in us as we abide in Christ. (See John 15:1-11.) Our relationship to God as daughters and sons is not our doing; it is God's. In our baptism God adopts us as God's children. Now that is good news!

SUGGESTION FOR MEDITATION: As we begin this week of preparation for the celebration of Jesus' baptism, sit quietly and picture the scene of Jesus' baptism. Next, attempt to picture the moment of your baptism. Recall yourself as an infant, as a youth, or as an adult and hear God's words spoken to you: "This is my child, the beloved, with whom I am well pleased." How does your life reflect that unbelievable reality?

"The Holy Spirit work within you, that being born through water and the Spirit, you may be a faithful disciple of Jesus Christ."**

---

*Episcopalian clergyman, church educator, conference and retreat leader; living in Cleveland, Ohio.

**From The Baptismal Covenant I, *The United Methodist Hymnal* (Nashville, Tenn.: The United Methodist Publishing House, 1989), 37.

TUESDAY, JANUARY 5 • Read Isaiah 42:1-9

The beautiful text from Isaiah provides insight into the significance of Jesus' baptism, while helping us understand our own baptism as well. The God who "created the heavens and stretched them out" is the same God who calls us at baptism. This text explicitly lays out the job description of the baptized. We are to be a "light to the nations." We are to "bring out the prisoners from the dungeon."

Scholars disagree about the identity of the *servant* in this passage. Does the term refer to an individual or to all of Israel? Christians have come to understand and interpret the passage as a specific reference to Jesus. Certainly Jesus incarnated this powerful text with his whole life. He healed the blind. He announced the dawning of God's new day with every word and action.

This week the church invites us to take this passage personally. We are the servant. God has called us and sends us into the world to be a "light to the nations." At baptism we enter into this call for servant ministry. No wonder the church has concern for the suffering, the oppressed, the sick, the ill-housed, and the ill-clothed. We have no choice! We are called as servants to take on God's agenda in the world.

SUGGESTION FOR MEDITATION: **Keep this text in mind today as you reflect on what is happening across the world and across town. Into what specific servant ministry is God calling you and the church today?**

"Through baptism you are incorporated by the Holy Spirit into God's new creation and made to share in Christ's royal priesthood."*

---

*From The Baptismal Covenant I, *The United Methodist Hymnal* (Nashville, Tenn.: The United Methodist Publishing House, 1989), 37.

WEDNESDAY, JANUARY 6 • Read Matthew 3:13-17
FEAST OF THE EPIPHANY OF THE LORD

Today we celebrate the Feast of the Epiphany of the Lord. The word *epiphany* comes from the Greek word meaning "appearance." The church proclaims that God revealed God's self to the world in Jesus. God appeared in the life, death, and resurrection of Jesus.

The church's celebration of Epiphany recalls three events of Jesus' life. First, the coming of the magi from the East signifies the universality of God's self-revelation. The magi symbolize the whole world that God has come to save. Jesus' baptism is the second event. Matthew tells us that God speaks from the heavens, and the Holy Spirit descends like a dove. The third story from the Epiphany tradition tells of Jesus' first miracle at a wedding in Cana (John 2:1-11).

The church is to be a continuing "appearance" of God's presence in the world. The gifts the magi bring us are the practical gifts for ministry.

Rulers appeared upon their palace balcony to reveal their presence to the people. The ruler "made an epiphany" before the people: "This is who I am. This is what I offer you. This is what I ask of you." Using the palace balcony as a metaphor, God in Jesus made an appearance (epiphany) on the world's balcony. We are to stand on the balcony of our own time and reveal the presence of God through our lives.

SUGGESTION FOR MEDITATION: **Participate in a celebration of Epiphany in your own congregation or in an ecumenical service. What gifts do the magi bring you for ministry? How are people "seeing" God through the actions of your congregation?**

THURSDAY, JANUARY 7 • Read Psalm 29

A ravaging storm provides a poetic description of God's powerful presence in the natural elements and in the realm of human life. God speaks "over the waters" through the thunder that accompanies the flashes of lightning breaking across the sky. The power of God revealed in a storm leads the psalmist to proclaim God's power over creation and human destiny: "The Lord sits enthroned over the flood; the Lord sits enthroned as king forever." God's presence is humbling. When natural and personal storms beset us, we recognize and acknowledge our human frailty.

Just as Psalm 29 affirms God's speaking powerfully through events of nature, so during our celebration of Epiphany we affirm that God spoke through Jesus of Nazareth. God spoke in that calmer scene at Jesus' baptism. God spoke through Jesus on country roads, at mealtimes, and in healing times. God spoke on the road to Emmaus and in the upper room. Even death could not still the voice.

SUGGESTION FOR MEDITATION: **When has the voice of God touched you over the years? Let the psalm stimulate your imagination. Remember with thankful praise voices from your life who have spoken God's word to you. What do these memories say about your calling as a baptized Christian? Out of the waters of his baptism, Jesus heard God speak. Out of the waters of baptism in the church today, God speaks through the pastor who says, "The Holy Spirit work within you, that being born through water and the Spirit, you may be a faithful disciple of Jesus Christ."***

---

*From The Baptismal Covenant I, *The United Methodist Hymnal* (Nashville, Tenn.: The United Methodist Publishing House, 1989), 37.

FRIDAY, JANUARY 8 • Read Acts 10:34-43

Peter thought he had his role as an apostle all figured out. He was to carry the good news of the risen Christ to the Jews. Anyone living beyond the borders of Judea was unclean. We know from the Gospels that Peter frequently seemed a bit slow in his understanding of Jesus' mission.

It takes a heavenly vision to shock Peter into a new awareness. (Acts 10:9-16). A voice from heaven orders Peter to "kill and eat" all the unclean animals falling to the ground in a great sheet. "What God has made clean, you must not call profane." Surprise! Surprise! God shows no partiality. Jesus came for all people!

Today's text picks up the story. Peter outlines the good news of Jesus to the Gentiles. This reading from Acts continues the theme of Jesus' baptism with particular reference to Jesus' being "anointed with the Holy Spirit and with power."

SUGGESTION FOR MEDITATION: What new visions has God unfolded for you over the years? How would you succinctly state the good news for those who might be considered in today's world "unclean" and not worthy? Using the Acts passage as a guide, write a brief statement of your own baptismal ministry. "After the anointing of my own baptism, I...." Think of the everyday opportunities for "doing good and healing," and believe that the Holy Spirit truly is working through you.

"Do you confess Jesus Christ as your Savior, put your whole trust in his grace, and promise to serve him as your Lord, in union with the church which Christ has opened to people of all ages, nations, and races?"*

*From The Baptismal Covenant I, *The United Methodist Hymnal* (Nashville, Tenn.: The United Methodist Publishing House, 1989), 37.

SATURDAY, JANUARY 9 • Read Isaiah 42:1-9

Until recent years, many congregations celebrated baptisms on Saturday or Sunday afternoon. Today there is growing ecumenical consensus on the centrality of baptism and the Lord's Supper in the life of the church. Baptism is not a private affair. Baptism is a public event that leads us to a public life of proclaiming God's presence and love for the world. As mentioned earlier this week, the Isaiah text describes the nature of our ministry as the baptized.

Notice the political implications of the Isaiah text: "He will bring forth justice to the nations." The Torah (first five books of the Old Testament) establishes God's claim for justice. In Exodus we read that God entered intimately into the lives of the Hebrew slaves of Egypt. "Then the Lord said, 'I have observed the misery of my people who are in Egypt….I know their sufferings, and I have come down to deliver them'" (Exod. 3:7-8). God's servants—that's us—enter into the struggle for justice in the world today. As outlined in today's reading, we are to carry out our ministry gently. We are not to cry out in the street, but our staying power must not be in question. We are to hang in until God "has established justice in the earth; and the coastlands wait for his teaching" (Isa. 42:4).

By holding this great Isaiah text before us, we will find direction for involvement in God's world. For example, a Saturday spent working at a Habitat for Humanity construction site may uncover other opportunities for servant ministry. Always look for ways to seek justice as well as service. New doors open as we discern God's word for us today.

SUGGESTION FOR MEDITATION: **Pray for those being baptized tomorrow or in the coming weeks. Pray for your own discernment. How are you being called as God's servant today?**

SUNDAY, JANUARY 10 • Read Acts 10:34-43

Today is the First Sunday after the Epiphany, the Baptism of the Lord. In the early church, this Sunday and the Easter Vigil were the primary times for baptism, and this practice is increasing in the church today.

We read that the Holy Spirit descended upon Jesus "like a dove and alighted on him" (Matt. 3:16). Luke tells us that "God anointed Jesus of Nazareth with the Holy Spirit and with power" (Acts 10:38). Later in the chapter, the Gentiles' receiving of the Holy Spirit leads to their baptism (Acts 10:44-48).

All week we have been thinking about our calling into ministry through baptism. Today we emphasize the other side of our calling: God empowers us with the Holy Spirit for ministry! We are not out there alone. Think of times you've used the words *inspirational* and *enthusiastic* to describe an experience. Remember the moments when you've said, "The words I needed just came to me when I walked into the room." Such moments give us glimpses of the deep significance of our anointing at baptism.

At the service of baptism in The United Methodist Church, the pastor lays hands on each person being baptized and prays that the Holy Spirit may "work within you,…that you may be a faithful disciple of Jesus Christ." That is our moment of the dove, our receiving of the Holy Spirit! Our baptism proclaims that the Holy Spirit has empowered us for ministry.

SUGGESTION FOR MEDITATION: **Think about those times when you have felt inspired and filled with words and understanding. Share those experiences with others who are using *The Upper Room Disciplines* as their guide through the year.**

God's Purpose for Our Lives
January 11–17, 1999 • Costa Stathakis*

MONDAY, JANUARY 11 • Read Psalm 40:1-11

This week we want to concentrate on God's call and purpose for our lives. To do what God requires is to fulfill God's purpose for our creation. We live in an age of instant answers; we want the Lord to reveal God's plan for us immediately in response to our prayers. The psalmist suggests just the opposite. The psalmist speaks of waiting on God: "I waited patiently for the Lord." The psalmist, like many of us, was probably not very good at waiting. The psalm's last words indicate a desire for immediate relief: "O my God, do not delay" (Ps. 40:17, NIV).

God's purpose for our lives unfolds gradually as a tree grows into fullness. It cannot be forced or achieved overnight. Jesus himself pointed out that the beauty of lilies does not result from their own efforts, for "they neither toil nor spin." Their growth comes about by their yielding to the friendship of the sun and the rain in purposeful waiting.

Only as we wait patiently upon the Lord will God unfold the riches of God's glory to us. God has made us for a purpose and wants nothing more than to disclose that purpose to us.

Verse 8 reiterates the psalmist's delight in doing the will of God and keeping God's teaching in his heart. This delight in God's loving purposefulness can enable patient waiting.

SUGGESTION FOR MEDITATION: Wait patiently on the Lord and ask for the unfolding of God's divine purpose for your life.

---

*Superintendent of the Johannesburg North Circuit in South Africa; senior minister of The Bryanston Methodist Church.

TUESDAY, JANUARY 12 • Read Psalm 40:12-17

The psalmist struggles with iniquities that seem to be overpowering. The writer feels inadequately equipped to cope with them and cries out to God for deliverance.

In the opening chapter of his letter, James gives us hope by reminding us that our life's difficulties, trials, and temptations give us an opportunity to grow. However, we need to stop and reflect on our situation: Are our present difficulties of our own doing? In what ways might these circumstances build our character? We cannot accomplish life's purpose through the attainment of ease or luxurious comfort. We accomplish life's purpose only in the achievement of Christlike character.

Christians can count it all joy when we encounter various trials. These test the mettle of our faith in God's purpose; when met with courage, these trials produce steadfastness of character. Everything that we have learned through our suffering, hardship, and related experiences rests on our assured conviction that God supports our lives.

Despite God's deliverance, the psalmist has not yet come to realize that the difficulties, trials, and temptations of life sharpen all of our God-given characteristics: our spiritual gifts, our personality, our abilities, our passion. The psalmist cannot yet affirm that he can garner good from these experiences. Yet, as Christians, we acknowledge that God uses all of life's experiences to our benefit. No hardship or difficulty is ever wasted. It all works together for good in God's design as we find ourselves being formed into the image of Jesus. Often only in retrospect as we emerge from difficulties and trials do we discover our spirituality deepened and our purpose refined.

SUGGESTION FOR MEDITATION: When have you felt overwhelmed by trials and temptations? How did this time of testing contribute to your spiritual life?

WEDNESDAY, JANUARY 13 • Read Isaiah 49:1-3

"You are my servant, Israel, in whom I will be glorified." Isaiah is to be God's servant, and his mission is to glorify God in the world. Jesus is the message of the glory, salvation, and the light of God. Jesus says "I have brought you glory on earth by completing the work you gave me to do" (John 17:4, NIV). Paul says, "I only want to complete my mission and finish the work that the Lord Jesus gave me to do" (Acts 20:24, TEV). Every person who comes into the world is a "message" from God.

Mother Teresa brought the message of God's complete acceptance of each one of us. Her life affirmed God's message that no person is beyond the limits of God's love. One of Mother Teresa's admirers journeyed to Calcutta to meet this hero of the faith. At the end of her brief visit she asked Mother Teresa what kept her going amidst the poverty and squalor in India. Mother Teresa replied that her work was sheer joy.

When I am doing what God requires, it is sheer joy. For this reason God created me.

God wants to say something to the world through you. It's a unique message, and only you can say it. God shaped you for this purpose from conception.

Despite God's self-sufficiency, God asks that we communicate God's glory to the people of the world. Peter states, "Each one, as a good manager of God's different gifts, must use for the good of others the special gift he [or she] has received from God" (1 Pet. 4:10, TEV).

SUGGESTION FOR MEDITATION: What message is God communicating through you? What message might God want to communicate through you?

THURSDAY, JANUARY 14 • **Read Isaiah 49:4-7**

The author's spiritual effort throughout life seems to be futile: "I have labored in vain." Have the servant's words fallen on deaf ears? Is there any reason to carry on? Those who genuinely seek to fulfill God's purpose in their lives may experience this kind of disheartenment. The disheartenment is not a physical weakness that comes about as a by-product of work; disheartenment comes from a lack of visible results of labor.

If you build a house, you can see the result of your labor. Gardeners can see the value of their efforts. But even the most saintly grow weary when nothing comes of their labors on God's behalf.

The Lord responds to the servant by offering the vision of an even greater work than anticipated. God gives this discouraged servant an even bigger task. And God's vision lifts the servant's sights from the small and lesser troubles to the immense work God has prepared.

The servant feels honored to be chosen by God for this work. This affirmation releases the servant to rise above disappointment and discouragement to a level of confidence and purpose again.

Many Christians today do not experience God's power because we have set our sights on the mundane rather than on the great adventure for which God has created us. We miss the opportunity to manifest God's mighty power. Only as we move by faith toward fulfilling the Great Commission do we experience the truth of God's abiding power and presence.

Only when the Israelites stepped into the Jordan did the water subside, enabling them to enter the land of milk and honey.

PRAYER: Lord, in my moments of disheartenment help me refocus my sights on the bigger picture and discover your purpose for me in it. Amen.

FRIDAY, JANUARY 15 • **Read 1 Corinthians 1:1-5**

"Called to be an apostle of Christ Jesus by the will of God" (1 Cor. 1:1). Paul acknowledges God's call and affirms God's purpose for his life. The other apostles were drawn to Jesus during his early ministry, but Paul's apostleship came after Jesus' death. Paul describes himself as one "untimely born."

Paul had persecuted Jesus' disciples, impelled by his conscience to destroy the followers of the new way. But then Someone more powerful than himself had taken hold of him, claimed him, set him apart, and fashioned him for a purpose far greater than he had ever imagined—to be an apostle. Paul discovered his destiny as he responded to the call.

God has called and shaped you and me for a purpose. In Job we read, "Your hands fashioned and made me" (10:8). Made in God's image and likeness, we are the work of God's hands. Each of us was put on this earth for a purpose; God does not create without reason.

God has been working in our lives since our conception, shaping our personality, giving us specific and unique abilities, and guiding us through experiences to prepare us for our life's call. Discovering God's call in our lives and responding in faith will enable our full expression of who God created us to be.

PRAYER: Lord, you shaped my being. Help me, by the power of the Holy Spirit, to discover my unique purpose. Amen.

SATURDAY, JANUARY 16 • Read 1 Corinthians 1:1-9

The people of Corinth are "called to be saints," to be Christ's ambassadors manifesting his Spirit. These saints come from all walks of life. Christ needs all kinds of people, differing gifts and graces to accomplish his redemptive purpose. To this end, these saints in Corinth find that Christ has strengthened them and enriched their lives.

In normal situations we tend to fall into grooves of routine. However, when the Spirit is at work, we find ourselves enriched —caught up in a world enhanced by God's infinite variety of creation, a creation in which no two snowflakes are alike. Christian fellowship makes a place for everyone.

The members of the Corinthian church have found themselves enriched "in speech and knowledge of every kind." This enrichment has come as the result of the strengthening of Christ's testimony among them. Paul's preaching of the gospel has led to the members' preparation to receive these spiritual gifts. Yet these Christians find themselves in a posture of waiting until "the revealing of our Lord Jesus Christ."

Our spiritual gifts may require preparation and cultivation. Perhaps we need to strengthen Christ's testimony among us. Perhaps we need to place ourselves in a posture of waiting before God.

God calls us to be saints, to discover our place in enriching the world. As we draw closer to Christ and make him the center of our lives, our purpose and mission in life become clearer.

PRAYER: Lord, prepare me and cultivate me. Help me wait before you until my purpose becomes clear. Amen.

The writer of John's Gospel conveys his meaning on two levels, which are evident in everything that is said. He uses expressions that have both a physical reality and a spiritual reality. Jesus' dialogue with John and Andrew makes sense in their question-and-response mode, but on a deeper level, the author is asking, What are people seeking when they follow Jesus?

Two disciples follow Jesus. On one level, they literally trail after Jesus, yet the verb used here meaning "to follow" also implies discipleship. They ask him, "Where do you live?" (John 1:38, TEV). On the first level they are asking for a physical address. But the question goes deeper: "Where is your home? Where are you abiding?"

Jesus abides in the Father. In John 15, Jesus uses the image of the vine and the branches to explain his sense of "home."

For Christians, "home" means abiding in Christ. To fulfill our God-given purpose we must abide in him. We take deliberate steps to do so: Christ's presence must fill our thoughts and be evidenced in our actions, our speech, and our mission. We consciously make time each day to review our life's mission, arranging specific times of prayer and silence to evaluate our fulfillment of our call.

Jesus responds to the disciples' question with the words "Come and see." He issues an invitation for them to take their following of him seriously. He invites them to see with the eyes of faith.

The writer of John does not name these two disciples—perhaps intentionally, so that we too may follow and hear Jesus' words as an invitation to us: "Come and see" (John 1:39).

PRAYER: Lord, help me respond to the challenge to come and see. May I never weary of abiding in you, and may I create space this day to be at home with you. Amen.

Faith in the Balance

*January 18–24, 1999 • Bonifacio B. Mequi Jr.**

MONDAY, JANUARY 18 • Read Isaiah 9:1-4

Christianity's astonishing claim is that the gospel is not a story we Christians made up but the core of a faith we inherited. Our reading from Isaiah reiterates that claim.

Isaiah's oracle could be a liturgy of enthronement for a new Davidic king from Galilee. It could also be a formula of longing for a messiah to come and redeem God's people, Israel. Christendom has understood the oracle in both cases not only as a prophecy long fulfilled in Jesus' birth, but that Isaiah's historical messiah is in truth the Christ of faith—the light, as it were, to those in deep darkness. Christmas stands as the great reminder to such a claim.

We know what it is like to walk in darkness. In oppressed societies and police states, when the gospel is preached and undercover agents listen in to determine whether the preacher lives or dies, that experience breaks the boundaries of the familiar to fathom the wrenching reality of darkness. I know. I have been there. Some still are. Darkness is part of the human condition: A man loses his job; a woman loses a spouse; a child loses to cancer.

So we long, with a craving in the abyss of our soul, for some light in our darkness. When the light comes, it is like the first day of life again: In God we see a great light, increasing our joy and breaking the yoke that burdens us.

PRAYER: Come, O God, come. Descend deep into the dark corners of my life and lift me out with the wings of faith to welcome the light of Christ. Amen.

---

*Filipino-American pastor in The United Methodist Church, Iowa Annual Conference; first ethnic district superintendent in Iowa United Methodism.

TUESDAY, JANUARY 19 • Read Psalm 27:1, 4-9

With the stark realities of life being as they are, the naked truth is that we could be the writer(s) of today's text. Two apparently independent psalms (vv. 1-6, 7-14) have mysteriously joined by virtue of a common truth in both to which we all attest: that even in conditions of healthy assurances of trust in God (v. 1), further in the dark lie the deeper concerns and anxieties that attend every human experience (vv. 7-9). Even in moments of great faith in God, we sense with foreboding the fear of being left and forsaken by God. One breath expresses a ring of confidence in the Lord. Yet the same breath gives rise to a sense of missing out on the shelter of the Almighty.

The Bible stares us in the face with unabashed frankness. We identify with the trust and the fear because we are beings both of darkness and light. All of us experience an ongoing struggle between two inclinations striving for mastery: the inclination to evil and the inclination to good. This is the universal human predicament. Both inclinations represent essential elements of human nature, which are inseparable from a truly free human will. Because God created us with such inclinations, we are free to do both evil and good.

Thus, with the psalmist, we need to stay rooted and grounded in God, to remain in God's shelter and cover. Without this "rootedness" we could fall prey to distrust and fear and become perpetrators of the very evil which the psalmist fears and from which he seeks divine deliverance.

SUGGESTION FOR MEDITATION: **What is your perception of life? In what ways do you sense the irresistibility of sin upon the individual to the extent that the human soul experiences both torment and glory? When beset with fears and anxieties, where do you turn to find grounding and shelter?**

WEDNESDAY, JANUARY 20 • Read Psalm 27:1, 4-9

It is said that experience shapes character, that tests of struggle, a nagging sense of doubt, and perhaps a deep-seated fear or two can transform a person of faith. If so, we can step into the psalmist's sandals with feet of clay but with the same resolve. Despite pain, trouble, and ordeal, we can stand firmly, grounded in our trust in God and convicted of ultimate divine vindication.

Like little children in their frailty, we want One who is constantly available so that we can affirm, under any circumstance, a more confident, capable, and trusting self. If our despair drives us to God, we can believe that God is righteous enough to vindicate us.

So it was with me in one of the darkest political times in my homeland's history. A friend, waiting for me to help bury his still-born child, was gunned down in full view of his wife and three children. A church leader in his prime, my friend had been entrusted with a mission to implement the government's most promising land reform program ever conceived. The oppressed and the wretched of the earth began to see in him a new day dawning and a sense of hope reborn. Yet, in the twinkling of an eye, he was gone—a victim of a classic political hit. Some stranger whispered in my ear that I might be the next to go; I was numbed just to hear it.

Such an experience helped shape who I am today. It etched in my memory this truth of faith: We can manage to go through the worst of times when we know deep down that God's righteousness will vindicate us in the end. Eventually God's light overcomes our darkness and that of the world.

PRAYER: **Take the life-and-death issues of my life, Creator God, and use them as refining fire to transform what is dead or dying in me into a purer mint of faith that endures above my pain. Amen.**

THURSDAY, JANUARY 21 • Read 1 Corinthians 1:10-18

As with every person, the church is not immune to the ominous threat of darkness. One of the most insidious manifestations of darkness is the onset of dissension, disunity, and discord. Nothing damages a young, fledgling community of faith more than factious allegiances to individual leaders against the party spirit. Jesus addressed this issue with his familiar words: "No...house divided against itself will stand" (Matt. 12:25).

The issue of divisiveness within the faith community in Corinth alarmed Paul. Chloe's band of slave converts has brought Paul disturbing news about the Corinthians' allegiances to individual missionary teachers: to Paul, to Apollos, to Cephas. Paul appeals to the Corinthians to cease their quarreling for the sake of one above whom there is no other: Jesus Christ. No leader can stand in Christ's place. Each must say, "I belong to Christ," and follow through in word as well as in will and purpose.

The appeal remains the same today. Rampant partisanship has no place in Christianity's witness to unity in Christ. The sharp rebuke divisiveness deserves takes no more telling form than the non-Christian's refusal to listen to the Christian message when the behavior of the messengers disavows the message they purport to proclaim.

Thank God, we can explain Christianity's story of rapid growth in Asia and Africa in part by the Christians' unmistakable image of being one in Christ. This unity stands against cultures' tribal divisiveness and regional conflicts between dialect or language groups. Third World citizens like myself carry part of that story with us, and it has marked us for life.

SUGGESTION FOR MEDITATION: What dilutes my loyalty to Christ? In what areas of my life and the world have I witnessed the unity of Christ overcoming division?

FRIDAY, JANUARY 22 • Read 1 Corinthians 1:10-18

The light of Christ must overcome the darkness of discord. In many far countries, and sometimes here at home, the solitary beacon proclaims the gospel like no other: The visible, united fellowship of Christ's church stands out as one of Christianity's major calling cards.

As Paul puts it, the cross of Jesus Christ is foolishness to those who see it as a symbol of weakness. But to those who see it as the power of salvation, it is none other than the power of God (verse 18). This affirmation may sound too vague to inspire us or too abstract to connect with the realities of life in a discordant world. But dramatic changes left by the gospel in its wake throughout the world tell a different story.

What better witness to the claim that God's power to save is real than the credibility of the church proved by its life and work? Is not a hospital in the middle of a depressed inner-city area salvation to those least able to afford it? Or a college in the hinterland salvation to the ignorant or uneducated? Or modern farming salvation to the "hand-to-mouth" poor? Yet these are Christianity's most eloquent testimonies to societies torn apart by class or caste—its single-minded, unified effort, a magnetic pulling force of light to a world in darkness. When asked, "Why do such things for us?" only then does the church say, "Because we belong to Jesus Christ. Would you care to know more about him?"

Being a Christian is a way of life whose sole purpose is to follow Christ and live in a Christlike way. This is the testimony of the faithful, the difference as to whether or not the church makes believable God's light to those groping in the dark.

SUGGESTION FOR MEDITATION: **What tangible testimony of the church do you see in your community? How does your community of faith offer light to a world in darkness?**

SATURDAY, JANUARY 23 • Read Matthew 4:12-17

Now we return to Monday's opening thought: Jesus is the fulfillment of Isaiah's prophecy, eternity invading time, to proclaim that God's reign has come in flesh and blood. Today's text offers a clearer picture of what has been said so far: that life's tragic darkness is bearable and faith's sense of hope is sustainable only because Jesus Christ has embodied in a unique way the promised and unrelenting supportive presence of God. Jesus is the light to those who sit in darkness; through him "the kingdom of heaven has come near" (vv. 16-17).

This promise of God's presence with us lies at the heart of Christianity. It helps us make sense of the seeming senselessness of our trying, troubled days and restless, sleepless nights: "It is the Lord who goes before you; he will be with you, he will not fail you or forsake you; do not fear or be dismayed" (Deut. 31:8). Suddenly, we can believe these words more easily.

Yet for Christ to become our light, we must do one thing: "Repent." Repentance always requires us to turn around, change directions, quit walking away from God and begin walking the walk of faith toward him who is God-with-us. Our continued efforts to stay on God's side and to go in God's direction encourage us in our living until that way of life becomes as natural as breathing. Our life in Christ takes a lifetime both to learn and to live out.

PRAYER: God of my life, turn me gently with firm resolve and let me truly come to know the living Christ through you. Amen.

SUNDAY, JANUARY 24 • Read Matthew 4:18-23

If repentance requires our turning around and changing direction, clearly the divine expectation is to follow Christ, to respond to his call, and to throw our lot in with him. As the early disciples did, so must we. We are not an especially gifted people, either with wealth or power or influence. Jesus' first disciples certainly were not. Jesus called them from the ordinariness of their lives as fishermen so that, by giving themselves to him, he could do something extraordinary with them.

Current times are no different. God in Christ calls us from the ordinariness of our lives, expecting to do something extraordinary with us. We must actively participate so the light of the world may overcome life's darkness. The world may perceive that there is no greater fool than God who expects to win the world with weaklings like ourselves. Yet that has been God's curious way as revealed in Jesus Christ, a carpenter in a workshop, a peasant teacher putting God's mind into the many to make them fish for people. "And I," said Jesus, "when I am lifted up from the earth, will draw all people to myself" (John 12:32).

So it is. Jesus calls; we respond. Jesus chooses us; we choose him and say with Paul, "I belong to Christ." We lift Christ up when we help remove the sting of shame or abuse or prejudice inflicted upon people, and they retain their human dignity and sense of worth. We lift him up when we side with the outcast or the lonely, overcoming boundaries that divide people from one another. Belonging to Christ is not a matter of feeling warm and fuzzy; it is a way of living and acting as Christ-called people. So be it.

PRAYER: **Lord of the dance, ordinary and clumsy as I am, I praise you for supporting me joyfully when I do the right steps to the music I hear as a follower of your way. Amen.**

What Does the Lord Ask of You?

January 25–31, 1999 • *Apelu T. Po'e**

Remember the source of your life

These verses from the writings of Micah, an eighth-century prophet, give us a deeper insight into God's controversy with Israel, God's chosen people. The key question here is, What is the main reason behind this controversy?

The passage suggests that the main reason behind this dispute is that the people of Israel have turned away from God, forgetting what God has done for them. One gathers from the prophet's words in verses 3-4 that the people of Israel have been raising accusations and complaints against God.

Certainly the tone of God's words reflects the deteriorating relationship between God and Israel. Historically the people of God are experiencing the disintegration of the heart of their own community because of the corruption of Israel's political and religious leaders.

What then is God's intention in expressing anger over this people? God intends to get the people of Israel to rethink the meaning of their divine vocation. Only then may they remember the source of their life and the expectations of them as God's chosen people. Despite Israel's sin and the numerous accusations the people have raised against God, God remains faithful to them.

Do you remember who the source of your life and salvation is? Do you remember what God required of you at your calling?

PRAYER: O God, you have called and sustained me with your grace. Keep me forever mindful of the source of my life. Amen.

---

*Pastor of Fetu Ao United Methodist Church, Torrance, California.

TUESDAY, JANUARY 26 • Read Micah 6:6-8

Live out God's justice

Israel's sin, the corruption of her political and religious leaders, led to the disintegration of the heart of the whole community. How then can we, as church and community leaders, find the road to a new sense of harmony and wholeness? a new sense of shalom within us? How can we know what God expects of us as we begin our walk with God in this new year?

Today's scripture reminds us that God already has told us what is good and what the Lord's requirements are. A Hebraic legend says that when God wanted to create the world, God thought, *If I create the world with mercy alone then sin will abound. But how can the world endure if I create it by justice alone? Therefore, I will create the world both by mercy and justice.*

Sometimes we take it for granted that we are living up to God's standard of justice and mercy. The truth is, we must admit that Micah's call for us is not easily put into action. Only when we carry out our calling with a sense of righteousness and mercy will we become a holy nation. That defining characteristic is the only thing that interests God. God only wants to know if we have the courage to carry out our vocation as a sign of our steadfast adherence to God.

When we know God's expectations of us and when we have the courage to carry out our commitment, then God will continue to sustain us and be gracious to us. God will forgive us of all the sins that we have committed with premeditation, all the sins that we have committed in a spirit of rebellion, and all the sins that we have committed unconsciously.

PRAYER: O God, I know how difficult it is to walk humbly with you. Give me the courage to do your will. Amen.

Be true to your calling

In ancient Israel people regarded religion and ethics as one entity. This insight may help us understand why the people of Israel have always looked upon their community as if it were a living organism. What happens in politics, economics, or any other sphere of life affects one's family and one's religious life. Everything in heaven or on earth is God's. Therefore, one's relationships with God and with others are important.

Today's scripture vividly describes a person who is truthful in dealings with others in the community. According to the psalmist a godly person integrates his or her religious faith with all the other aspects that affect one's community life.

"O Lord, who may abide in your tent? Who may dwell on your holy hill?" The psalmist's answer is all-inclusive. It includes Christian ethics (vv. 2b-3a); political ramifications (vv. 2b-3a); community relationships (vv. 3b-c); and economics (vv. 5a-b).

What is the point of the psalmist's opening question? The psalmist intends that the question encourage the reader to reflect on his or her own religious life, which encompasses relationships with God and others in the community.

God's requirements force us to be mindful of the true nature of our Christian calling: to make God's presence known in church, in politics, in economics, in every sphere of human life. They force us to work together with politicians, economists, scientists, technologists, and community leaders to create a loving and a just community. Within this community, we relate to one another not on the basis of force and coercion but on the basis of our mutual relationship in God's human family.

PRAYER: You have searched me and known me, O God. Help me be faithful and truthful to you at all times. Amen.

THURSDAY, JANUARY 28 • Read 1 Corinthians 1:18-25

Reach out to the world

Today's scripture comes from one of Paul's most profoundly ethical writings, his letter to the church at Corinth. This letter helps us learn something about the apostle Paul himself: What sort of character does this man have? What is his source of strength? It also depicts life and problems of the church at Corinth: What action does the apostle take to resolve those problems? Finally, it challenges us to continue to reach out to the world with the gospel of Christ.

The call to reach out to the world is not a personal agenda. It is God's agenda. Jesus said, "Go therefore and make disciples of all nations, baptizing them in the name of the Father and of the Son and of the Holy Spirit" (Matt. 28:19).

Paul understands Jesus' desire very well. Paul realizes the importance of fulfilling Jesus' call in his life. Confronted by the Lord face to face on the road to Damascus, Paul recognizes what God requires of him: to become an apostle to the Gentile world, making known the good news about the living God whose self-disclosure to the world comes through the person of Christ.

Some people expressed doubts and suspicions about the apostle's work, just as many today question the church's ministry. But such skepticism did not stop this man. Why? Because Paul knows who called him and what the Lord requires of him. He states the source of his power and the power of others who are called: "Christ the power of God and the wisdom of God."

Can you imagine where we would be today if Paul had not brought the gospel out of Jerusalem into the Greco-Roman world and to us here?

PRAYER: O God, help me reach out to the world with the gospel of Christ. Amen.

FRIDAY, JANUARY 29 • Read 1 Corinthians 1:26-31

Accept God's salvation in Christ

One of the basic teachings of Christianity affirms human inability to save our souls from the power of sin. No matter how hard we try we always end up committing sin. Chronic sin not only leads to the collapse of our moral discipline, but it leads to an impure spirit. The end result: We become prisoners of our own sin and lust. For this reason Christianity maintains that our salvation rests in having faith in God through Jesus the Christ.

The apostle Paul understands this teaching well, and he reflects on it in this letter: Those who are saved are not the wise of this world. No, they are not even the powerful or the noble. They are simply the ones who actually believe that our only hope for salvation lies with God through Jesus Christ.

Many people in the church at Corinth did not share this truth about the Christian life and faith. Some allowed their false assumptions about worldly standards and wisdom to deceive them. So Paul writes to the church at Corinth, trying to convince nonbelievers that Christ is their only hope. As far as their salvation goes, they have nothing left to achieve. Everything required for their salvation already has been done by God through Jesus' death on the cross.

How good it is to know that the merit of our own deeds does not determine our salvation; our salvation comes through God's own gracious divine initiative. Our salvation was made possible only by the precious blood of God's sacrificial lamb, Jesus Christ. No wonder the apostle says, "Let the one who boasts, boast in the Lord."

Are you aware of the cost of your salvation and mine?

PRAYER: I give you thanks, O God, for the redemption price that you have paid for my salvation. Help me accept your gift of salvation with a grateful and loving heart. Amen.

41

SATURDAY, JANUARY 30 • Read Matthew 5:1-8

Behave responsibly

Any successful business or organization has clearly defined goals, which it sets out to achieve. Therefore, the responsibility of all staff, particularly those in positions of management or leadership, involves keeping these objectives in mind and aiming continually for their accomplishment. Without such goals that integrate a company's vision statement, personnel, resources, and capital, much effort would be wasted.

The necessity of setting goals is also true in an individual's life. How meaningful are the lives of those who have no vision of what they can do for the future of their family, church, community, or country? How purposeful is the existence of persons who have no sense of responsibility for what they do?

Jesus' action in the opening verses of today's passage reminds us of the importance of having a sense of responsibility for the lives of those to whom we are sent. In today's reading, Jesus sees the crowds, goes up the mountain, and sits down to teach. Jesus takes the required action because of his sense of responsibility for their salvation. Surely Jesus knows the harsh reality of life that we experience today because many of us do not want to be held accountable for our actions.

Each decision we make, each action we take—even the things that we elect not to do and our failures—all have consequences. With a sense of responsibility for what we do and what we do not do, church ministry will experience genuine and honest change.

PRAYER: **Give me, O God, the sense of responsibility for what I do and do not do. Amen.**

SUNDAY, JANUARY 31 • **Read Matthew 5:9-12**

Rely on God's power

Our human nature encourages us to think that we can rely completely on our own personal power or strength. Many of us today are searching for the key to personal power so we can live independently. Some of us think that money and education make us self-sufficient.

Today's scripture, however, teaches us that as Christians we cannot depend entirely on our own personal power or strength; we are to rely on God as the source of our life and strength.

We live in a tough world, a world characterized by hatred, jealousy, and discrimination—not only among individuals but also among ethnic groups, races, nations, and religions. In order to be God's instruments in making this world a better place for all of us to live in, we need to depend on God's power. Without God's power we will not have the strength to endure the harsh reality of today's violent and unjust world. But perhaps more important is that without God's power and guidance, we will be unable to restore a just order that the world desperately needs today.

Jesus says, "Blessed are the peacemakers....Blessed are those who are persecuted for righteousness' sake....Blessed are you when people revile you and persecute you and utter all kinds of evil against you falsely on my account. Rejoice and be glad, for your reward is great in heaven."

God calls us to heavy tasks, responsible duties. When we cast our burdens and our heavy loads on the Lord, we receive power to endure.

PRAYER: O God, you have promised to sustain me and be gracious to me. You have also assured me that you will show me your goodness and give me a heritage. I continue to trust in your power. Amen.

Called to Live and Teach God's Commands

February 1–7, 1999 • Linda J. Vogel*

MONDAY, FEBRUARY 1 • Read Matthew 5:13-16

Called to be salt; called to be light

This week's readings help us discern what it means to be called to journey toward God's "kindom" ("kindom" denotes a world in which we recognize that we are related, that we are "kin" in God). That kindom is both here and now because of the crucified and risen Christ and will be filled full at the end of time. Today I invite you to read prayerfully these four verses from our Gospel lesson.

To journey toward God's kindom calls each of us to "let your light shine before others, so that they may see your good works and give glory to your Father in heaven." Our good works are not an end in themselves; we do not earn our own salvation. Our good works are our way of giving glory and praise to the One who creates all things. Our gift of praise and glory may lead those who witness our act to praise this great God themselves.

The image of being salt speaks powerfully to me. While salt is necessary in the baking of bread, it does not call attention to itself. It permeates the whole loaf, yet we are unaware of its presence; only when salt is missing do we realize how flat and lifeless the loaf is.

We are called to be salt, to bring life to a hurting world that may be unaware of what is necessary to turn "no longer good for anything" lives into a meaningful and hopeful existence.

SUGGESTION FOR MEDITATION: What is God calling you to be and do as salt and light in the place where you live and work?

---

*Deacon in The United Methodist Church; teaches Christian education at Garrett-Evangelical Theological Seminary; member of St. Luke's United Methodist Church in Dubuque, Iowa; active participant of Epworth United Methodist Church, Chicago, Illinois.

Called away from false worship

Being called toward God's "kindom" means being called away from false worship. Today's passage from Isaiah places a harsh reality before us. God does not desire fasting (or any of the other spiritual disciplines or favorite worship forms to which we cling) unless it leads us into justice-doing and compassion-bearing.

God's people ask, "Why do we fast, but you do not see? Why humble ourselves, but you do not notice?"

God's response to Israel's questions and to our questions is clear. Fasting or worshiping in whatever way we judge to be right and proper is not an end in itself. If we leave church to serve our own interest and to oppress others, God will ask us the question Isaiah proclaimed in his day: "Will you call this a fast, a day acceptable to the Lord?"

False worship is as alive and well today as when this passage was written: around the time when Babylon fell to Cyrus, king of Persia, and God's chosen ones hoped that their exile would end, and they would be able to return to Judah.

Many voices in our day seek to entice us to focus on the forms of our worship. If you will only do this or that, your worship will be vital and alive, and more people will come. Our focus must remain on our journey toward God's "kindom." Our worship must grow out of God's call as our response to God's gracious gift of love and salvation.

False worship leads us away from God. How are we to recognize its many forms? Tomorrow's passage contains many clues to the answer we seek.

SUGGESTION FOR MEDITATION: If God were to call you "to announce to my people their rebellion," what would God want you to proclaim?

WEDNESDAY, FEBRUARY 3 • **Read Isaiah 58:6-12**

Called to worship truly by doing justly

These verses from Isaiah invite us to remember our Gospel passage on Monday that called us to be salt and light. That call to us immediately follows Jesus' teaching on the mountain: "Blessed are the poor in spirit..., those who mourn..., the meek..., those who hunger and thirst for righteousness..., the merciful..., the pure in heart..., the peacemakers..." (Matt. 5:3-9).

Isaiah's words surely must have been in Jesus' heart as he taught the crowd that day in Palestine: "Is not this the fast that I choose: / to loose the bonds of injustice, / to undo the things of the yoke, / to let the oppressed go free, / and to break every yoke? / Is it not to share your bread with the hungry, / and bring the homeless poor into your house; /...and not to hide yourself from your own kin?"

Those who choose to answer the call to journey toward God's "kindom" know clearly what their response must mean. They choose a pathway of justice-doing and compassion-bearing, a pathway to be shared by the poor and all who are cast out and oppressed.

God's call requires that we lead lives of inclusion, not exclusion; to share God's love, not hoard. If we say "yes" to this call to worship truly by doing justly, Isaiah proclaims an amazing promise: "Then your light shall break forth / like the dawn, / and your healing shall spring up quickly; /...Then you shall call, and the Lord will answer; / you shall cry for help, and [God] / will say, Here I am."

SUGGESTION FOR MEDITATION: What do you need to do to claim God's promise that "the Lord will guide you continually, / and satisfy your needs in parched places, / and make your bones strong; / and you shall be like a watered garden, / like a spring of water, whose waters never fail"?

Called to trust God

Those who love God "rise in the darkness as a light for the upright"; their attributes include grace, mercy, and righteousness. The psalmist reminds us that the desire of the wicked comes to nothing; the psalmist emphasizes the lasting rewards that come to those who delight in God's commandments.

Trusting God means acting generously and conducting our affairs with justice. The psalmist, like Isaiah, knows that journeying toward God's "kindom" brings great responsibility. Whenever God's people focus more on the privileges that come with being chosen than on God's call to be a light in a dark and hurting world, they run the risk of joining the false worshipers and cutting themselves off from God's "kindom."

Trusting God calls us to share with the poor, believing that wealth is transitory while righteousness endures forever. Those who trust God are upright, blessed, gracious, merciful, righteous, generous, and just. Because they trust God, their hearts are steady and they do not fear.

As we reflect on the Isaiah passages and today's psalm, we might remember Jesus' admonition: "Not everyone who says to me, 'Lord, Lord,' will enter the kingdom of heaven" (Matt. 7:21). Worship is false when not connected to right living as proclaimed both by the Law and the Prophets.

A call to trust God is a call to lead lives that bring light to dark places and hope to the poor and oppressed. This call to righteous and just living gives God the glory and praise.

SUGGESTION FOR MEDITATION: What will it mean for you and your faith community to conduct your affairs with justice?

FRIDAY, FEBRUARY 5 • **Read 1 Corinthians 2:1-5**

Called to faith in God's power

Paul writes this letter to the church in Corinth about the middle of the first century. In these verses Paul clearly states that the heart of his message does not rely on human wisdom. It rests squarely on Christ, and him crucified.

Christ crucified is the ultimate expression of God's power to save. Paul can hold his own among the rabbis, teachers, and orators of his day. But here he chooses to take a different route and to stand firmly on God's power.

Paul must have recalled these words from the prophet Jeremiah: "Thus says the Lord: Do not let the wise boast in their wisdom, do not let the mighty boast in their might, do not let the wealthy boast in their wealth; but let those who boast boast in this, that they understand and know me, that I am the Lord; I act with steadfast love, justice, and righteousness in the earth, for in these things I delight, says the Lord" (Jer. 9:23-24).

Paul recognized that human wisdom could never comprehend or explain the mystery and power of God that God makes known in Jesus Christ, and him crucified. Paul proclaims in his message that God demonstrates justice-seeking, compassion-bearing power in response to the most dehumanizing form of execution known to humankind. God's power turns the world's power upside down. We cannot explain this marvelous saving act of God. Our only possible response is to come in faith and gratitude, worshiping truly and doing justly.

SUGGESTION FOR MEDITATION: **How do you respond to Jesus Christ, and him crucified? What does it mean for you to rest your faith on God's power?**

SATURDAY, FEBRUARY 6 • Read 1 Corinthians 2:6-16

Called to be taught by the Spirit

Paul continues to stress that *knowing* God does not result from human wisdom. This kind of knowing permeates our whole being—our minds, hearts, and souls. Knowing God is a gift of the Spirit, which God gives to those who open themselves to the teaching of the Spirit. God's Spirit comprehends and relays those things that are beyond human knowing, beyond sight and hearing, to those who love God.

The Spirit's teaching enables us to discern our God-given gifts. In the meeting of our gifts and the world's need, we discover our Christian vocation. The Spirit's teachings speak to our hearts of things spiritual. Indeed, in verse 16 Paul sheds light on what it means to be spiritual when he says, "we have the mind of Christ."

Having the mind of Christ enables us to use our senses and our minds in disciplined and faithful ways; we are open to discern God's justice and God's compassion. Having the mind of Christ means thinking, loving, and caring beyond the boundaries of human time and understanding.

Discerning goes beyond using our minds to figure things out. It goes beyond what our senses convey to us. Discerning is opening our hearts and minds to God's Spirit so that we may understand the gifts that God bestows on us.

SUGGESTION FOR MEDITATION: **What is the Spirit of God seeking to teach you and give you? Where do your gifts and the world's needs intersect? How can you open yourself more completely to receive God's gifts?**

SUNDAY, FEBRUARY 7 • Read Matthew 5:17-20

Called to live and teach God's commands

Journeying toward God's "kindom" means doing and teaching God's commands. Both doing and teaching find their grounding in God's righteousness. The journey toward our relatedness to all creation must reflect the mind of Christ.

Jesus implies that getting caught up in the letter of the law is not the answer. Our righteousness must exceed that of the scribes and Pharisees. The point is not to ignore or abolish God's law and the witness of the prophets; we are to fulfill or fill full the Law and the Prophets in ways that reflect the mind of Christ.

Sometimes Christians focus on certain verses of scripture as dogma (like the scribes and Pharisees before them), forgetting that the Spirit of God continues to instruct and teach those who remain open to the gifts God chooses to bestow on them and others today.

This week's readings call us to be salt and light in an unsavory and dark world. They remind us that worshiping truly and doing justly go hand in hand. This week's scriptures call us to trust God and to have faith in God's power; only then are we open to being taught by the Spirit.

Today's reading provides the context for all we have seen and heard—all that has been given to us. God's great gifts for us and for all people fill full the Law and the Prophets.

What does the Lord require of us? The prophet Micah asserts that we are "to do justice, and to love kindness, / and to walk humbly with your God" (Mic. 6:8). Jesus responded to a similar question by summarizing the Law and the Prophets in this way: "You shall love the Lord your God with all your heart, and with all your soul, and with all your mind....You shall love your neighbor as yourself" (Matt. 22:37-39).

SUGGESTION FOR MEDITATION: **What does it mean today for you to continue journeying toward God's "kindom"?**

Encountering Divine Transcendence

February 8–14, 1999 • John Killinger*

MONDAY, FEBRUARY 8 • Read Mark 9:2-8

This strange event, generally known as the Transfiguration, appears to have three important elements: (1) It prefigures the Resurrection. (2) It links Jesus with Moses, the giver of the Law, and Elijah, the most popular of the prophets, thus "legitimizing" Jesus' messiahship. (3) It provides a second occasion (the first was Jesus' baptism) for God to pronounce Jesus as beloved Son.

For us, perhaps the passage's significance lies in providing a moment of transcendence in Jesus' earthly life—a glimpse of heaven's touching earth and normal, everyday existence receiving a brief blessing from that connection to the eternal.

Many of us have experienced inexplicable "otherworldly" events—either personally or through others: A dead friend or relative made a momentary appearance. A psychic message proved to be true. An angel came during a time of prayer. A physical object was eerily levitated or transported.

We usually dismiss such occurrences, eventually forgetting them. But if we give these events much thought, they might offer us a different view of reality—a view that includes mysterious, unexplainable experiences as well as ordinary ones.

The Transfiguration is an unexpected window through which we glimpse more than ordinary life. Surely this singular event on the mountain better prepared those disciples who were with Jesus to later meet the resurrected Christ.

PRAYER: Help me, dear Lord, to be less hardheaded about physical reality and to realize that spiritual reality is just as real and just as close to my life. Amen.

---

*Minister of The Little Stone Church, Mackinac Island, Michigan.

TUESDAY, FEBRUARY 9 • **Read Luke 9:32-36**

Luke gives us a more detailed picture than either Matthew or Mark of the human reaction to Jesus' transfiguration. Luke alone points out that Peter doesn't really know what he is saying when he asks if he and his companions may build three dwellings on the mountain, one for Moses, one for Elijah, and one for Jesus.

It's a natural reaction, isn't it? In the days of the Exodus, when the Jews traveled through the wilderness, they carried with them a crude building known as the tabernacle. It contained the ark of the covenant, the tablets of the Law, and, in their thinking at least, the holy presence of God.

Jesus and the disciples are in a wilderness setting, and the disciples find themselves overwhelmed by the holiness of their experience. Peter can't help thinking it would be fitting to build dwellings to house the great figures gathered there.

We probably would have responded the same way. Human beings tend to want to solidify spiritual experiences by building things around them, by erecting monuments to them, by establishing something that says for all time to come, "A very important event happened here."

But Jesus knows that we don't hold on to spiritual experiences that way. We may memorialize them, but they evaporate, fade into other experiences, become forgotten. The importance of such an experience comes through its serving as an impetus to our spiritual living. We begin to live in such a spiritual manner that we continue to have new spiritual experiences all the time.

PRAYER: **Dear God, help me not to fasten upon the few special experiences I have had but to live so devoutly and sensitively that there will be many of them. Through Jesus Christ. Amen.**

To derive the full impact from our study of the Transfiguration, we need to consider this passage that relates what happened immediately following the event. Jesus and the disciples have come down from the mountain. They come upon a man beside himself with grief for his son who has seizures. These seizures convulse his son and throw him to the ground. In the idiom of the day, the man understands the disease as demon-related.

"I begged your disciples to cast it out," the man says, "but they could not."

Apparently Jesus has been trying to lead his disciples into the gift of healing, but they are slow to learn; he turns on them with an irritable rebuke. Then he himself does what they were unable to do and gives the healed son back to his father.

Jesus and a few of his disciples have just experienced an extraordinary act of transcendence. But here, only a few hundred feet away, life goes on in its grubby, sordid way. People are ignorant, diseased, hungry, unimaginative. These two poles of reality exist for all of us—the sublime and the absurd—and we must live with both.

Perhaps the experience of the mountain equips and sustains us for dealing with what lies at the foot of the mountain. Had the disciples who failed been to the mountain and witnessed what happened there, possibly they could have healed the boy.

PRAYER: Lord, teach me to deal with the problems of life by spending time in high places with you, for you have the answer to everything. Amen.

THURSDAY, FEBRUARY 11 • Read Exodus 24:12-18

When we think about the commandments God gave to Moses, we tend to forget the setting in which they were given: on the mountain, clouds everywhere, and then a devouring fire.

The very setting denotes holiness and transcendence. It is awesome, as befits the God of all gods and Lord of all lords.

The orientation of our age toward technology causes us to forget the importance of holiness. Henry Adams, the great American writer and educator, attended the World Exposition in Paris in 1893. He went out to Chartres to see the cathedral he loved best in all the world and was surprised to find few people there. The people were all gathered around the great dynamo at the Paris exposition, a sign, he said, that people's interests were turning in the wrong direction.

Perhaps the weakness and confusion of our civilization indicates our having followed the dynamo and materialism; we have forgotten holiness. Yet commitments to the dynamo and materialism offer little deep understanding of humanity.

In a day of general apostasy, it is all the more important for us to seek the rarer atmosphere of the mountains, a place where we may experience the glory of the Lord. Only then may we live with clearheadedness and decisiveness.

PRAYER: Help me always to seek you in the heights, dear God, that I may know your glory and live with proper humility and faithfulness in the world. Amen.

FRIDAY, FEBRUARY 12 • Read Psalm 2

This psalm gives deeper understanding to our earlier reading of the Transfiguration scripture. In this "dialogue" psalm, God addresses the son, much as God addresses Jesus from the cloud at the Transfiguration. When the psalm was written, God may have been addressing the psalmist or perhaps David, the king of Israel. But the early Christians surely saw a connection between this psalm and the voice that came from the clouds, both at Jesus' baptism and on the mountain, to endorse his messiahship.

The psalm as a whole reminds us of the importance of national humility before God. God looks at the plots and conspiracies of the nations to get ahead and laughs at them. All these nations, God says, will serve God's king, the king God puts in place—David, in the great days of Israel; and Christ, in latter times, when the kingdoms of earth become the kingdom of our Lord.

E. Stanley Jones's visit to Moscow depressed him, particularly the evidences of the Soviet state everywhere. He returned to his hotel room and read his Bible. In the Book of Hebrews he came across the promise that "we are receiving a kingdom that cannot be shaken" (Heb. 12:28). *How wonderful!* he thought. *Regardless of what happens among the kingdoms of this world, our heavenly kingdom will last forever. Nothing can topple or destroy it!* Jones's depression left him, and he returned to the world with a new confidence in life itself.

PRAYER: **In a world where nations rise and fall and freely brandish force on every side, I thank you, O God, for a kingdom that can be neither shaken nor destroyed—the kingdom of your Son. Amen.**

SATURDAY, FEBRUARY 13 • Read 2 Peter 1:16-21

"Cleverly devised myths." Peter, the leader of the early Christian community, denies that the stories of the believers' faith are such things.

How could they be? Who would have thought to build a world religion around the figure of a man rejected by his own people and then raised from death by God? Paul calls Jesus' death a *skandalon*, in the Greek—a "stumbling block," something neither Jews nor Greeks can easily accept.

Real myths—structured ways of seeing the world—don't emerge suddenly or carelessly. They evolve over the ages and remain true for people because they have great credibility.

The Christian story didn't happen overnight. Its fashioning began in the prophecies of the ancient Jews. When Christ came into the world, the truth of various prophecies became self-evident. Clearly the prophecies pointed to Jesus.

Not only that, but God vocally endorsed Jesus as God's son in the presence of the disciples. Peter himself had heard the voice. It nearly frightened him out of his wits, but he had heard it—an unforgettable experience.

How restrained this writer's language is: "You will do well to be attentive to this as to a lamp shining in a dark place, until the day dawns and the morning star rises in your hearts." These words are reminiscent of the language of the prologue to the Gospel of John, about the light's shining in the darkness. But again, both writers are alluding to an experience they have had with Christ. They are not devising clever myths. They are bearing witness to what they have seen and heard.

PRAYER: Let the certainty of Christ grow strongly in my life, O God, until the great day dawns and the Morning Star rises in my heart. Amen.

SUNDAY, FEBRUARY 14 • Read Matthew 17:1-9

We come full circle for the week, back to another version of the Transfiguration account, this time the one recorded in the Gospel of Matthew. We have considered some of the Old Testament references that give added meaning to the story's details. We have read about Moses and the elders going to the mountain where they received the Law while standing in the cloud, blinded by the great and devouring fire. And we have read Psalm 2, in which God speaks to his beloved Son, promising him victory over the nations of the earth.

All of our reading supports the fact that our Christian faith did not come about in a vacuum. Its preparation began hundreds, even thousands, of years ago by a God who constantly interacted with human beings, promising life and support but asking for loyalty and devotion in return.

God is still God. God still offers life and support while asking for loyalty and devotion. Most of us will not hear this. We will go on as the masses did in olden times, worshiping idols and following the dictates of our own hearts. But those of us who go to the mountain, occasionally catching glimpses of holiness through the fire and the cloud, will know the truth.

And it is up to us to live that truth and to proclaim it in our time. God has not changed. The truth has not changed. But every age requires new witnesses, and the mantle now falls upon us. If we have seen something, felt something, heard a voice on the mount of Transfiguration, the message is ours to deliver. And Jesus says to us, as he did to the disciples who witnessed this awesome event, "Get up and do not be afraid."

PRAYER: Thank you, O blessed God, for the experience of the mountaintop. Help me to absorb it and live out of it this day and all my days. Through Jesus, your beloved Son. Amen.

Joy in Forgiveness

February 15–21, 1999 • *Walter W. Westbrook**

MONDAY, FEBRUARY 15 • **Read Genesis 2:15-17; 3:1-7**

In the beginning God set forth one rule. The rule was clear, easy to understand, easy to obey: Do not eat the fruit from the tree of the knowledge of good and evil. Very simple.

In today's reading, we find Eve and the serpent involved in a theological discussion about the real meaning of the rule. The serpent implies that the man and woman may eat no fruit from *any* tree in the garden. Eve corrects him, adding that the fruit of this particular tree and the tree itself is off-limits. Eve goes on to add that they may not even touch the tree for fear of death. Neither debater quotes the rule correctly.

As it turns out, subtle interpretation of the rule doesn't matter. Adam and Eve willingly eat the forbidden fruit when the serpent suggests that eating the fruit will make them "like God, knowing good and evil." The original sin seems to be the desire to be like God. Yet we today have discovered that all the knowledge in the world will not make us God, or even godlike.

Yet, as Christians, our aspirations are to be like Christ. This quest involves deepening our relationship with God through Jesus Christ rather than pondering ethical gray areas.

The better our relationship with Christ, the more Christlike we become. Our desire to be like God untwists to become our desire to serve God. We give up our need to control in order to offer ourselves freely to God. We trust God's ability to make us into the image of Christ, to bring forth our true blessed humanity.

PRAYER: O Creator, help me desire to be less "like God" and more like Christ. Amen.

---

*Pastor of Bethany United Methodist Church; chair of the Virginia Annual Conference Division of Spiritual Formation; spiritual director, juggling instructor.

TUESDAY, FEBRUARY 16 • Read Romans 5:12-19

According to Paul, Jesus Christ is the New Adam. How does Paul come to that conclusion? He states that Adam's original sin demanded judgment that led to condemnation. That condemnation resulted in death, not only for himself and Eve, but for the whole human race. Not only did we inherit death, we inherited the curse of sin.

For Paul, Christ short-circuits the current that runs from sin all the way to death. Christ offers God's grace in response to our sins. If we accept the offer of grace by repenting, God forgives us. Repentance leads to justification, then to righteousness, and on to life.

The Christian view of life does promote a sort of inherent pessimism: We are sinners. That is human nature. After countless generations since Adam, after Moses brings the Law, after God speaks through the prophets, we find ourselves helpless to save ourselves from our bent to sinning. This interpretation stands in strong contrast to those believe that if we just try hard enough with the right herbs, the right crystals, the right diet, we can fulfill our total human potential.

As Christians, we acknowledge our sinful nature and our inability to change ourselves. Every day we choose again to let God transform us, to allow God to work with us as we become less prone to sin and more prone to lives of service in the name of Jesus Christ. John Wesley described this process as "going on to perfection." We need to accept the gift of God's grace, repent of sin, and let Christ enter our hearts and minds. May our neighbors find the image of Christ to be more prominent in us than the image of Adam or Eve.

PRAYER: **God of love and transformation, remind me daily that I can fulfill my human potential only through reliance on you. Amen.**

WEDNESDAY, FEBRUARY 17 • **Read Joel 2:1-2, 12-17; Psalm 32**
ASH WEDNESDAY

Joel's prophetic activity spanned the years from around 400 B.C. to 350 B.C. During this time Joel witnesses a plague of locusts that absolutely decimate the crops of Judah. He describes the locusts' thorough devastation as "a nation" with teeth like "lions' teeth" (Joel 1:6).

Joel interprets this plague as a warning from God. The people need to repent before worse things befall their nation. He warns of the forthcoming Day of the Lord, a day to be feared by the unrepentant.

Joel respects the Temple rituals but calls for a deep, sincere, personal repentance: "Rend your hearts and not your clothing." Clearly repentance involves more than being sorry for one's sins. Repentance involves turning from sin and self toward God. It requires a change in behavior. Once repentant, the children of God may genuinely anticipate the Day of the Lord.

Psalm 32 sings the joys of repentance as expressed in confession. Before the psalmist confessed to the Lord, his body was wasting away; his groans were constant; his strength dried up.

But with confession, the psalmist receives God's forgiveness. God becomes a refuge in times of distress. The psalmist discovers new confidence in knowing the ways of God. His life becomes full of gladness in the Lord. The psalmist rejoices and shouts for joy.

If the fruits of a forgiven life are so wonderful, why do we resist? Why do we hesitate to repent? Why do we refuse to confess?

Today on Ash Wednesday, as the ashes mark our foreheads and remind us of our fallen nature, let us confess our brokenness to ourselves, to God, to brothers and sisters in the faith. Then as the "upright in heart," let us be glad in the Lord and rejoice.

PRAYER: Lord, help me embrace your forgiveness with joy. Amen.

THURSDAY, FEBRUARY 18 • Read Psalm 51:1-17

Tradition attributes this psalm to David who may have composed it in response to Nathan's rebuke of David. David had stolen Bathsheba from Uriah the Hittite and then had had Uriah killed in battle.

David asks for God's mercy. He does not ask for God's gentleness, leniency, ignorance of sin, or looking the other way to give David a break. No, David asks God to make him pure. David desires washing, cleansing, purging. He knows the process will not be easy, but he realizes that God wants "a broken and contrite heart." David approaches God fully aware of his sinfulness and his inability to rise above that sinfulness by himself.

David recognizes that a dramatic change must occur deep within himself. He knows of his guiltiness from birth, and he acknowledges this sinful nature. Despite his lifelong closeness to God, David now desires a powerful transformation that only God can effect.

So David offers God his greatest gift: his willingness to be transformed. He now seeks the joy of God's salvation. He will respond by sharing his experience of God's wonderful forgiveness and glory with others. And with the proper motivation, David will offer right sacrifices once again. Offering heart and soul to God can fill the empty ritual of worship with new meaning.

What is our response to God's offer of transforming power in our lives? How do we recognize our need for God's creation of a new heart within us? David, a man after God's own heart, needed divine transformation. Might we not as well?

PRAYER: **God of David, purge me, wash me, and cleanse me. Give me a clean heart and a right spirit. Affirm my openness to your transformation, while restoring my joy. Amen.**

FRIDAY, FEBRUARY 19 • Read Matthew 4:1-11

Immediately after his baptism, Jesus is led by the Spirit into the wilderness. His life has just taken a major turn with God's acknowledgment of Jesus' role as God's Son, the Messiah. Jesus fasts for forty days in the wilderness before the devil comes to tempt him. Weak from lack of food, Jesus finds that the devil approaches him at a critical time in his life and ministry.

The devil sets before Jesus three staples in the earthly concept of "kingdom." We can translate them into current terms of *economics*, *entertainment* (or *distractions*), and *political power*. None is inherently evil, but none represents the agenda of God's kingdom.

Sometimes our most compelling temptations are not evil. Sometimes they are actually good things. We find ourselves more and more attached to these things. We find ourselves devoting more time, energy, and money to them. One day we discover that they have become our gods. We awaken to find them at the center of our lives, replacing the Lord. Family, job, home, respectability: all good things that we can turn into idols, little gods.

But they are not God. They cannot support the entire weight of our souls. To make that demand is unfair and unrealistic. The weight will destroy our idols, and their collapse in the center of our lives can devastate us.

Jesus resists temptation because he knows who he is and Whose he is. Such self-knowledge will help us resist even the most beautiful temptations. And we have more support: Our Savior faced his own temptations and triumphed. He enables us do the same. With Christ's help, we can face any temptation and emerge victorious, just as he did.

PRAYER: **O God, in this time of penitential wilderness, help me know who and Whose I am. May this knowledge sustain me in my times of testing. Amen.**

SATURDAY, FEBRUARY 20 • Read 2 Corinthians 5:20*b*–6:10

In today's scripture passage attributed to Paul, the writer pleads for his readers' reconciliation to God. But to whom is he writing? Paul is writing to the Christians in Corinth. The Christians! Aren't Christians supposed to be reconciled to God already? Isn't that part of our identity as Christians?

Well, maybe in the next world Christians will need no such reconciliation. But in the first-century church and in the twentieth-century church, we find our ranks full of unreconciled Christians.

Paul quotes Isaiah 49:8 when he addresses the "acceptable time" and the "day of salvation." This day is not one in the distant future. The time for reconciliation is now.

Reconciliation implies repentance and the life that follows. Reconciliation is the proper response to the Crucifixion, to the love that drove Jesus to that cross. In reconciliation, we accept God's grace and our whole lives change.

Paul worries that some readers may have accepted "the grace of God in vain." This vain acceptance can take many forms. It always conveys the tragic sense of someone's catching a glimpse of the kingdom and failing to act upon it, either by ignoring it or by settling for the glimpse rather than living a kingdom life.

Let's not lose sight of the urgency of Paul's message. Almost 2,000 years later, *now* is the time to accept God's grace. *Now* is the time to respond to God's love. *Now* is the time to enter a new day. Then we, like Paul, can survive the world's attacks. We will find ourselves to be strong, resilient, and rich in all the ways that truly count.

PRAYER: God of grace, move me to respond to your love and reconcile myself to you. Remind me that the here and *now* offers me new possibilities to respond to your love. Amen.

SUNDAY, FEBRUARY 21 • Read Matthew 6:1-6, 16-21

During the Sermon on the Mount, Jesus talks about almsgiving, praying, and fasting. Not surprising topics since all three practices provide common ways for people to express their devotion to God.

But Jesus does not congratulate the generous, prayerful, fasting Jews in his audience. He suggests that some Jews pursue pious practices to gain attention and respectability for themselves. They blow a trumpet to attract attention to their almsgiving. They pray long and loud in the synagogues and on the street corners. They make sure they look dismal during a fast so people can glimpse the depth of their holy suffering.

This emphasis on appearance rather than substance indicates a materialistic, rather than a spiritual, worldview. And a materialistic worldview would make sense if God did not exist. In such a world, all that would matter is what feels good right now. Even storing up earthly treasures can give us that kind of pleasure.

But the Christian understanding of reality includes not only the material world but the spiritual as well. And the spiritual world is just as real and much more important. It is, after all, eternal.

Jesus would never discourage our giving or praying or fasting. We may even indulge ourselves in worldly pleasures on occasion. But we need to do these things for the right reasons. We give, pray, fast, attend church, study the Bible, serve the poor, support missions, and do other kingdom work out of love for God and for neighbor. If this can be our motivation, God will certainly be able to use us mightily.

PRAYER: Lord, as I move through this season of Lent, help me do the right things for the right reasons. Amen.

Sojourners in Faith

February 22–28, 1999 • Susan Gregg-Schroeder*

MONDAY, FEBRUARY 22 • Read Genesis 12:1-4a

Called to move

The Bible is full of stories of persons called by God to move. These people aren't looking for God, but God is looking for them. That's often how it works. We don't go out and find God; but through our openness to life and our humility before its mystery, God finds us.

God asks Abram and Sarai to pack their bags, leave their home and country, and venture to an unknown land. God calls Abram and Sarai to move. God calls us to move, but how we respond to that call is up to us. Many of us, having heard God's call to move, come up with myriad reasons for not doing so at this time.

But Abram does not offer excuses, and his response to God's call makes him a model of faith for Jews and Christians alike. Abram and Sarai, as the "first family," become the parents of a new nation and the bearers of a promise of salvation for "all the families of the earth." Their story begins a history of salvation because God's call to move comes with a promise. Like Abram and Sarai, we are called by God to be a pilgrim people, a people on the move, a people who have received a promise of blessing.

SUGGESTION FOR MEDITATION: Come along with me as a sojourner in faith. Bring along a sense of expectancy, a vision of high hope, a glimpse of future possibility, and a vivid imagination, for God's creation is not finished.

---

*Minister of Pastoral Care and Spiritual Formation at First United Methodist Church, San Diego, California.

TUESDAY, FEBRUARY 23 • Read Romans 4:1-5

Faithful obedience

When Abram, later renamed Abraham, leaves home, he is not sure where he is going or what is going to happen to him. But he knows God accompanies him on the journey, and he trusts God's promises. For this reason, the apostle Paul looks to Abraham as an example of faithful obedience. Abraham responded to God's call even when the path ahead was unclear and uncertain. The Bible tells us that God changed Abram and Sarai's names to Abraham and Sarah to symbolize the covenant relationship of trust and faith.

The opposite of faith is fear. Fear holds us back, allows us to get stuck, keeps us from taking risks. Perhaps our fear of change renders us immobile; many of us resist change. We feel it is less painful to remain as we are than to open ourselves to the growth and pain that change may bring. We may choose change freely like Abraham, or we may have change forced upon us. Change requires that we step out in faith, that we risk the pain.

The Hebrew word for *obedience* literally means "to hear," and the Greek word for hearing often means "to obey." Faithful obedience requires that we listen with our heart to discern God's word for us. In that understanding, obedience is not an external demand that requires strict adherence to a law. Rather, obedience springs from within, encouraging us to respond to God's word freely. When we hear or discern God's word, our response is to follow in faithful obedience.

SUGGESTION FOR MEDITATION: God says to each of us, "You are my chosen one. I love you. I'm proud of you. Know that I have forgiven you. I call you by name. You are mine. I have entered into covenant with you and will stand by you in all times and places. Dare to live fully the life to which I have called you."

WEDNESDAY, FEBRUARY 24 • Read Romans 4:13-17

God keeps promises

God's call to us comes with a promise—a promise of blessing. The Hebrew Scriptures understood blessing as concrete and tangible items such as descendants, fame, land, crops, and herds. Today we still measure our blessings and our worth in terms of concrete, tangible items. Instead of counting our sheep or our descendants to determine our value, we look to bank account balances, to stock market reports, or to the number of degrees we hold. Too often we feel that we need to earn God's blessing by our "works."

Remarkably, the promised, tangible blessings never materialized in Abraham's lifetime. He never saw his descendants. In fact, in his radical obedience to God, Abraham willingly offered his son, Isaac—the only one who could give him descendants—on the altar of sacrifice as an act of faith in God.

Blessing in Hebrew means "to sustain life." We discover the real blessing through faithful obedience to God and in the companionship of God who shares our travels. Through the journey of faith we experience transformation. During the journey of faith we become new persons. We cannot earn God's blessing; it is a gift freely given. Being in relationship with God is the real blessing. Abraham received blessings along the way as he responded "yes" to God's call to move.

PRAYER: Loving Creator, all of life is a call and a response. I thank you, O God, that your call is also a promise, a promise to be with me on my journey. For this promise I give you thanks and praise. Amen.

THURSDAY, FEBRUARY 25 • Read Psalm 121

On the move

Psalm 121 is part of a collection of psalms pilgrims used when journeying to Jerusalem for the celebration of various festivals. This psalm is a litany that the pilgrims assembled in the village might recite prior to their departure. The pilgrims usually would gather in a central location and spend the night together before beginning their journey to Jerusalem. Probably the pilgrims sang verses 1-2 and those left behind or the leader of the group responded with verses 3-8. These verses convey a blessing to the pilgrims who face the dangers of the journey, offering the assurance that God travels with them and holds each person in protective care. The God who keeps Israel "will neither slumber nor sleep."

As with many journeys upon which we embark, risks and uncertainties may always present themselves. So the pilgrims begin their journey with an affirmation of faith that when they lift up their eyes to the hills, their help will come from the Lord, Creator of all.

This beautiful psalm continues with words of assurance of God's protection and care for the pilgrims. A number of images relate to travel: sturdy footing, shade to protect the pilgrims from the daytime sun, and God's keeping of the pilgrims in their "going out" (departure) and their "coming in" (returning home).

When our personal pilgrimages seem difficult, may the assurance of God's guidance and protection comfort us.

SUGGESTION FOR MEDITATION: **Consider your life pilgrimage. What do you fear? Where do you need to step out in faith with the assurance that God's presence guides and protects you?**

Faith and works

Sometimes God's call requires that we physically move from one place to another. Like Abraham, we may be called by God to leave the security of the familiar behind and move to new lands or new cities. But sometimes God calls for more than physical movement; God may call us to move ahead in our spiritual journey of faith.

So it was with Nicodemus, a man we come to know exclusively in the Gospel of John. Nicodemus, a leading Jew and Pharisee, believed that righteousness consisted of careful obedience to detailed rules of conduct. Nicodemus, like many of us, sought signs and proofs for his faith. He comes to Jesus in the darkness of the night. This passage records a snatch of one conversation.

Jesus states that "no one can see the kingdom of God without being born from above." Nicodemus does not understand that Jesus is referring to a spiritual rebirth, not a physical one. Jesus continues to elaborate and explain. Nicodemus still does not grasp Jesus' invitation to embark on a spiritual journey of faith that will challenge his legalism. But his open-mindedness led him to risk the encounter, and he came to Jesus with difficult questions. As a seminary professor of mine once said, "Questions are answers in embryonic form."

Biblical witness testifies to Nicodemus's support of Jesus in the Sanhedrin. And Nicodemus joins another learned Jew, Joseph of Arimathea, in laying Jesus' crucified body to rest. We do not hear the end of the story. Did Nicodemus overcome his timidity of faith to affirm publicly the man who offered spiritual rebirth?

PRAYER: Loving God, help me overcome my timidity of faith so that I can ask the difficult questions and live into the answers. I yearn for spiritual rebirth. Amen.

SATURDAY, FEBRUARY 27 • Read John 3:11–17

Faith and hope

Today's reading contains the much quoted John 3:16, "For God so loved the world that he gave his only Son, so that everyone who believes in him may not perish but may have eternal life." Indeed verses 16 and 17 summarize the theology of John's Gospel. Because of the familiarity of these words, we often forget their radical nature.

While verses 1-10 specifically relate a conversation between Jesus and Nicodemus, verses 11-17 offer words of hope to all who need the reminder that our relationship with God does not depend on our achievements. The writer of John takes this opportunity to give us a little sermon. In this season of Lent, these words are but a foretaste of our hope that all who have faith receive eternal life. For the Gospel writer, eternal life is both a present reality and a future hope. Eternal life means living life the way life is supposed to be.

Like Nicodemus, we active church members need to be reminded that our work will not earn us points with God. Verse 17 assures us that Christ did not come into the world to condemn the world but to save the world. Our lives are a gift from God. We can participate in eternal life right now, just as we are, if we simply accept the gift through faith that God gives us in Christ.

PRAYER: **Loving God, you call me to pioneer a future yet unnamed. As I venture forward, I leave behind my desires for a no-risk life, worldly accumulations, and certainty. Let me travel light in the spirit of faith and expectation toward you who hold my hopes and dreams. Amen.**

Responding in faith

Many of us today focus too much on a destination, goal, or end result rather than trusting God's presence in the journey itself. As a person of faith, Abraham trusted that God would appear in unlikely times, among unlikely people he might meet along the way. When we journey in faith we are often surprised.

Just as God called Abraham, God continues to call unlikely, unsuspecting persons like you and me to journey forward in faith. Real faith comes when we respond affirmatively to that call, either as individuals or as communities of faith, without absolute certainty as to the destination or the ultimate outcome. We realize that we become partakers of God's promise of blessing when we respond in faith, when we take those creative risks, when we move forward and keep going despite the obstacles.

This is God's call to us: to say yes to a lifelong journey of really going someplace with our faith and with our lives; to recognize the sacredness of all of life and to develop a sensitivity to all of God's creation. The God who calls us to move accompanies us. God's presence enables us.

Our openness to God's presence in our simplest daily tasks allows us to recognize God in our midst—God encouraging us, sustaining us, guiding us, and strengthening us for the journey. We truly live by faith when we realize that we are already on a journey, and we trust God in our travels.

PRAYER: Come along with me as a sojourner in faith, secure in the knowledge that we never travel alone. Amen.

Beyond the Surface to the Depths
March 1–7, 1999 • Diane Luton Blum*

MONDAY, MARCH 1 • Read Exodus 17:1-7

When our sons were quite young, the eternal questions punctuated our eighteen-hour drive to visit a grandparent: "Are we there yet?" "How much longer will it be?" In every journey—even a rapid airline flight—every step and stage follows upon the previous one. In a journey of faith we continue to experience stages of unfamiliar surroundings. Often we receive no immediate answer to our urgent questions: How much further? How will our needs be provisioned? Are you still with me, God?

The barren appearance of Rephidim, the new Israelite campsite, seems to attest to the lack of a water source. The Israelites begin complaining as soon as they arrive. They demand, in a most quarrelsome and threatening way, that Moses give them water. They too raise questions about the journey: "Why did you bring us out of Egypt, to kill us and our children and livestock with thirst?"

So, at this stage of the journey, Moses asks some questions: God, are we in the right place? If we are, how can we live as your people? With the trusty tool of earlier liberation, God leads Moses to strike the rock, releasing the water hidden beneath the barren surface.

As we move by divine leading to new places by faith, our fear of the unfamiliar can be displaced by our trust in God's provisions: cleansing, living water and grace sufficient for today's stage of the journey.

PRAYER: God, dissolve my homesickness, release me from slavery to the familiar, guide me by your grace. Amen.

---

*Associate Pastor of First United Methodist Church, Franklin, Tennessee.

TUESDAY, MARCH 2 • Read Psalm 95

Read verses 8-11 again and hear God's disappointment and disgust with the Israelites' behavior as remembered in Exodus 17 and Numbers 20. The wilderness journey toward the Promised Land of rest had grown longer than any of these Israelites had imagined. They were tired, dusty, and mad. Whatever their ages, they behaved like impatient children. They had forgotten their wondrous redemption from bondage; and they had, for the moment, lost sight of their journey's purpose. With lowered sights they had quarreled with God, with Moses, and with Aaron, as if these providential allies had become their enemies. The heat of these moments kindles even God's anger.

The God of love and liberation remembers who we are and who we can be. This Divine Artist sees beneath the surface of our worst behavior: the depths and heights of our actions, the light and shadow of our motivations, and the length and breadth of our capacity for compassion and love.

Now, read verses 1-7 again. On this day, if you and I will only listen to this amazing God, we will discover God's great care for us. We are the flock of God's own keeping. We are the creation of God's own hand. Come quietly into God's presence. Envision the natural world through which we journey. Offer to God your own unique echo of the music of the seas and the weather; join in the celebration of the birds and the fields. Raise your sights to the stars and the galaxies. Just beneath the surface of our daily routine runs the living water of an everlasting spring. Strike it in faith. Drink deeply. Draw strength for today.

PRAYER: God of the oceans and the skies, rivers and mountains, open my eyes to your distant Promised Land of rest. Lead me today, for your sake. Amen.

WEDNESDAY, MARCH 3 • Read John 4:5-15

Jesus' journey led through foreign territory. Given the fierce hatred between generations of Jews and Samaritans, this stage of Jesus' journey sounds like God's leading rather than a human preference. Jesus travels across religious taboo and social segregation and rests at a well. Thirsty, Jesus encounters a Samaritan woman with the means to draw water for them both. He dares to draw her into the shared task of satisfying his need for water. The noonday sun is hot. She questions and hesitates but relents in the face of their common necessity.

Jesus invites the woman to move beyond the surface of this water's meaning and depths. He already has led them both across the boundaries of their people's enforced separation. Jesus offers her life, the eternal life that the well water only begins to signify. *Look beneath the surface*, he urges her and us. *Look beyond the edge of this encounter with life's wellsprings. Look across the boundaries of race, sex, religion, culture, geography, economics, and social barriers.*

Dare today to look for water that is more than water; dare to live beyond the bondage of material gains and losses; dare to move out from the superficial exchange of consumer transactions. What a daring conversation Jesus and the woman enter on that day's travel stop. Allow him to meet you in this moment. What will he push you to accept? What will he challenge you to share?

Dare to move today in the presence of Jesus' love: from the surface of your life to the heart of God's concern, from water in a bucket to living water offered for all.

SUGGESTION FOR PRAYER AND MEDITATION: Place a vessel of water before you. Touch the water; remember all it means in your life— cleansing, renewal, refreshment, life, and death. Look beyond it to the living water of life in Jesus Christ.

THURSDAY, MARCH 4 • Read John 4:16-26

The woman has come alone to the community well, not in the cool of daybreak but in the bright heat of noon. Perhaps she is "hiding" at this hour from her peers; given her marital history and status, the other women of the village may no longer have welcomed her as they shared this early morning work. Jesus knows the woman beyond her own telling and asks a probing question about her husband. Jesus tells her information about herself, relating history she preferred to hide. By verse 19, she compliments his prophetic abilities and quickly changes the subject, moving away from her own story.

At times we hide. We change the subject to more comfortable topics. Often we hide what we know about ourselves not only from strangers but from people we love. In our hiding places we may find ourselves isolated or alienated from others, even those who love us. Eventually we may hide what we know about ourselves from ourselves. We fear that others may withdraw their love from us, "If they only knew...."

Jesus does know. Although we may change the subject many times, he does not desert us. Dare to welcome God's intimate knowledge of all you are, of all you have done. In knowing and being known, we are invited to receive the truth, the whole truth about ourselves in the light of God's grace. The truth of Jesus Christ crosses the boundaries of our hiding places to offer us mercy and grace. Grace breaks the surface of our disguises and releases us from the bondage of our fear of being fully known.

PRAYER: God, reveal the truth you need me to claim about myself. Cover me with your love and grace that I may have the courage to come out of hiding, that I may become the person you have created and redeemed me to be. Amen.

FRIDAY, MARCH 5 • Read Romans 5:1-5

Five years ago my husband and I restored an old wooden sailboat. We purchased replacement timbers from a remarkable fellow who dealt largely in well-seasoned white oak, which he sold to boat builders across the U.S. We learned that this kind of wood is especially resistant to rot at sea, and the years of seasoning successfully expose the timbers to extremes of temperature and moisture. We trusted this wood's reliability for our boat.

Living by faith in God's grace provides believers with the trustworthy foundation for life and ministry. If God's grace is our core building material, we may expect our faith to be tempered and seasoned by the storms and extremes of life, not destroyed by them. A sailor who sets out in a well-built vessel can weather most any storm. Our confidence and joy, our hope and perseverance grow as we weather new conditions. Our confidence is not built on the "luck" of missing life's storms. Our confidence grows with every faith-testing experience, every failure and loss.

At the heart of our faith is the work that Jesus Christ has already done for us through the cross. That work is God's reversal of what we humans are tempted to believe about failure: that out of death life can triumph, that in the face of evil love can prevail, and from crucifixion God has raised Jesus up for our salvation.

You and I are invited to live and serve beyond the safe waters of life's harbors. Trusting in God' gracious presence, we can venture into deep waters and strong winds. As we learn to trust God's leading, our afflictions serve to temper and shape our character until God's divine image in Christ can be seen in the record of our faith journey.

PRAYER: **God of grace, let your love light my way and guide me through life's storms and sufferings. Amen.**

SATURDAY, MARCH 6 • Read Romans 5:6-11

When does God's love for us begin? Paul declares God's love for us began while we were still sinners, even before we could attempt to earn God's favor. God's love is not a reward for good behavior. God's love comes to us incarnate in Jesus Christ, in the very midst of our bad behavior. God's love comes, already knowing us, to make peace with and among us.

There's no hiding the childish behavior of the recently freed slaves when Moses brings them to Rephidim. Did God know how mean and furious they could become? Yet while they were still full of sin, God's strong hand saved them from bondage; God's steadfast presence provided food and drink for their long journey to claim their freedom and God's promise.

The Samaritan woman at the well could not hide her life's failures from Jesus. In the face of all Jesus knew about her, he shared his identity in God's purposes and offered her the living water of his presence and divine love.

God already knows us, even better than those who see us every day. Our families, our coworkers, our sisters and brothers in Christ see and know the many ways we do not merit God's grace or their patient love. This is the wonderful news: God sent Jesus to express divine love to me and you, long before we recognize how little we deserve this saving gift. When such unmerited love meets us, and we receive it, everything changes. This love is the source of the courage we need to yield our willful decisions and impulsive actions to God-given direction and Christlike actions.

PRAYER: Gracious God of unconditional love, become for me the source of courage I need to desire that your will, not mine, be done. (*Pray the Lord's Prayer.*) Amen.

SUNDAY, MARCH 7 • Read John 4:27-42

On the surface of things, the disciples have to be embarrassed—even dismayed—by what they see: Jesus talking to a woman, a Samaritan. It is a fearless encounter with an untouchable woman, an enemy people. The disciples' reputations are at stake. Saying nothing about the most important encounter of the day, they hold to their surface agenda: "Jesus, have something to eat."

Jesus reminds them that the real nourishment for their souls goes beyond the food they eat. Real nourishment comes from doing God's will and completing God's work. We find this food (like the living water that a jar cannot contain) when we go beyond the surface of our hunger for "things" to the need we all share for that which lasts, for that which is eternal.

Imagine the disciples' amazement at the crowd coming from the town to meet Jesus at this well. The woman, releasing her embarrassment and basking in the acceptance and hope that Jesus has offered, has spread the good news quickly. Many will meet Jesus for themselves. They come to see and to know, to be known and to be loved for themselves.

At this well, Jesus draws up the living water of God's mercy and grace and offers it for them all. The crusty surface of alienation between peoples has broken open. Painful divisions are healed. Jesus invites us to come to this well to release our own doubts and fears in the face of God's unconditional offer of grace. Will we leave this spring of living water unmoved, or will we go with the Samaritan woman to tell and to share what is joyfully ours?

Boldly enter the landscape of the unfamiliar; cross boundaries of distrust with divine love and forgiveness; seek the completion of God's work in your journey.

PRAYER: **Lead me, Lord, in your ministry of reconciliation and evangelism. Amen.**

Opening Our Eyes to God
March 8–14, 1999 • Jan Johnson*

MONDAY, MARCH 8 • Read 1 Samuel 16:1-13

As Samuel dries his eyes and starts from scratch looking for a new king for Israel, the outward appearances of Jesse's first seven sons impress him plenty. But God tells Samuel what we often forget: "The Lord looks at the heart." So attentive Samuel asks for the missing son and in David finds God's irregular choice of a leader.

When we're asked to choose leaders—to evaluate our supervisor or to serve on a church committee or to choose a neighborhood committee chair—we tend to look for someone with good ideas and energy to carry them out. We notice the messages their dress and mannerisms convey. This passage encourages us to overlook people's style and to focus on their substance instead. We look for a character that reveals a heart that listens to God—a heart full of kindness, humility, and serenity.

Passages such as this one also turn our eyes back on ourselves: What does God see when God looks at my heart? Does God see a person whose continual conversation with God is so rich that I frequently surrender difficult people and situations? Does God see a heart that mourns for the voiceless? Does God see a heart that cares about advancing justice and showing compassion? In this reflective way, we train our eyes to look at the heart as God does.

PRAYER: O God, I confess that I am stunned by the outward ambience of people and have overlooked those whose heart is strong for you. Teach me to value what you value in myself and others—a heart that is devoted to you. Amen.

---

*Retreat leader and author, living in Simi Valley, California.

TUESDAY, MARCH 9 • Read Psalm 23

Keeping our eyes open for the presence of God is something we're better at in campgrounds and cathedrals than in boardrooms and bank lines. God is always with us (Matt. 28:20), but our absorption of that reality needs frequent check-ups. In tricky situations such as the one Psalm 23 mentions—sitting across the table from an opponent—the last thing we ponder is the presence of God.

Yet the psalmist sees and perceives God's presence so clearly that he speaks of God's anointing his head as if he is someone special and filling his cup to overflowing. The psalm implies that the enemy is impressed to see his opponent honored in God's eyes. This enemy may even decide to acquiesce!

As I overhear gossip about myself or plead the case for my child or homeless friend, I see God's strong hand resting on my head. God lays more than enough resources before me. I continue in my struggle because the shepherd of my soul is a skillful one.

The psalmist also provides us with detailed images to bind and settle our fear. The shepherd steers him to the serenity of green pastures and quiet waters, restoring his soul in a demanding and soul-wrenching time. In the deep valleys—the crucial interview during lengthy periods of unemployment, the grueling medical test, the abandonment or death of the one most cherished—the Presence abides. Yes, this is a terrible table at which you have to sit today, but God's presence can be so strong that it's as if you're dwelling in the house of the Lord—nurtured, guided, restored.

SUGGESTION FOR MEDITATION: Picture Psalm 23 and place yourself at that table. Imagine also your opponent and God's grace for you in that place.

WEDNESDAY, MARCH 10 • Read Ephesians 5:8-14

Life gets confusing, and sometimes we're not sure where God is in a situation. Are the people I know helping this person or ganging up on her? As a parent or caregiver or supervisor, is this a moment to admonish or encourage, to discipline or excuse? Does the accepted way of doing things (which I'm expected to do) reflect the compassion and fairness of God?

To live as children of light in the daily moments of life at work, rest, and leisure requires that we ask Christ to come and show us what pleases God, to illumine the dark places for us. Christ brings clarity through a fuller understanding of how goodness, righteousness, and truth can play themselves out in the situation. Goodness checks our heart; righteousness weighs our values; truth helps us see our true selves. Our confusion about where God is in any situation fades.

This process changes us, bathing us in the light of God's character and glory and love so we delight in living as children of light. Infused with light, we learn to see and surrender the fruitless words, attitudes, and actions that darken the soul—things that often confuse us and bury our better selves. Instead, we focus daily on what pleases God whom we love, and we find in that focus interesting ideas about how to behave in a good, righteous, and truthful manner. Through the singing from the heart to God and training ourselves to give thanks in even the most rigorous circumstances, we become drawn to God's light and to God's purposes even more (Eph. 5:15-20).

SUGGESTION FOR PRAYER: **Consider a situation in which you need discernment. Ask God to show you how to be a child of light in that circumstance.**

81

THURSDAY, MARCH 11 • Read John 9:1-7

Have you ever been around people who see possibilities for God everywhere they go? (Often these are the most senior of citizens.) They have a knack for noticing the seeking spirit or wandering soul and loving that person.

When the disciples spot a congenitally blind man, they cite him as a case study in their traveling seminary education with Jesus, and they want to know why bad things happen to good people. Jesus addresses their theological question but moves on to point out the possibilities for glorifying God. It's as if Jesus says, *But look what is possible with God! See what God can do!*

So after Jesus offers the culture's style of healing (gritty and tactile), the man quickly follows Jesus' instructions to wash in a well-known landmark location, a place where the water issues from a conduit into the city. When Jesus invites this man to taste and see God and to experience God's healing, the man pursues the invitation.

When God offers us opportunities to experience God, these opportunities may look strange (washing in a pool from a water conduit?) or take too long (why couldn't Jesus just *do* the healing?). Yet in the strangeness and delays, we acquire the warm, tactile experiences we need; or we're moved to a landmark setting where others might benefit. The key is to have our eyes open for what God is calling us to do, to hear the richness of God's suggestions, and to refuse to disobey the heavenly vision.

Like Jesus, we can also develop the knack of seeing a little heavenly vision for others. What is God teaching this person or helping this person to do? How can we be involved in others' spiritual development?

PRAYER: **Healer and Redeemer, keep my eyes open to the ways you are calling me to your side. Amen.**

FRIDAY, MARCH 12 • Read John 9:8-17, 24-29

When you know what's right and you have a system in place for implementation, someone with a different agenda can untidy things. The Pharisees, who organized to reform and purify Judaism, have a system: Don't work on the Sabbath. Their rules hold more fascination for them than God does apparently. As a result, they don't recognize God when they see God. They are blind to God's compassion or the results of God's work in this world.

Jesus knows the Pharisees' system but heals on the Sabbath anyway, doing forbidden work as he makes clay from mud and saliva. The Pharisees have stated that medical attention on the Sabbath is forbidden unless life is in danger. Jesus riles them because their religion is not a religion of the heart. Their rigidity also prevents them from recognizing God's truth in unexpected sources, so they view this compassionate healing as work instead of glorification of God. Besides, Jesus isn't the sort of messiah they are looking for.

In the same way, we don't expect to hear the voice of God in the words of the waitress who serves us breakfast, the rebellious teenager who offers her scathing opinion, or the whining man who sits at the back of the church. But to a spirit akin to God, the voice will resonate until we turn around and understand that we have heard from God the admonition, encouragement, or direction we have most needed. A child of light learns to recognize goodness, righteousness, and truth in the oddest containers.

PRAYER: O God, I know that often you speak to me from unexpected sources. Soften the rigidity of my heart and teach me to seek you and to hear your voice. Amen.

SATURDAY, MARCH 13 • Read John 9:18-23

Facts become obscure in the face of fear and intimidation. The formerly blind man's parents, fearing they will be cut off from their lifeline with God and their community (the synagogue), reduce their testimony to basic admissions: He's our son; he was born blind. No further comments. They refuse to discuss what may have been the most wonderful event of their lives: to see a dream come true, to see the boy they nurtured receive the gift they most wanted for him.

The irony is that in their fear they do the very thing they most want to avoid: They cut themselves off from God by distancing themselves from Jesus. Christ offers a renewed connection to God.

When the people we trust—parents, mentors, leaders, super-visors—discredit someone, we tend to go along with them. We may not be as fearful and intimidated as the man's parents were, but we trust the wisdom of those we revere. We take ourselves out of the loop of communication by saying, "Don't ask me. Ask someone else," as the man's parents said. In so doing, we miss important encounters with God in which we seek God's counsel and guidance and see people and circumstances according to God's light.

Like the man's parents, we also may miss out on the joy of seeing our dreams come true. At the moment we could be cele-brating a movement forward—a breakthrough in the church, a restoration of a relationship, a financial recovery—we're backpedal-ing because we're afraid. In those situations, we escape the penalty, but we fail to win the prize of the knowledge of Christ.

SUGGESTION FOR PRAYER: Ask God to show you who intimidates you and to show you how that intimidating relationship blocks your communication with God and God's transformation of your behavior.

SUNDAY, MARCH 14 • Read John 9:30-41

Perhaps the man's lifelong lack of eyesight has made him so sharp; he thinks clearly with simple logic. He tells the Pharisees the truth: Jesus did a miracle—he must be from God. The man's indomitable spirit is so refreshing in this story because this ecclesiastical squabble is enough to make you want to wash your hands of political intrigue and fly to Tahiti.

In this dispirited moment of being thrown out of the synagogue (supposedly losing his lifeline to God), this man finds Jesus. In our lives, we may acknowledge that when the people who are supposed to know what's going on and on whom we have relied for counsel temporarily absent themselves from their heart and ours, Christ comes to us. Christ breaks that isolation and reassures us that indeed we have gazed on him and spoken with him. In those needy moments, we may worship, enjoy, and draw strength from God's presence.

Like the newly sighted man, we can step aside and let God fight the battle for a while. God knows the hearts of the people around us and has insightful ways to break their rigidity and soften their spirit. In the meantime, our pleasure is to know Christ and speak to him, surrendering the chaos around us and praying for truth and grace to triumph.

This connection with Christ fuels our ability to overcome our Pharisaic blindness. In that connected place, Christ transforms our motives and hearts and makes us persons whose eyes continually focus upward.

SUGGESTION FOR MEDITATION: **Picture yourself in a troublesome situation, perhaps a situation of misunderstanding and dismissal by people you value. Imagine Christ's coming to you in this situation and speaking quietly to you.**

Out of the Depths
March 15–21, 1999 • Emilio Castro*

MONDAY, MARCH 15 • Read Ezekiel 37:1-14

Ezekiel, a member of a priestly family, is taken into exile in the first wave of people deported from Judah to Babylonia, as early as 597 B.C. He understands his vocation: "You shall speak my words to them, whether they hear or refuse to hear; for they are a rebellious house" (Ezek. 2:7). Ezekiel records today's reading after the fall of Jerusalem. The prevailing mood is one of total despair.

The spirit of the Lord sets the prophet down in a valley of dry bones and asks the question: "Mortal, can these bones live?" "O, Lord God, you know," is the prophetic answer—total readiness to listen to the word of God in such a desperate situation.

We know something of the despair of peoples around the world. Life can look like a valley of dry bones, with no signs of life and no hope of new life. Yet in the middle of these valleys of tragic reality, God calls the prophet, the church, and each one of us to announce that God's reconstructive power will breathe upon this dry reality and inspire new life, new beginnings, new hope. The prophet, siding with those who suffer, can proclaim a deeper reality: This brutality prevalent in the world will not have the final word. "Say to the spirit"—let us appeal to God's resources. Let us start with the reality of dry bones, but let us go forward to the reality of the life-giving Spirit. During Lent we walk with Jesus toward the horrible tragedy of the cross, but we know the secret: through that cross new life is coming.

PRAYER: From the profound reality of despair, we call on your life-giving Spirit. Come, Holy Spirit, renew the whole creation. Amen.

---

*Methodist pastor in Uruguay; former General Secretary of the World Council of Churches.

TUESDAY, MARCH 16 • Read Ezekiel 37:1-14

The valley of dry bones portrays quite well the self-awareness of the exiled community in Babylonia and also of the scattered Hebrew community in Palestine. Valley of dry bones, death, death, death. The prophet enters into that somber mood, living in solidarity with the human reality of historical defeat. He does not rejoice in the fulfillment of his warnings and predictions of judgment. His central vision is the living God who calls him to prophesy to these bones, "O dry bones, hear the word of the Lord."

The resources of God are brought to bear on a closed historical situation. The opening toward a different reality does not depend on human resources but on God's powerful handling of history to open new possibilities: "I am going to open your graves, and bring you up from your graves, O my people; and I will bring you back to the land of Israel." The good news to these people who perceive themselves as scattered and powerless is this: God is still alive, opening the future. The miracle of faith resides in its ability to risk. Faith is "the assurance of things hoped for, the conviction of things not seen" (Heb. 11:1).

We recall the sad times of slavery in America and the power of spiritual songs to keep faith and hope alive; we think of the Orthodox Christians in former socialist countries singing "Christ is risen, is risen indeed" as the only simple and powerful answer to ideological propaganda. Or we see children singing God's praises in refugee camps in the heart of Africa. God's message is clear and historical: "'I will put my spirit within you, and you shall live, and I will place you on your own soil; then you shall know that I, the Lord, have spoken and will act,' says the Lord."

PRAYER: O Servant Lord, who participated in profound human despair on the cross, help me look beyond my closed reality to the power of resurrection, to the new heaven that is coming. In Jesus' name. Amen.

WEDNESDAY, MARCH 17 • Read Psalm 130

"**O**ut of the depths I cry to you, O Lord. Lord, hear my voice!" This psalm provides the theme not only for this week but for all of Lent, taking us with Jesus to the cross and the Resurrection. The psalm expresses both penitence and trust in God.

"Out of the depths" of our human situation and totally naked before God, we come to pray, to search for God's company. These words serve as a passionate confession that our whole being, our feelings, our body, our soul all aspire to intimacy with God. We call to God out of our profound need. And even if we have everything we consider to be important, we know that nothing matters if God is not there. The psalm invites us to look for the essential.

Out of the depths, *de profundis*. We come to God out of the depths of our whole being; in God's presence we realize the seriousness of our sin. Prayer requires no argument to bring forth the recognition of our sinfulness and the assurance of our forgiveness. The recognition comes in the miracle of the presence of the living God. The encounter with God brings us to our knees and we confess "there is forgiveness with you, so that you may be revered."

On the human side, our prayers could begin with any sense of need: material, psychological, historical, political, spiritual. Through prayer we attempt to connect to the sources of our lives; prayer is a cry for the hidden treasure of the mysterious and wonderful reality of Godself. In that search for God, we discover our profound need of forgiveness as we simultaneously discover God's graciousness, the graciousness of a God who comes to rescue, filling us with an overwhelming sense of God's presence. The profound encounter of prayer awakens our admiration, wonder, and reverence.

PRAYER: Such as I am, O Lord, I come to you. Blessed be your name. Amen.

THURSDAY, MARCH 18 • Read Psalm 130:5-8

We would like to recover the sense of expectation the psalmist describes. The nightwatchers, those who keep the peace of the city, ensuring that nothing disturbs the sleep of the population, look toward the mountains for the first rays of morning. With the coming of day, their night duty ceases, and they may relax. In Latin American cities, the watchmen traditionally would walk down the street shouting from time to time, "The night is calm and serene," in that way giving confidence to those who might be awake.

This sense of expectation, anticipation, assurance that the morning will come for the biblical poet describes our prayer attitude. We cry for the Lord's presence; we anticipate that encounter; we are assured the encounter will take place just as surely as the sun rises. The Christians of the first generation would summarize their prayers in the expression *Maranatha*, "Come, Lord Jesus." They looked to the future in eager anticipation of his coming. Christians worshiping in the catacombs, hiding from the dangers of the outer world, eagerly anticipated the coming of the new day, when the presence of the Lord would be a living reality.

We walk today in the same expectation of a daily encounter with the living God, and at the same time we anticipate the liberation for our church, for our people, for the whole of humanity. We continue to walk the road of the cross in this Lenten season. We anticipate, we enjoy already the assurance of the promised liberation. But we will look for more at the banquet of the Lord.

Yes, we already have encountered the living God; our prayer has been answered with the full taste of God's presence. We will look for more assurance, and we eagerly hope for the day in which the Lord will be fully manifested.

EXHORTATION: "Pray in the Spirit at all times in every prayer and supplication" (Eph. 6:18).

FRIDAY, MARCH 19 • Read Romans 8:6-11

The letter to the Romans describes the broken situation of humankind. Our separation from God has produced not only conflicts and war with fellow human beings but also profound disruption in ourselves. We are beings at war with ourselves. Paul recognizes the profound nature of the rupture: "I do not do the good I want, but the evil I do not want is what I do" (7:19). He uses the categories of *flesh* and *spirit* to indicate the dichotomy, the schizophrenic division in ourselves. Life in the flesh is life according to what is usual: following the values and convictions of the majority and allowing them to control our lives. Life in the spirit is the very same bodily life, but this life centers itself in conscious relationship to God in Christ, awaiting the fulfillment of the Spirit of God to infuse our own spirit. The life of the spirit holds out the possibility of reconstituting a new humanity to overcome the brokenness of our sinful condition.

The crowning verse of this Bible passage is verse 11: "If the Spirit of him who raised Jesus from the dead dwells in you, he who raised Christ from the dead will give life to your mortal bodies also through his Spirit that dwells in you." God's Spirit redeems not only our spiritual life but also our human body. The action of the Spirit inside our very being reconstructs our total personality.

The affirmation that in the resurrection of the dead our life will be given back to us is not just an end-time promise. That regaining of life also stems from our current awareness of God's power at work in our lives, rebuilding internal peace and enabling us to reconstruct relations of peace with neighbors.

PRAYER: Heavenly Father, send down your Holy Spirit to indwell my whole being so that body, soul, and mind can celebrate your glory joyfully and offer you the praises of my total life. In Jesus' name. Amen.

SATURDAY, MARCH 20 • Read John 11:1-16

Jesus receives the news of the illness, and later the death, of his dear friend Lazarus. He explains to his disciples that "this illness does not lead to death; rather it is for God's glory, so that the Son of God may be glorified through it." And then Jesus adds, "Let us go to Judea again."

The disciples respond, "Rabbi, the Jews were just now trying to stone you, and are you going there again?" The disciples realize that going back to Bethany or Jerusalem will mean facing opposition, even death. Yet for Lazarus, Jesus readies himself to confront death on the cross. He will provide consolation for the family and share in the death of Lazarus through his own cross. The resurrection of Lazarus will be the ultimate revelation of God in Jesus and an affirmation of God's love at the very moment in which the powerlessness of the cross is coming clear on the horizon.

Because Jesus wants to save his friend, he doesn't consider his own safety. I think of people who offer themselves as volunteers for peace missions: those in the jungles of Central America who witness for peace or those in central Africa who help alleviate the plight of the refugees and affirm that life and love are stronger than death and hate. Many vocations involve the surrendering of our well-being, the risking of our privileges as part of our faithfulness with Jesus in our way to the cross and to the resurrection.

It is important to hear Thomas's words, "Let us also go, that we may die with him." In the relative comfort and security of our modern life, we do not envision life-threatening situations, but the option is real for each one of us. Are we looking for the manifestation of God's glory in our life, ready to surrender our existence for the cause of the kingdom?

PRAYER: **Merciful God, who in Jesus Christ gave us a savior who offered his life for our salvation, recruit me on your road to service so that I share in the glory of the cross and the resurrection. In Jesus' name. Amen.**

SUNDAY, MARCH 21 • Read John 11:17-45

Many Jews had come to Martha and Mary to console them about their loss. The Gospel of John often describes the Jews as Jesus' enemies. In fact, a superficial reading of the Gospel may create an anti-Semitic feeling, which may have been at the root of much Christian prejudice against the people of Israel through time. So let us emphasize that here in the hours of mourning, the Jews came to console Martha and Mary on the death of their brother, Lazarus. The Jews in the house followed Mary because they thought she was going to the tomb to weep; they accompanied her to the encounter with Jesus. When Jesus saw her "and the Jews who came with her also weeping, he was greatly disturbed in spirit and deeply moved." Jesus began to weep, and the Jews recognized in those tears Jesus' profound love for Lazarus.

Jesus' weeping takes us into the depth of human suffering and human emotions, giving us one of the most revealing pictures in the Bible. The God of Israel and the God of Jesus is not a far away God, undisturbed by human emotions. As a father, a mother, God suffers with us. *De profundis*, out of the depths of human suffering and anguish, God calls Lazarus from the grave.

This is the *skandalon* of the Christian faith: God's sharing our suffering, God's dying on the cross. In the Gospel of John, the most intellectual of all the Gospels, we see Jesus sharing in human suffering and inside that suffering bearing witness to the power to bring new life from the grave. In the depths of the cold suffering of humankind resides the hope and power of God. Jesus offers glimpses of eternal life, a life that overcomes the grips of despair and calls us into a living vocation.

PRAYER: **Out of the depth of shadows of death I cry to you, O Lord. I am overwhelmed. You weep with me. You call me through the cross to the resurrection. Thank you, O Lord. In Jesus' name. Amen.**

Let Our Eyes Be Opened

March 22–28, 1999 • *Alvin B. Deer**

MONDAY MARCH 22 • Read Matthew 21:1-11

In our reading to start this week, we see Jesus preparing to enter Jerusalem on a colt as a triumphant king. The Gospel of Matthew intends that we not only see the king but see the king "lowly, and sitting on a donkey" (NKJV). Contrast this image with the one presented in Revelation 19:16 where the "King of kings and Lord of lords" appears on a white horse, coming in righteousness to judge and make war. Matthew's image bears witness to the "dispensation of the fullness of the times" (Eph. 1:10, NKJV). Jesus, as he enters Jerusalem, fulfills this dispensation of time. He will gather "together in one all things...in Him" (NKJV) through his death.

Many scholars will suggest Zechariah 9:9 as our link to today's reading. I would suggest that we read Matthew 20:29-34. In this prelude to our reading, Jesus has just left Jericho, "the city of palm trees" (Deut. 34:3). In Jericho, Jesus has responded to the cry of two blind men: "Lord, let our eyes be opened."

Jesus leaves the city of palm trees and enters a city on a road strewn with palms. He leaves a city where two blind men sat along a road and cried for mercy and enters a city where a multitude of the spiritually blind cry, "Hosanna to the son of David!" Jesus leaves a city where he expressed compassion for the blind and touched them to enter a city where his overwhelming compassion enables him to lay down his life—touching all and changing humankind forevermore.

PRAYER: O God, open my eyes as I enter this week of celebration, that I may remember Jesus' victory over sin and death. Amen.

---

*Executive Director of the Native American International Caucus, Oklahoma City, Oklahoma; clergy member of the Oklahoma Indian Missionary Conference.

TUESDAY, MARCH 23 • Read Psalm 118:1-2, 19-29

Our theme still emphasizes the victor's entering the city. Psalm 118:19-20 states,

> Open to me the gates of righteousness,
> that I may enter through them and give thanks to the Lord.
> This is the gate of the Lord;
> The righteous shall enter through it.

Jesus' entry into the city does not bring with it the annihilation of the city or the destruction of the enemy. Jesus conquers the enemy by dying for their sins! The Hebrew word for "righteous" can also mean "just." The psalmist addresses our faithfulness with these words: "The stone that the builders rejected has become the chief cornerstone." We have withstood the test, and "this is the Lord's doing." God takes action, and our reliance upon God brings us through. The thought for today is that a "just " person, one who has stood up for justice, may expect the "gates of righteousness" to open to her or to him.

Today our secular society measures success by annihilation and obliteration. The way we look at our athletic events reflects this measure. We have "slam dunk" basketball and a "blitzing" football game. In business, industries "maximize" profits at the expense of social justice; and in the political arena, opponents destroy one another's character in order to win. But in the midst of this world, God calls God's people to be different. Jesus enters Jerusalem offering peace and wholeness; Jesus enters our lives offering peace and wholeness. As Christians, we offer our broken world peace and wholeness. We are to do justice; and as we do, the gates of the righteous swing open.

PRAYER: Lord of my liberation, as I ponder your mission in Jerusalem, help me always to choose righteousness and justice as my road to salvation. Amen.

WEDNESDAY, MARCH 24 • Read Isaiah 50:4-9*a*

The Passion week hymn, "Hosanna, Loud Hosanna," proclaims,

"Hosanna in the highest!" that ancient song we sing,
for Christ is our Redeemer, the Lord of heaven our King.
O may we ever praise him with heart and life and voice,
and in his blissful presence eternally rejoice.

Passion week is a time we use all our senses to offer praise and to rejoice. Our reading today states,

The Lord God has given me the tongue of a teacher,
  that I may know how to sustain the weary with a word.

To speak compassionately is a gift from God; "The Lord God has given me," the text says. Compassion does not come naturally to many of us, particularly compassion for those beyond our family or immediate circle of friends and coworkers. Compassion springs from our willingness to serve God with our whole being. We must be willing not only to sing that ancient song, "Hosanna," but we must open our voices and speak life to a person who is weary from the journey.

God touches all the senses of those who are willing, making those persons more acutely attuned to the world around them—even in awakening. We most often perceive awakening as a sense related to sight. But our reading today says our ears awaken first. In reflection, we realize that this ordering of perception is truly what happens. We *hear* the radio or the alarm long before we *see* the light of a new day. Our word today affirms that willing servants, sensitive to the awakening voice of God, will put themselves in tune with God's perfect will.

PRAYER: Awaken my senses, O God. May I not only sing "Hosanna" to the Lord, but may you awaken my sense of compassion, morning by morning and day by day. Amen.

THURSDAY, MARCH 25 • **Read Psalm 31:9-16**

About one year into my ministry, I began to visit a woman in the nursing home. She was the only Native American resident. When I met this Cheyenne lady, only a year had passed since the time of her accident—a fall from her porch that broke her neck and paralyzed all four limbs. As I entered her room I saw a picture of Jesus, a Bible, and a wall plaque with a scripture quotation. She had a smile on her face, yet her hands had atrophied and curled up. She had no feeling below her neck. "Have mercy on me, O Lord, for I am in trouble" (NKJV).

Over the years, this wonderful lady has ministered to me in more ways than I could have to her. She could have gone the way of her body. She could have said, "My bones waste away....I am like a broken vessel." But instead, she has become a prayer warrior for her native people.

I helped her get a motorized wheelchair, and she visits other residents in her nursing home, bearing witness to God's love. She has brought hope to people who could get out of bed on their own and walk out of that nursing home—something she cannot do. Surely God's word echoes through her ministry: "My times are in Your hand" (NKJV).

As we reflect on these days leading up to Passion/Palm Sunday, call to mind other examples of Christ's ministry—dynamic, yet manifested in broken vessels.

PRAYER: "Deliver me from the hand of my enemies,
       And from those who persecute me.
       Make Your face shine upon Your servant;
       Save me for Your mercies sake" (NKJV). Amen.

FRIDAY, MARCH 26 • Read Philippians 2:5-11

As we come closer to Calvary, we come over the last hill on our journey; and we begin to see our destiny unfold before us in the distance. We see the cross silhouetted against the next horizon. We are almost home—victory at last! God the Son was born in "human likeness" and became "obedient to the point of death." For this obedience God the Father exalted him and gave him a name above every name.

A church in downtown Los Angeles was called "The Church of the Open Door." Above it, a twenty-foot neon sign with the words *Jesus Saves* shone in all four directions. How many other times have you seen the name of Jesus scrawled across a city wall, or on boulders facing lonely travelers as they traverse the interstates?

In Oklahoma City a few years ago, someone decided that this name that is above every name should be before everyone who traveled into downtown Oklahoma City. Many convenient spaces gave way to the words *Trust Jesus*. Someone else decided to make an editorial change and rubbed out the T in front of *Trust*. Now the message simply reads *rust Jesus*. As we consider today's reading, the danger is that our minds will rust, if we don't trust: "Let the same mind be in you that was in Christ Jesus." Many of Paul's teachings speak of transcending the mortal you and putting on the likeness, or mind, of Christ.

These words introduce verses 6-11, a passage considered to be one of the earliest witnesses and reflections on the nature and mission of Jesus. This "Christ hymn" reminds us that just as Christ humbled himself, so must we value humility. I invite you today to let this mind also be in you.

PRAYER: Lord, thank you for your obedience. Today let your mind be my mind. Amen.

SATURDAY, MARCH 27 • Read Matthew 27:11-25

We find a little-known scripture in Matthew 27:19: "While he was sitting on the judgment seat, his wife sent a message to [Pilate], saying, 'Have nothing to do with that just Man, for I have suffered many things today in a dream because of Him'" (NKJV).

Whenever we study the events leading up to Calvary, we never hear about Pilate's wife and her message to her husband. As a matter of fact, if we removed verse 19 from the Book of Matthew, few people would know the difference! I have checked a few commentaries; and little, if any, mention is made of this warning from Pilate's wife. The parallel Gospel writings in Mark and Luke do not mention the warning. What might have been Matthew's reason for including this warning?

This passage looks at the testing of Pilate's conscience. The message from his wife confirms Pilate's belief that the cries of his conscience are right: Jesus is a just man! Pilate tries to satisfy the cry of his conscience, yet comes to a tragic decision by washing his hands of the whole ordeal.

How often is your conscience tested? How do you stop your conscience from crying out for justice? Do you turn your head? Do you assign responsibility to someone else? Do you try to salve your conscience with token gestures?

As we reflect on this scripture, particularly verse 19, let us remember that the still small voice of God comes to us in many different ways, empowering us toward justice and righteousness.

PRAYER: O God, you speak to me in many different voices. Let me hear you today. Amen.

SUNDAY, MARCH 28 • Matthew 27:45-56
PASSION/PALM SUNDAY

Today is Palm Sunday, the beginning of Passion week. In our Monday meditation we contemplated Jesus' entry into Jerusalem as a victorious king. Today we look beyond the crowds and hosannas, the time of enthusiastic endorsement, to a time of loneliness and isolation. Today our scripture reading focuses on Jesus' crucifixion. The crowd's jubilant hosannas at Jesus' entry become a centurion's confession at Jesus' death: "Truly this was the Son of God" (NKJV). What a wonderful confession to make on a day we call the Lord's Day. As we reflect on that first Good Friday, the cross reminds us that only through obedience to God did Jesus win the victory.

The celebration of that victory began on the palm-covered road that first Palm Sunday. As we look beyond to the cross, the cheers are not forgotten; the palms laid before Jesus are not in vain. The Son of God, hanging between heaven and earth, is obedient even to the point of death.

Perhaps the signs and wonders that accompanied the death of our Savior moved the centurion to utter his confession. Perhaps we are tempted to discount his confession, to value it less because the centurion actually *saw* the son of God. We easily suggest that the centurion made his confession *only* because he *saw* signs and wonders. But in John 12:32 Jesus says, "And I, if I am lifted up from the earth, will draw all peoples to Myself" (NKJV).

Our scripture doesn't tell us what the centurion did with his confession. Did it change his life? Today as we reflect on Jesus' being "lifted up," our confession of Jesus as Son of God can become a new way of being and living.

PRAYER: Jesus, I confess that you are truly the Son of God. Amen.

Holy Week

March 29–April 4, 1999 • *Vigen Guroian**

MONDAY, MARCH 29 • **Read Isaiah 42:1-9; John 12:1-11**

The promise of new and everlasting life

We enter Holy Week greeted by a fresh beginning in the natural cycle of the seasons. April beckons us to shake off the torpor of winter. The sun warms the earth, and the sweet scents of lilacs and hyacinths flood the air. All of our senses are awakened; life seems more real. God helps us believe in the resurrection of the Son and the renewal of our own lives. The prophet Isaiah is not the first or the last to express the hope: "Behold, the former things have come to pass, / and new things I now declare" (RSV).

Somehow Mary knows that her friend Jesus has fulfilled that prophecy. After all, just the week before, she and others had witnessed a miracle: Jesus brought her brother Lazarus, four days dead in the grave, out alive into the light of day. On this day the impact of his deeds moves her to do something that perhaps she had not contemplated. Mary takes expensive oil, anoints Jesus' feet with it and then wipes them with her hair. What meaning does this act of humility and love hold? Among Jews, one meaning was clear: such is done for a king or the Messiah. Does Mary suspect what Jesus quickly tells his disciples—that she is honoring his death and burial that soon will come? How can this be when the house is filled with the sweet fragrance of the ointment and Mary's love poured out?

SUGGESTION FOR MEDITATION: "Today the Holy Passion shines forth upon the world with the light of salvation....He who holds all things in the hollow of His hand consents to be hung upon the Tree to save [hu]mankind" (from an Eastern Orthodox hymn).

*Professor of Theology and Ethics, Loyola College, Baltimore, Maryland; Orthodox Theologian of The Armenian Church; author.

TUESDAY, MARCH 30 • Read Isaiah 49:1-9; John 12:20-36

Holy Week is when the Father calls on us to assess our lives by the life and death of the Son. During this week, he whom the prophet describes as the one God gives "as a light to the nations, / that... salvation may reach to the end of the earth" endures his dark night of the soul. His passion has begun. John's Gospel asks us to enter into this passion and make it an example for our own lives.

In his last public speech, Jesus assesses his own life and his ministry. To complete his service to the Father, he must give himself over to his Father's will—even if that means dying on a cross. He who in the previous week had raised Lazarus from the grave will willingly meet his own death. The lesson is spoken in a great metaphor of the Christian faith: "Truly, I tell you, unless a grain of wheat falls into the earth and dies, it remains alone; but if it dies, it bears much fruit" (RSV). During Holy Week we must permit these words to penetrate our hearts and minds. If we surrender our lives to God for the sake of others, we join in God's kingdom.

How will we conduct our lives from this moment on? God has loved us into being and called us into God's service while still in the womb (Isa. 49:1, 5). We cannot ignore this calling and still lay claim to the eternal life that the Father grants through the death and resurrection of the Son. But how can love embrace death and still live? Christ shows us how in these last days of his life. God has created us all as seeds of eternal life. A seed, however, is not the source of its own being nor is it able by its own power to grow into a new plant. This week we are being asked to walk in the light of the Son along the path that only he could have chosen. We must let his light come inside of us so that, even in the darkness of our graves, our inert seeds have the energy to reach for the light in the midst of the garden that the Lord has prepared.

SUGGESTION FOR MEDITATION: "I am the resurrection and the life" (John 11:25).

WEDNESDAY, MARCH 31 • Read Isaiah 50:4-9*a*; John 13:21-32

God made us for the light. "God is light and in him is no darkness at all" (1 John 1:5, RSV). But some of us choose darkness anyway. It is a indeed a profound mystery, this evil in the hearts of men and women that moves them to walk toward shadow and darkness rather than substance and light. This evil is not moved to repent even when looking into the face of the purest goodness.

I do not doubt that Judas believes just as much as the other disciples that Jesus is the Messiah. Yet Judas chooses the darkness. What does he hope to gain? He has kept the greatest of all treasures—the Creator—in his heart. And yet he willingly exchanges this treasure for a few silver coins. Jesus gives Judas opportunities to repent and change his course. While preparing to wash the feet of the disciples, Jesus announces that not every one of the gathering is clean. "For he knew who was to betray him" (John 13:11, RSV). At the table, Jesus states, "Truly, truly, I say to you, one of you will betray me" (RSV). Jesus breaks the bread and gives a piece of it to Judas, but Judas remains unswayed by this love.

God's mercy is inexhaustible. However, God honors our liberty and hopes that we will come to the light freely. The one who willingly went to the cross permits Judas, who set this fate in motion, to finish his wicked deed. This act is one of great love that contains a terrible judgment. As Jesus gives Judas the bread, he says to him, "Do quickly what you are going to do." The other disciples are confounded. Immediately after taking the bread, Judas "went out. And it was night." What darkness must have greeted him.

SUGGESTION FOR MEDITATION: A painting by the artist G. Bashindjaghian (1857–1925) entitled "Judas's Remorse, Golgotha" hangs in the museum of Holy Etchmiadzin. It depicts Judas paused in the darkness of night before the three crosses, illumined only by the moon, all in shades of gold and brown and faded aqua blue, earth and sky desolate. His head hangs down; we see only his back.

THURSDAY, APRIL 1 • **Read Psalm 116:1-2, 12-19; John 13:1-17,**
31b-35

MAUNDY THURSDAY

The Eastern Orthodox mattins service for Maundy Thursday picks up the theme of Judas's betrayal, asserting avarice as the primary motivating factor. Certainly greed is partially responsible for Judas's betrayal of Christ, but tradition also recognizes the large part that pride plays. We cannot help but contrast this pride with the great humility of Jesus in washing his disciples' feet.

"All who exalt themselves will be humbled, and all who humble themselves will be exalted," Jesus says in Matthew's Gospel (23:12). And what a shameful and desolate death Judas dies. He hangs himself, presumably in utter despair, displaying the opposite of the faith and hope with which his companions will die their deaths. Judas's pride is his ruin; their obedience and humility permit them to share in the Son's glory.

Christ teaches a profound lesson of humility when he washes the feet of the disciples. They have been tempted to think of him as a king with claim to earthly authority. However, he needs to persuade them that his kingdom is not founded upon such pride or power. The memory of Jesus' triumphant entry into Jerusalem is still fresh in the minds of the disciples. Is Jesus thinking of this event when he speaks? "What I am doing you do not know now," he says to them, "but afterward you will understand"(John 13:7, RSV). He means that the Lord of heaven and earth will be nailed to a cross. The foundation of God's kingdom is love expressed as service to one another rather than a pursuit of power and domination. The path that the disciples—and all Christians afterward—follow they tread with feet washed with the blood of Christ spilled on the cross.

SUGGESTION FOR MEDITATION: **Consider these words of Saint John Chrysostom: "Humility is the root, mother, nurse, foundation, and bond of all virtue."**

FRIDAY, APRIL 2 • Read John 18:1-17
GOOD FRIDAY

On Good Friday Christians remember Jesus' crucifixion and death on the cross. But let us for a moment direct our attention to the subplot of Peter's denials that the writer of John's Gospel weaves into his story. It serves as a counterpoint to the tale of Judas's betrayal of Jesus. Like Judas, Peter abandons Jesus and leaves him to suffer at the hands of his enemies. Peter's apparently bold gesture of cutting off the ear of the high priest's slave may be empty bravado that masks his great fear. Soon thereafter as he secretively follows Jesus and his captors through Jerusalem, Peter denies three times that he is a follower of the Nazarene.

Also like Judas, Peter wanders into the night. But unlike Judas Peter does not allow his bitterness and despair to swallow him up. His remorse leads to repentance. Luke's Gospel reports that Peter weeps bitterly after the cock crows.

After the meal and foot washing, Peter asks Jesus where he is going. Jesus assures Peter that he cannot follow Jesus' path. Peter responds, "Lord, why can I not follow you now? I will lay down my life for you" (John 13:37). Jesus understands Peter's strengths and weaknesses, as he understands yours and mine. Now is not the time of Peter's strength. But at the right moment Jesus will exact the promises he needs from Peter. After his resurrection, Jesus reveals himself to the disciples at the Sea of Tiberias. Having broken bread and breakfasted with them, Jesus asks Peter, "Do you love me?" (John 21:17). Peter affirms his love, and Jesus asks him to tend and feed his sheep. Jesus asks three times: Three affirmations replace Peter's three denials. And we receive those same opportunities.

SUGGESTION FOR MEDITATION: **"Wishing to pardon, Christ came to the earth. Wishing to pardon, he was nailed to the Cross. In pardoning, he made death submit to those who cry, 'Hasten, Holy One, save your flock'"** (an excerpt from Saint Romanos the Melodist's chanted sermon "On Peter's Denial").

SATURDAY, APRIL 3 • Read Job 14:1-14; Psalm 31:1-14;
1 Peter 4:1-8

In Orthodox Christianity the icons named "The Harrowing of
Hades" and "The Spice Bearing Women" are brought out on Easter
to celebrate the Resurrection. Nevertheless, the Eastern Christian
liturgies for Holy Saturday concern themselves especially with the
mysterious events of Christ's descent to the dead. First Peter 3:18-19
mentions this: "For Christ also died for sins once for all,...but [he
was] made alive in the spirit;...he went and preached to the spirits
in prison" (RSV). First Peter 4:6 continues, "For this is why the
gospel was preached even to the dead" (RSV).

The Orthodox tradition attaches great significance to these
Petrine verses. And the depictions of these mysterious events are
appropriately dramatic: Christ stands above the dark abyss of Hades,
surrounded by an emanating radiance, usually in light shades of
slate blue, often with stars set on the outer edges of the oval. This
luminous, heavenly Christ reaches down with strong arms to lift up
Adam and Eve from their tombs. The doors of Hades form Christ's
platform, and we see Satan trapped under these doors in utter
blackness. Behind Adam and Eve, to the left and to the right, stand
ancestors of the faith: David, King Solomon, Moses, and others.

Christ's descent to the dead represents the fulfillment of Israel's
hope as expressed by David in Psalm 31 and in the Book of Job.
Even on Holy Saturday, which is such a dark day because the Lord
of Creation has been laid in a tomb, we still may take heart in Job's
yearnings for new life: "There is hope for a tree, if it is cut down,
that it will sprout again....If mortals die, will they live again?"

SUGGESTION FOR MEDITATION: **"Through your burial in a new
tomb, bring me, who am buried in sins, out. By descending into
the pit of sin, raise me up from the pit of my sins"** (verses from the
Armenian hymn "This Ineffable Day" of Saint Nersess Shnorhali).

SUNDAY, APRIL 4 • Read John 20:1-18

EASTER SUNDAY

Even in the darkness before dawn, Mary Magdalene can see that the great stone has been removed, revealing the empty tomb. And in that darkness, Mary's dread must have turned to terror. Without a second thought she runs to find Peter and "the other disciple."

In tears Mary cries out to them, "They have taken the Lord out of the tomb, and we do not know where they have laid him." All of them race back to the tomb. The other disciple goes in first, and Peter follows. While Peter notices the napkin used to cover Jesus' head rolled up neatly and separate from the linen wrappings, it is not he but the other who believes. But just what is this belief? The Gospel does not say. It adds only that neither disciple quite comprehends the meaning of the scripture, "that he must rise from the dead." The two men return home with much to ponder. Mary, however, remains frozen in her grief.

Then as Mary stoops to look in again, two angels greet her. They glisten in white raiment, but they are not the true revelation. The true revelation is yet to come. Mary turns and sees a man who asks, "Woman, why are you weeping? Whom do you seek?" (RSV) Then Jesus speaks her name: "Mary." Instantly she recognizes him and cries out, "'Rabboni!' (which means Teacher)."

Jesus' resurrection is not an object of scientific proof; rather it is in the order of personal knowing. Jesus calls Mary's name, and she recognizes him. Her relationship with Jesus in life and death opens her eyes and her heart in faith to his resurrected presence. With our eyes we shall see him in his resurrected body. With our hearts we will know him as our Lord. And there will be no more tears, only joy. For he is risen! He is risen, indeed!

SUGGESTION FOR MEDITATION: "He [or she] who has it not cannot believe in it: how should death believe in life, though all the birds of God are singing jubilant over the empty tomb?" (from a sermon by George MacDonald)

Rejoice and Believe in the Resurrected Christ

April 5–11, 1999 • Nan Duerling*

"**Y**ou show me the path of life," writes the psalmist. These words express confident trust in God. Indeed, "there is fullness of joy" and "pleasures forevermore" for the one who takes refuge in God. The psalmist writes with the same fervent passion about God's ability to protect the faithful from the places of death—Sheol and the Pit—as John, Peter, and Luke will later write about God's ability to raise Jesus from the dead.

We can journey on "the path of life" too. Yet, like the author of Psalm 13 who had asked God how long he would have to suffer, we find this path is neither straight nor smooth in our own faith journeys. Challenges, grief, and pain often force us to wrestle with questions of belief. Does God really love me? Will God truly "protect me" ? Is God always "at my right hand," present in the most difficult moments of my life and as I face death?

The psalmist answers these questions with a resounding yes. Our loving God is present, faithful, and trustworthy. Belief in God is not a matter of agreement with theological or doctrinal statements. No, we take refuge in God because we have *experienced* the joy of close communion and fellowship. Consequently, our hearts are "glad" and our souls "rejoice." How does your experience assure you of God's saving presence?

PRAYER: Hold me close, saving God, for in you I experience the joy of life. Amen.

---

*Writer and editor of church school resources for denominational publishing houses; adult education leader, Linthicum Heights United Methodist Church, Linthicum, Maryland.

TUESDAY, APRIL 6 • Read Acts 2:14a, 22-32

Filled with the Holy Spirit, Peter preaches amazing good news to the Jewish pilgrims who have come to Jerusalem to celebrate Pentecost, an important feast day commemorating God's gift of the Law. Peter testifies that Jesus, to whose messiahship God attests "with deeds of power, wonders, and signs," has been raised from the dead. The apostle proclaims his message with eloquent boldness, for he has witnessed the event and cannot keep silent about God's unprecedented action.

Peter quotes Psalm 16:8-11 in his sermon (Acts 2:25-28). His source is the Greek translation of the Hebrew Scriptures, known as the Septuagint, which varies from the one we read in our Bibles. Peter notes that King David, who has been dead and buried for about a thousand years, had expressed in these verses a hope in a "Holy One" who will not experience the corruption of death. According to Peter's understanding of Psalm 16, David foresaw the Messiah's resurrection. Peter asserts that God raised Jesus up because death could not hold him.

What do you believe about Jesus' resurrection? During this Easter season, ponder how your belief informs and transforms your faith journey. Also consider the ways you share your witness about who Jesus is with others. Perhaps God has called and equipped you, like Peter, to speak courageously. Telling others about the Messiah is surely important, but faith in action is just as essential. The cup of water given to the stranger, the visit to the sick or imprisoned, and the meal served to the hungry evidence God's grace working through ordinary humans to witness to the love the resurrected Messiah has for all.

PRAYER: I give you thanks, O God, that you freed the crucified Jesus from death so that he might become the risen Lord in whom I hope. Amen.

The scene of today's scripture passage opens just hours after Mary Magdalene's announcement that she has seen the Lord. Night has fallen on Easter Sunday. Fearing for their lives, the disciples have locked themselves in the house. Their fears certainly are not unfounded. If Jesus had so threatened the religious leaders that they had turned him over to the Roman authorities for crucifixion, surely those same persons might be anxious to stamp out his followers. Even though Mary has reported Jesus' words to the disciples, they probably find them more mystifying than comforting. How can they understand what has happened to Jesus? We can only imagine the terror and confusion that races through their minds.

In the midst of their mental turmoil, Jesus appears to them. John does not explain how Jesus comes to them in a locked room; the importance of the "why" far outweighs the "how." Jesus comes to bring his friends peace and reassurance. He identifies himself by showing them his hands, which had been nailed to the cross, and his side, which had been pierced by a soldier's sword. This One who stands before the disciples bears the marks of suffering and is indeed the crucified Jesus. That they do not doubt. Jesus' tangible presence proves that death cannot hold God's Beloved.

The disciples respond with great joy. Jesus is alive! How do you respond to that incredible news? Where in your own life do you need the peace that only the Resurrected One can give?

PRAYER: Lord, let me hear the comforting words, "Peace be with you," as I confront the challenges of this day through the power of the risen Christ. Amen.

THURSDAY, APRIL 8 • Read John 20:21-23

Jesus again offers the gift of peace to his followers. Had Jesus stopped with this simple offer, the Christian life surely would be much easier. But Jesus continues, saying, "As the Father has sent me, so I send you." These words are much harder for us to hear. Jesus bears the marks of suffering and death because he was willing to be sent by God. If we are to be sent to others just as God sent Jesus, then we too must be prepared to suffer.

The good news is that we do not face the suffering and challenges of discipleship unequipped. John records that Jesus breathes on his followers and says, "Receive the Holy Spirit." Just as God had breathed life into Adam (Gen. 2:7), Jesus breathes new spiritual life into his disciples. John's account of the coming of the Holy Spirit differs from Luke's story of Pentecost in Acts 2, part of which we read yesterday. Yet the outcome is the same. The Spirit empowers people for mission and ministry. We go forth and serve God as new creatures in Christ. How has God called and equipped you to serve? To whom do you think God is sending you? How have you responded?

One way we serve is by offering God's forgiveness to others, just as Jesus forgave. After commissioning Peter to be the rock on which Jesus founded the church, he authorized the church to forbid and permit certain actions (Matt. 16:18-19). In John's account, the risen Christ calls the church to a ministry of forgiveness. As we go forth to minister, we take the gift of forgiveness with us. How do you offer this gift to others?

PRAYER: **Risen Christ, send your peace upon me this day that I might go out and serve you by the power of the Holy Spirit. Amen.**

Thomas the Twin certainly subscribed to the adage that "seeing is believing." John's Gospel does not explain Thomas's absence from the other disciples. All we know for certain is that he is away when Jesus comes. We can only imagine the disciples' mind-boggling conversation with Thomas when he returns after Jesus has left. Surely his friends give detailed descriptions of Jesus' words and physical appearance. They declare that they have "seen the Lord." Yet Thomas insists that he will not believe their reports. These eyewitness accounts do not persuade him. No, Thomas will have to see Jesus firsthand. Even more, Thomas actually wants to touch the places where Jesus' side has been pierced and nails driven into his hands. Then—and only then—will he believe that Jesus is alive.

A week later, Jesus returns a second time to his friends. The scene resembles the first visit, with one important exception: This time Thomas is present. Jesus invites Thomas to touch his wounds and "not doubt but believe." Immediately Thomas acknowledges Jesus as his Lord and God. He believes because he has seen unmistakable proof. Jesus, however, blesses those of us who will not have this concrete evidence and yet still choose to believe.

In what ways are you like Thomas? Must you see, hear, touch, smell, or taste before you will believe? If so, why do you think those sensory experiences make something "real" for you? What challenges do you face in trying to balance your need for "proof" with your willingness to believe by faith?

PRAYER: I believe, O God. Help my unbelief. Amen.

SATURDAY, APRIL 10 • Read John 20:30-31

As John draws his Gospel to a close, he announces his purpose for writing: "So that you may come to believe that Jesus is the Messiah, the Son of God, and that through believing you may have life in his name." This statement appropriately follows yesterday's reading in which Thomas declares his belief in the risen Christ, who in turn affirms those who believe in him. John tells us in verse 30 that his Gospel does not include everything he knows about Jesus. Rather, he has selected stories concerning signs that point to Jesus as the Messiah. Page through this beloved Gospel to recall passages that strengthen your own belief. John's Prologue (1:1-18) is a favorite among many Christians. So too are the records of Jesus' conversations with Nicodemus (3:1-21) and the Samaritan woman at the well (4:7-42). John paints unforgettable images of Jesus as the bread of life (6:48), the light of the world (9:5), the good shepherd (10:11), and the true vine (15:1).

Across the centuries, John's written word has fulfilled his purpose, for it has spoken to "those who have not seen [Jesus]" and called them to "come to believe." God used John's gifts as an eloquent author to bring countless numbers of seekers to believe in Jesus. What gifts has God given you to help others come to believe? Can you speak or sing or dance? Maybe you can teach a class or serve on a committee. Possibly you are gifted to see with compassionate eyes, hear with empathetic ears, and respond with a loving heart. How can you use your gifts to bring others to Christ, just as John did through his writing?

PRAYER: **O God, empower me to use whatever gifts I have so that others may come to believe that Jesus is your Beloved Son, the Messiah. Amen.**

SUNDAY, APRIL 11 • Read 1 Peter 1:3-9

"Rejoice with an indescribable and glorious joy, for you are receiving...the salvation of your souls." These words must have come as incredibly good news to the recipients of this letter, residents of Asia Minor being persecuted for their faith. The author reminds the readers that God has given them new life through the death and resurrection of Jesus. Faith is indeed tested, but hope comes in the midst of these crises and trials. That Christian hope, rooted in the resurrection of Jesus, becomes the act in which we recognize God's intentions for all who believe. We too will be saved, but we must believe. First Peter 1:8 echoes the theme of John 20:24-29: the importance of believing in the Messiah even though we have not seen him.

Although we live in this world as "exiles," God assures us an inheritance in heaven that is "imperishable, undefiled, and unfading." In short, nothing can destroy or damage that inheritance. We have experienced a "new birth" in this life because of our relationship with Jesus, but we have yet to receive our inheritance. In the meantime, God's power protects us through faith

These words sound reassuring—until real suffering comes our way. Probably we do not suffer because of our faith, but all of us suffer physical, spiritual, or emotional pain and grief. How do you understand and appropriate First Peter's teaching in your own life? Do you really believe that God will be present, protecting you until such time as you receive your inheritance of the promised salvation? If not, what does God need to supply to strengthen your faith?

PRAYER: **Your resurrection has blessed me with the hope of a new future, O Christ. I give humble thanks and rejoice. Amen.**

Easter Reflections

April 12–18, 1999 • John C. Purdy*

MONDAY, APRIL 12 • Read Luke 24:13-35

As we read today's passage, let us free our imagination and walk with these disciples on the road as they encounter the risen Jesus. We may discover that the disciples' encounter with Christ bears great similarity to our own.

Like those disciples whose "eyes were kept from recognizing him," you and I have no innate talent for receiving God's revelation. The Resurrection experience falls outside the apprehension of natural law. Our experience of the natural world may keep us from seeing the risen Christ.

Until someone has "interpreted…the things about [him] in all the scriptures," Jesus may remain for us merely an interesting historical figure. Our sophistication may hinder our recognition of the promised Messiah in a condemned and executed criminal.

And like those disciples, we need some physical sign to complement verbal and written testimonies to the risen Christ: the broken bread of the Eucharist, the feeding of the poor, the physical presence of the beloved community. We require visible signs alongside the word if we are to know the Lord.

In the richness of the Emmaus narrative, we must not ignore or forget these aspects of Easter. What we find hidden among the lilies is this central truth: Easter is not primarily about immortality or life after death; *it is the announcement of what God has done.* God raised Jesus from the dead; and God has opened our eyes, made good the promises of scripture, and given us signs of the divine presence.

PRAYER: God of all, open our eyes, minds, and hearts to the presence of Christ in every walk of life. Amen.

---

*Retired minister, Presbyterian Church, USA; member of First Presbyterian Church, Santa Fe, New Mexico.

TUESDAY, APRIL 13 • Read Luke 24:13-35

Luke's narrative of Christ on the road to Emmaus underscores a radical evangelical truth: *The goal of Bible study is the recognition of Jesus Christ.* Until Jesus "interpreted to [his own disciples!] the things about himself in all the scriptures," they did not recognize Jesus as "the one to redeem Israel." Jesus Christ unlocked for them their sacred writings, disclosing the meaning of Israel's history. We may find that Bible study that has a goal other than the recognition of Jesus Christ leaves us wistful and sad like the disciples on the Emmaus road.

But the converse is also true: The scriptures can lead us to the recognition of Christ! Reflecting on their experience, the disciples agreed: "Were not our hearts burning within us while he was talking to us on the road, while he was opening the scriptures to us?" Without the biblical witness, Jesus remains a mystery—shrouded in speculation and conflicting testimonies. Scripture can bring us to a recognition of Christ. Inscribed on the cornerstone of the Reformation are the words *Sola Scriptura*—"by Scripture alone."

The Emmaus narrative illustrates another Reformation fundamental: the priesthood of believers. Each needs the testimony of the other to discern Christ's presence. As Dietrich Bonhoeffer observed in *Life Together*, Christians need other Christians who speak God's word to them. They need the surety of another's faith to strengthen their heart in Christ. Every Christian must find a place for Bible study among the fellowship of believers.

Our hearts hunger for the presence of the risen Christ, a longing only Christ can satisfy. The Emmaus promise is that Christ waits to reveal himself. So we pray, "Break thou the bread of life, dear Lord, to me."

PRAYER: **Even as the loaf is broken for us in the Supper, O God, break open to us the blessed mystery of the scriptures. In Christ's name. Amen.**

WEDNESDAY, APRIL 14 • Read Acts 2:1-14*a*, 36-41

A layman who coaches preachers is a proponent of the cookie-cutter conclusion. "Sum up your sermon in a final sentence," he counsels. "Lay down the words of that sentence very slowly and very clearly—like a baker pressing cookies out of dough."

Read aloud, slowly and clearly, the closing sentence of Peter's Pentecost sermon: "Therefore let the entire house of Israel know with certainty that God has made him both Lord and Messiah, this Jesus whom you crucified." *That is the bottom line of apostolic preaching.* The risen Jesus is Israel's long-expected savior; more than that, he is the savior of the world.

But what are we to make of Peter's pronouncement that God has *made* Jesus both Lord and Messiah? Peter's statement contrasts human action with divine action: Humans judged Jesus to be a criminal and put him to death. God, by raising Jesus from death, declares him to be humankind's redeemer and ruler. The earliest Christian confession, "Jesus is Lord," roots and grounds itself in the experience of the Resurrection.

Peter's cookie-cutter conclusion reminds us that Jesus' ministry and his Resurrection are inseparable events. We cannot, as disinterested investigators, examine the words and works of "the historical Jesus" as we might the life and death of any political activist of the first century. "Therefore let the entire house of Israel know with certainty that God has made him both Lord and Christ, this Jesus whom you crucified." Those numbered among God's elect also bear responsibility for Jesus' death. God sent a savior; we killed him. But that was not the final judgment on Jesus. God raised him from the dead. Grace triumphed over sin. Can you remember the conclusion to last Sunday's Easter sermon? In what ways did it address God's vindication of Jesus as Lord and Messiah?

PRAYER: **Blessed are you, O God, who for our sakes opened the door to eternal life. In the name of Jesus Christ. Amen.**

Suppose that Peter—instead of being an apostle of Jesus Christ—was a messenger from Mount Olympus. The news that a divine being has been unwittingly killed by the populace would bring forth loud public lament. Cut to the heart, the people would wail, "What great sacrifice can we offer to propitiate the wrath of the gods?"

The listeners' response to Peter's Pentecost sermon is equally heartfelt: "Brothers, what should we do?" Yet Peter demands no act of sacrifice. Instead, he says, "Repent, and be baptized." How can repentance and baptism be a suitable response to the news that one has participated in slaying the King of Glory?

But Peter's message is not one of doom but of good news. God has triumphed over human depravity. God offers mercy, not punishment.

One Sunday morning my adult class discussed the question, Why did Jesus have to die? Members of the class held different theories. One woman referred to the story of Abraham and Isaac and the animal substitution for the son. The class leader vehemently declared that there never was a time when God was not forgiving. We all agreed on one point: All theories of the Atonement have as their bottom line the triumph of mercy over wrath. The guilty schoolchild holds out his hand for the teacher's punishing ruler. But the Christian believer holds out her hand to receive God's mercy. And with that same hand we hold out our children for baptism.

We assert that baptism is a sacrament. The secular meaning of the Latin word *sacramentum* refers to a soldier's oath of loyalty to the emperor. In like fashion, in baptism we acknowledge Jesus Christ as our rightful Lord.

PRAYER: Help us, O God, to open our hands and let go the guilt that so grievously occupies us. In Jesus' name we pray. Amen.

FRIDAY, APRIL 16 • Read 1 Peter 1:17-23

Some scholars think that First Peter is constructed of material that was originally a sermon. Not just your regular Sunday sermon, with three points and a conclusion—but a sermon delivered to new converts on the occasion of their baptism.

Certain phrases in 1 Peter 1:17-23 make that thesis plausible. We can imagine that Gentile converts living in the cities of Asia Minor had a great familiarity with "the futile ways inherited from...ancestors." Their joining the Christian community would commit them to living in "exile"—in the world, yet not of it. Like all newly minted Christians, they might need the reminder to practice mutual love.

However, 1 Peter 1:17-21 sounds more like a baptismal *symbol* than a sermon. The Apostles' Creed is such a symbol; and the words of 1 Peter 1:17-21 march across our consciousness like the phrases of a creed: "ransomed...with the precious blood of Christ ...destined before the foundation of the world...revealed at the end of the ages...raised...from the dead."

To appropriate these verses, we memorize them, learning them by heart. And then we recite them over and over, until—like the creed—they are planted deep in our consciousness.

The author of First Peter says that we are born anew of imperishable seed through God's word. The metaphor points to the new birth that faith occasions. As Jesus taught, the word is like sown seed, which—when it falls on fertile ground—brings forth much fruit. If we allow the Word to be planted in our hearts, surely it will bring forth fruit. And as the apostle Paul teaches, the first and most important fruit of the Spirit is love for one another—the "genuine mutual love" of which this letter also speaks.

PRAYER: Let our faith and hope be set on you, O God; and may faith and hope be joined to mutual love for one another. In Jesus' name. Amen.

SATURDAY, APRIL 17 • Read 1 Peter 1:17-23

A prominent image in many Holy Week hymns is that of the Lamb of God. Although rooted solidly in the biblical witness, the metaphor carries with it a danger. We might suppose that Jesus' death was like the killing of an animal as a substitution for our punishment. Many Christians find abhorrent the idea that God's wrath ever needed appeasement. A friend of mine quotes from Psalm 103 as a testimony to God's forgiveness throughout scripture:

> Bless the Lord, O my soul,
>   and do not forget all his benefits—
> who forgives all your iniquity (vv. 2, 3a).

First Peter speaks of Christ's death as "destined before the foundation of the world." That enables us to have it both ways: The death of Christ is a ransom for sin; even before there was sin, there was atonement!

The metaphor of the redeeming Lamb of God, who exists from before the foundation of the world, confronts us with the unimaginable and unthinkable. We cannot penetrate the mystery of God's eternal love and present it in precise formulations. Yet we cannot think of a time when the God who is our Creator was not also our Redeemer. And so we join our voices to those around the throne and sing,

> "Worthy is the Lamb that was slaughtered
> to receive power and wealth and wisdom and might
> and honor and glory and blessing!" (Rev. 5:12)

PRAYER: Blessed are you, O God, who forgives all our iniquity, heals all our diseases, and redeems our life from the pit. In Jesus' name we pray. Amen.

SUNDAY, APRIL 18 • Read Psalm 116:1-4, 12-19

During a twenty-four-hour choir retreat, we sang or read aloud sixteen psalms. We were led by the practice of the Benedictines who gather three times daily to recite from the Psalter. Those sixteen psalms touched upon most of the concerns and emotions common to human beings: peace, war, sorrow, death, poverty, aging, oppression, depression, joy, ethnicity—and many more.

We did not read Psalm 116. To avoid subjectivity in the choice, we selected the first and last psalms—and every tenth one in between. But like those others, this psalm touches on a common experience: The thought of dying terrifies the author, and he prays for deliverance. When the threat of death has passed, the grateful survivor vows to make a public show of thanksgiving in the midst of the congregation. The psalmist uses a liberation metaphor to describe God's deliverance: "You have loosed my bonds," a common Easter theme.

How many church members present on Easter Sunday returned the following Sunday to "offer to [God] a thanksgiving sacrifice and call on the name of the LORD"? Probably the returnee rate was higher than the ten percent of the lepers who returned to thank Jesus for their deliverance. But it probably fell far short of one hundred percent!

Might church attendance increase if we celebrated Communion the Sunday after Easter? The term *eucharist,* which we sometimes call the Lord's Supper, comes from the Greek word for thanksgiving. The Eucharist allows us to acknowledge publicly our gratitude for God's deliverance from death.

So often our kids ask, Why do we have to go to church anyway? Why not answer, To thank God for our deliverance from death. That might make them stop and think!

PRAYER: **Praise be unto you, O God, who has loosed the bonds of death through the resurrection of Jesus Christ our Lord. Amen.**

Our Way or God's Way?

April 19–25, 1999 • *Allan Waterson* *

Following

Today's scripture follows up the great events of the Day of Pentecost when the church's flags flew full mast. It was a real blowout: wonderful enthusiasm, altar call with thousands responding. But following that ecstatic event, the disciples face the routine business of running a church. They can't get stuck in the excitement of Pentecost; they have to get busy teaching, fostering friendships, communing with one another, and attending prayer meetings. In other words, they become obedient sheep who follow the inspiration of the Good Shepherd, while taking on the responsibility for shepherding the new and growing flock of Christians in their midst.

The disciples had dual roles: followers of the great "I AM" and leaders of new converts. They had to become students themselves, willing to be taught while devoted to teaching others. The burdens they bore and the stress they experienced in their new roles found perspective in the daily disciplines of prayer, sharing in fellowship together, and in the confession of the Holy Meal.

Those first disciples recognized the important of devotional habits in forming their lives as Christians. Praying together regularly contributed to the powerful witness of their lives and the dynamic nature of the early church. It empowered them to make a difference in the lives of others.

SUGGESTION FOR MEDITATION: **How may you become more intentional in your devotional habits? How are you allowing God's word to shape you? Seek God's direction as you pray today.**

*Senior pastor of Aldersgate United Methodist Church, Tustin, California.

TUESDAY, APRIL 20 • Read Psalm 23

Trusting

My favorite shepherding image occurred on the country roads of Scotland during my first visit to the land of my parents' birth. The plenteous gift of rain resulted in lush, green pastures. The ruddy complexion on the shepherd's face spoke volumes about his devotion to his sheep. That pastoral scene remains fixed in my mind as a Sabbath moment. I get that same sense of care and devotion when I read this psalm.

The Lord as shepherd conjures up pleasant images for me. But it also implies that I'm like a sheep! The pastoral scene of a Scottish countryside or the meditative image of Psalm 23 may dull our minds to the truth about this comparison, which is not very complimentary. We may even find it offensive.

Sheep aren't very smart. They wander into trouble and need to be rescued, led, cared for, and watched over. They get lost easily and are very dependent creatures. Who would want to be compared to sheep? Sheep really need a shepherd, but we're different!

We prefer to be in charge, self-reliant, dependent on no one for anything. Isn't that the attitude that really prevails in this world? Anything we need we can do for ourselves! And if we ever get stuck, help is as close as the volumes of self-help books that adorn our shelves.

However, the time comes when we realize our need for a shepherd. Some things we cannot do for ourselves! The night may be too dark to handle on our own. In times like these, we acknowledge our need for the nurturing love of the gentle Shepherd who anoints us with healing oil.

SUGGESTION FOR MEDITATION: Read Psalm 23 slowly. In what ways or areas do you need to be more trusting as you grow in your relationship with God?

Restoration

This shepherd's psalm presents God's loyalty and devotion to an individual sheep. That intentional caregiving goes so far as to insure that the sheep lies "down in green pastures," comforted with cool, refreshing water. The sheep finds itself restored to new life.

I couldn't believe my ears when the doctor said "cancer." Recuperation from surgery would take a month. My parched soul needed renewing. I had allowed the demands of ministry to take its toll. My rut had become familiar and far too comfortable. I had been grazing on parched land and drinking stagnant water too long. Now cancer had invaded my body.

While recuperative rest was forced upon me, I availed myself of the opportunity to lie down in God's pasture and feast on the rich banquet prepared for me. I drank from the cool waters of God's abundance. As I meditated on this psalm, I realized that God used this time for my healing to restore my soul, to renew my life.

Psychologist Erik Erikson defines adulthood as the developmental stage of generativity when we begin to wonder what we have to pass on to the next generation. Too often we discover generativity's opposite, which is stagnation. In stagnation, we do not fulfill our dreams, and we find ourselves involved in doing what we really do not enjoy or find rewarding. We're on life's treadmill, staying in motion without receiving life or giving it. We are empty.

In our emptiness, God calls us to a place of quiet to restore our souls. The place of quiet is safe and comforting. We vow to return often for refreshment and restoration.

PRAYER: Good Shepherd, take the stagnation of my life and make of it a resting place with you. Lead me to still waters that I may drink in safety. Amen.

THURSDAY, APRIL 22 • Read 1 Peter 2:19-25

Suffering

Today's scripture makes me bristle because it seems to condone abusive treatment of slaves. When viewed in its broader context, today's passage sets forward one example among three (2:11–3:7 examines the conduct of citizens, slaves, and marital partners) of the new ways Christians are to live and relate to one another in the world.

My ministry started in the 1960s, and I remember the young African-American pastor who carried a huge cross around our annual conference to remind us of racism's evils. That omnipresent cross stirred up a lot of emotion among the saints. And despite the suggestion from some scholars that New Testament slavery lacked the quality of racism, our historical knowledge makes it difficult to read today's text. And despite their context, these verses stand before us as part of the gospel with which we must struggle.

This text does not discuss the propriety of slavery, nor does Jesus deal with it in the Gospels. Here the writer of First Peter simply helps us understand the relevance of the gospel in the face of hostile circumstances. Now *that* understanding can speak to us. Have you ever felt powerless, impotent, or outcast? Are you in bondage to someone or something? Have you become weary waiting for the wheels of justice to set things right?

The good news is that God reaches out and touches all of us caught up in these conditions. Jesus' conduct during his Passion sets the example for all in situations of hostility. The writer's hope is that our faith may blossom even in the midst of persecution. May Jesus' example minister to us all, especially when we feel powerless, frustrated, or put upon.

PRAYER: May my suffering, O God, become a means of grace to strengthen me so that I may become a means of grace for others. Amen.

FRIDAY, APRIL 23 • Read 1 Peter 2:21, 25

Involvement

Yesterday's reading asked that we identify with slaves—the down-trodden, defeated or abused and those for whom life has been difficult. We acknowledged that God reaches out to us even under the most dire circumstances.

Identification with One who suffers, however, could give us cause to respond passively to the injustices of the world, to lick our wounds and accept the status quo. But if God is a just God, then injustice is not God's will. As Christ stood in solidarity with the defeated and oppressed as our "shepherd and guardian," we in the church can do no less.

The writer of First Peter reminds us: "For to this you have been called, because Christ also suffered for you, leaving you an example, so that you should follow in his steps." And at this point our commitment to Christ becomes more demanding. Following "in his steps" compels us to stand up and be counted, to serve as an advo-cate for those whose voice is not being heard.

Early in my ministry, I went to Haiti to "encounter mission." Nothing prepared me for this drastic introduction to poverty. My experience in Haiti quickly shattered my illusions about the poor and oppressed. These people needed a voice and a helping hand, not simply a handout. Grace Children's Hospital in Port-au-Prince serves as a monument to the work and involvement of many faithful Christians who chose to take a stand against the injustice of poverty. Sharing in this public health ministry has allowed me to follow "in his steps."

SUGGESTION FOR MEDITATION: **Which injustices of the world have you left unopposed and unaddressed? What are the sources of your discomfort? Where can you plug in so as to follow in Jesus' steps?**

SATURDAY, APRIL 24 • Read John 10:1-10

Obedience

The image of a caring shepherd who leads us through life provides comfort. As I write these words while vacationing under a peaceful Hawaiian sky, the news that one of my flock has taken his life radically shatters my serenity. I am reminded that life's pastures are not always pleasant.

Today's scripture affirms that God goes ahead of us and encourages us to follow as obedient sheep. Our Christian formation requires submission to God through obedience. The Good Shepherd "calls his own sheep by name." We know and are known. We recognize the voice of one we trust.

Occasionally our dark days mask the voice of God. In those times we may try to be our own shepherd, which results in further alienation, loneliness, and despair.

However, the discipline of obedience reminds us of that intimate place where, in times past, we have lain down and found nourishment. In the stillness we hear again the familiar voice of the Good Shepherd who leads us to graze in fresh pastures.

I have not experienced prolonged periods of God's absence in my faith journey. When God's voice becomes faint, usually I have wandered off to graze in a particularly appealing spot, a new "fast-food" diet that provides little spiritual nourishment and demands little personal discipline. Like a straying sheep, I finally look up and discover that I am all alone.

Nudged by the recollection of a more obedient season in my past, I know that I must cease my wandering and return to the fold. I have learned to listen, and I am not disappointed. I hear my name. The Good Shepherd gently leads me to communion with others. I willingly follow.

PRAYER: **Teach me to submit my will to you, O God, knowing you lead me. Amen.**

SUNDAY, APRIL 25 • Read Acts 2:42-47

Advocacy

The members of the new Christian community remain spiritually alert by devoting themselves "to the apostles' teaching and fellowship, to the breaking of bread and the prayers." The Christians gather often to share the sacred meal, thus reminding themselves of Jesus' sacrifice, the sacrifice that offers forgiveness and hope. This meal is central to their unity. Even today, breaking bread together is an intimate experience. As we ask God's blessing on our food, the meal takes on a sacred meaning.

In the early Christian community, any shared meal served to remind the Christians of God's vitality and life. Eating a meal or sharing the Lord's Supper brought folk from different walks of life together in Christian fellowship. The meal and the diversity of those gathered around the table reminded them in a tangible way that the God who raised Jesus from the dead also breaks down class barriers.

When Jesus stood in the synagogue and read from the scroll of Isaiah (Luke 4:18-19), he declared that he was anointed "to bring good news to the poor....release to the captives and recovery of sight to the blind." His ministry was bound up in his love for the poor. "[Jesus] had compassion for them, because they were like sheep without a shepherd" (Mark 6:34).

The model of the early church is a radical reminder that we must break down the walls of exclusion that separate us and become advocates for the poor. When we realize what we have received from God, that will not be such a struggle.

PRAYER: **Give me courage, O God, to be a voice for those whose voice cannot be heard except through me. Amen.**

Chosen for…

April 26–May 2, 1999 • Janet Wolf *

MONDAY, APRIL 26 • Read 1 Peter 2:2-10

In a world that pronounces so many of us "not good enough," what might it mean to believe that we really are chosen, precious, and beloved? In new members' class we talked about baptism: this holy moment when we are named by God's grace with such power it won't come undone.

Fayette was there—a woman living on the streets, struggling with mental illness and lupus. She loved the part about baptism and would ask over and over, "And when I'm baptized, I am…?" We soon learned to respond, "Beloved, precious child of God and beautiful to behold." "Oh, yes!" she'd say, and then we could go back to our discussion.

The big day came. Fayette went under, came up spluttering, and cried, "And now I am…?" And we all sang, "Beloved, precious child of God, and beautiful to behold." "Oh, yes!" she shouted as she danced all around the fellowship hall.

Two months later I got a call. Fayette had been beaten and raped and was at the county hospital. So I went. I could see her from a distance, pacing back and forth. When I got to the door, I heard, "I am beloved…." She turned, saw me, and said, "I am beloved, precious child of God, and…." Catching sight of herself in the mirror—hair sticking up, blood and tears streaking her face, dress torn, dirty, and rebuttoned askew, she started again, "I am beloved, precious child of God, and…." She looked in the mirror again and declared, "…and God is still working on me. If you come back tomorrow, I'll be so beautiful I'll take your breath away!"

PRAYER: Lord, baptize me in the waters of your grace that I might remember always who I am and the One to whom I belong. Amen.

---

*Pastor, Hobson United Methodist Church, Nashville, Tennessee.

TUESDAY, APRIL 27 • Read 1 Peter 2:9

We are chosen, beloved and precious in God's sight, *in order that* we may proclaim, talk about, witness to God's incredible grace and mercy. We are called and claimed *in order that* we may declare the marvelous acts of One who moved us from darkness into light. When folks look at believers, they know something about this wonderful love of God; look and see—among us, this motley crew of nobodies—signs of God's grace and glory here and now.

We can easily forget that we've been "blessed to be a blessing." We like the part about being chosen, but we often quickly assume that God has chosen us because we're wonderful. From that assumption, we easily become folks who make a list of those who are not as good as, worthy as, holy as we are. With that kind of thinking, we end up with churches singing "Amazing Grace" and then slamming shut the doors of hearts and minds and buildings to people from a different race, sexual identity, class, ethnic or educational background.

First Peter 2 sings this incredible song of grace and wonder: "Once we were nobodies but now we are God's somebodies. Once we didn't even know the meaning of mercy, but now we find ourselves immersed in the wideness of God's steadfast and never-failing mercy" (AP). And this is God's gift, which invites us to live into and out of God's good grace: to be the church, the body of Christ in and for the world.

PRAYER: Lord, remind me that we are chosen so that the world may see in us, through us, among us the light of your astonishing grace. May it be so!

WEDNESDAY, APRIL 28 • Read Acts 7:55-60

Stephen's eyes have seen the glory of God's resurrection power let loose in this world, glimmers of God's glory splintering the darkness. So he can live in defiance of death: loving in the face of hatred and anger, forgiving in a world hell-bent on revenge, testifying even while folks cover their ears and throw stones to silence his witness.

We too are Easter people, called to this subversive, transforming faith. In Acts, disciples are arrested for living out their conviction that resurrection is real. They face charges of turning "the world upside down," and their distinctive characteristics are their boldness and courage. They are Easter people, trusting in the Lord of life despite the powers of death and destruction.

Resurrection goes far beyond simply life after this life; it is life here and now, life not shaped, limited, or destroyed by the awesome powers of death. In spite of all that appears to be true, in spite of all who say they are in control, in spite of all the powers that be and their attempts to define who we are and how we live, Jesus Christ risen means we have been set free! The text invites us to live now as Easter people, folks who can move through the fear into the light of God's resurrection reality, claiming life in the midst of death, hoping in the face of despair.

Our congregation learned about living as Easter people from the children who showed up at our church—many coming without any adult, not having been part of a church before. The children—most of them struggling with poverty, racism, violence, and a school system that quickly writes them off—came dancing and dreaming, laughing and loving, singing and hoping. They brought with them their incredible capacity for joy and life, and they have taught us to be the church.

PRAYER: Holy and wonderful God, teach me to define my life not by death but by life in Jesus' name. Amen.

THURSDAY, APRIL 29 • Read Psalm 31:1-5, 15-16

Like Stephen, the psalmist moves through fear into the arms of God. In a time when life seems to be falling apart, when the soul seems almost silenced by incredible sorrow and suffering, the psalmist turns toward the God who waits with a grace that is always sufficient. The psalmist does not minimize the struggle but resoundingly affirms God's power and presence in the worst of times.

The psalmist sings of what God has done in the past, is doing now, and will surely make possible in the days ahead. "My times are in your hand!" Not in the hands of those who label me as an object of dread, a horror, a person to be scorned, but in the hands of One who is faithful and steadfastly loving.

In our congregation, the people on the edge—the homeless, those struggling with addiction and mental illness, those attempting to heal from deep wounds and a profound sense of "nobodiness"— have taught us how to praise God in good times and bad. Folks may be homeless, still struggling with poverty and racism, depression and underemployment; but they stand and praise God. They say thank-you for getting up in the morning, for being clean three days, for having a place where they belong. Every week folks share testimonies of God's work in the world, and the one giving the witness will declare, "God is good!" The congregation shouts back, "All the time!" Then the witness cries out, "All the time!" and we respond, "God is good!"

PRAYER: **Wonderful and gracious God, giver of life and all good things, teach me to praise your name in all times and places. In Jesus' name. Amen.**

FRIDAY, APRIL 30 • Read Psalm 31:1-5, 15-16

The psalmist leads the congregation in naming the hurt and celebrating the hope, in giving voice to the sorrow and struggle that might have silenced the singing of this song. The psalmist confronts the powers of death in the name of the Lord of life.

For a while, our congregation engaged in a fairly silent prayer time. Few people offered up either their joys or sorrows, choosing to keep those to themselves. But then the children came. "For what are we thankful?" I'd ask. And the answers would come tumbling out: "Trees, pretzels, flowers, birds, my shoes, sunshine, rain, sometimes my sister," and on and on until someone would suggest that we save some for next time.

As a way of really sharing our burdens and joys, we include an index card in each bulletin and invite folks to write down or draw pictures of celebrations and concerns. We gather the cards and then each of us takes someone else's card home so that we can pray each day for whatever is on the card.

One child, seven years old at the time, drew a picture of a boy lying on the ground with blood oozing out of his body; a young girl stood nearby with tears streaming down her face. As the girl offered up her card, she said, "I want you to pray for my friend who died and for me who almost did and for all the kids who aren't dead yet." She had been standing next to her friend when he was gunned down in the crossfire of a drug deal.

Like the psalmist, the child brought to God and to the church her hardest hurt and her deepest hope. That moment changed the prayer life of our congregation. It reminded us that the world waits for us truly to be the body of Christ in and for the world, engaging powers and principalities in the name of the One who came that all might find life.

PRAYER: Heal me, O God, that I might become a channel of healing for others. In Jesus' name. Amen.

SATURDAY, MAY 1 • Read John 14:1-14, focusing on verses 1-4

Jesus invites us home, believing there is room for all in the wideness of God's mercy. Would Jesus have told us if it were not so?

Our congregation was startled into the invitation of this text one morning during Easter baptisms. A young man, homeless, struggling with crack addiction and deep depression, hurting from old wounds of abuse and neglect, had gone through our new-member class to come to this moment. As he turned to face the congregation with tears streaming down his face, he whispered, "I always thought you had to die to get to heaven. But here it is; all I've ever wanted: a family that claims me, a place where I belong."

What does it mean to live out the love of Christ in a world where so many of God's children are hungry and homeless, uprooted and wandering with no place to belong? What does it mean to be the church, the body of the One who says, "There is room, a place, for you"? What does it mean to believe that God's powerful grace can create family from a group of strangers, community from isolated individuals?

Our congregation sees the sufficiency of God's grace every time we form our closing circle, hold hands, and sing "Shalom." For a moment we see a dramatically diverse community: black, white, yellow, red, and brown; old and young; rich and poor; gay, lesbian, and straight; folks who have been in the church forever and those brand new to the church; people with power and PhDs and folks who have never gone past the third grade; folks with two houses and folks living on the streets; and, as one person who struggles with mental health declared, "those of us who are crazy and those who think they're not." We are learning to dance on the common ground of God's most amazing and marvelous grace, accepting Jesus' invitation to come home.

PRAYER: Gracious God, thank you for being home for me and with me. Empower me now to become home for others. Amen.

SUNDAY, MAY 2 • Read John 14:1-14

This is one of the most beloved texts of the Bible, often used as words of comfort in funerals. And while the text surely offers comfort and healing words of hope, it also challenges us.

Jesus says, "You know the way...you've seen...so believe." The disciples respond, "We do not know...how can we know? We have not seen! Show us!" But Jesus is insistent, "You do know, you have seen, so believe! For you are called, not simply to follow but to do even greater things than I have done."

Rather shocking words, especially when most of us are in the same place as the disciples, arguing that we have not seen and we do not know, which is why we cannot quite believe. "To know" in the Hebrew sense of the word is to have an intimate relationship with. To know is not to accept an intellectual doctrine but to be immersed in the experience of this knowing, to have our heart and soul marked by the relationship. To know is to see, to recognize, become aware of and open to; thus, to believe, to live out the truth of what we know/see.

Today's text invites us to discover what God is already doing in the world around us; to come to know the God who loves, redeems, reconciles, makes new; and to live in the light of God's kingdom already breaking into this world here and now.

How might our worship and ministries change if we believed we were called to do all that Jesus did—and more? How is it that we are on "the way": becoming channels of healing and justice and hope, feasting with those who are left out, raising the dead, bringing good news to those worn out by poverty, setting prisoners free and breaking the yokes of oppression and injustice?

PRAYER: Holy God, set me free to be all you have called me to be. In Jesus' name. Amen.

A Post-Easter Perspective

May 3–9, 1999 • *David J. Lawson**

MONDAY, MAY 3 • Read 1 Peter 3:13-15

"In your hearts sanctify Christ as Lord."

Like the generation before them, the Christians of First Peter are under attack for adhering to a so-called "false religion." The persecution is beginning. Some say these Christians question the moral code of their culture. Others observe that they refuse to worship the Caesar. In this matter, Rome does not ask for much. Rome submits that they may continue to be Christians; they simply have to pay religious homage to the Caesar. Just a little pinch of salt on Caesar's statue or shrine and a muttering·of the words, "Caesar is Lord."

However, the Christians could not do this! Many died because of a little salt and those few words. They declared, "Jesus Christ is Lord, not Caesar!" Their declaration gave birth to one of the first Christian affirmations of faith: "Jesus Christ is Lord." They could have but one Lord. Any compromise at this point, no matter how empty the gesture, would strike a blow at the heart of their faith.

And we? Choosing Christ as the controlling center of our lives requires more than an intellectual decision or a guilt-ridden compulsion or a strong-willed effort to maintain control even in relationship with God. We belong to God; God does not belong to us. At the sacred center of our lives, we persevere in obedience to the will of God known in Jesus Christ.

PRAYER: **My Lord, in awe I hunger for a yielding of myself to you as I whisper, "Jesus Christ is Lord." Amen.**

---

*Retired United Methodist bishop, formerly served in Wisconsin and Illinois.

TUESDAY, MAY 4 • Read Acts 17:22-31

"I see how extremely religious you are in every way."

Paul waits for his traveling companions in Athens. While no longer at its political peak, Athens is still a center of learning and culture. Many shrines honoring Greek gods are scattered among its beautiful buildings. To avoid offending any god, the city has even erected a shrine "to an unknown god." The political correctness of such an action clearly indicates the extreme religiosity of the Athenians.

Some people say that our society is decidedly secular. If by "secular" they mean no affirmation with or participation in organized religion, then many in our society fall into that category. Yet a general spiritual hunger haunts us. The religious book market's expansion (angels have become a hot topic), rising coverage of religious issues in popular media, and the reappearance of values and ethics in college curricula indicate spiritual hunger among the populace. Many of us attach religious feelings and behavior to political positions, sports, and material acquisition. Even persons who vigorously deny the title "religious" do so with religious fervor.

Perhaps deep down all of us are religious. For a moment lay aside traditional beliefs and honestly consider what claims your highest loyalty. What guides your decisions and determines your use of resources? What gives meaning to your ordinary days?

I recently commented on the remarkable faithfulness of many African Christians. Despite poverty and danger, they hold to the faith and continue to worship God. One of them replied, "David, you live in the more dangerous place. Your people can desert the faith and assume it will cost them nothing."

You may be faithful, but in whom or in what do you trust?

PRAYER: O God, forgive me and help me. It is so easy to slide into faithlessness. Amen.

WEDNESDAY, MAY 5 • Read Psalm 66:8-13

"I will pay you my vows."

A few years ago, my wife and I spent a night in a Scottish bed and breakfast. Such a lodging! It was a small castle refurbished with style and furniture faithful to its ancient period. The new owner, a Scotsman from Australia, returned home after long absence. How does one make these arrangements from such a distance? He said he did it all over the phone: made the purchase, arranged for financing, contracted the reconstruction. He was never in Scotland until he moved home.

I, being an American, asked, "How is such an endeavor possible?" The innkeeper replied simply, "I am Scottish. Our word is our bond. If you cannot trust my word, what can you trust? A piece of paper would mean nothing."

With joy the psalmist promises to pay the vows he has made to God. A vow is an oath, a bond, promise, covenant, commitment, troth, or one's word. Our familiarity with vows includes their presence at our baptism, as we join the church, marry, pursue consecration to office and responsibility or ordination In holy settings we make promises to God.

Today review the vows you have taken, your promises to God. Find a copy of the wedding service, the ceremony of church membership or confirmation, the services of consecration or ordination. Remember not just the vow itself but its context: holy place, sacred space, holy ground. God present with us! Holy, awesome, mysterious, loving God! God known to us in Jesus Christ. We promised God we would pay our vows.

PRAYER: **Holy God, I meant those vows the day I pledged them. I mean to pay them now. Please help me. Amen.**

THURSDAY, MAY 6 • Read John 14:21-22

"They who have my commandments and keep them are those who love me; and those who love me will be loved by my Father, and I will love them and reveal myself to them."

Walking down the hall of the Christian education building one Sunday, I heard the voice of the fourth-grade teacher. This class had a reputation. Each teacher told the next of "trouble on the way." This skilled teacher was obviously losing it when she said in a loud voice, "You boys behave yourselves, or God won't love you." She knew better than that, but sometimes fourth-grade boys have a way of causing us to lose touch with our theology.

It is tempting to view today's scripture in that same deal-making light. With no effort at all, we can turn the message around until it says, "If you keep my commandments, I will love you. If you do not, I will not." Suddenly good news becomes bad news.

In this passage, Jesus tells us that our keeping of his commandments signifies our love for Christ, rather than being a precondition for receiving that love. "We love you, O Christ, and with joy and gratitude we seek to understand and follow your teachings. You have loved us, and now we offer our commitment to your Way as a grateful expression of our love for you."

So how do we keep Jesus' commandments? How do we exemplify our commitment to his Way? We become students of scripture. We worship in company with other Christians. We conference with others as we seek to expand our grasp of Christ's way. God's grace frees us to experiment, even to fail, in our hunger to be pilgrims of the Way. At the conclusion of each day we offer that day's discipleship to God with these words, "This day's life and yearning signify our love for you, O God."

PRAYER: God of love, I love you. I yearn to be your faithful disciple. Amen.

FRIDAY, MAY 7 • Read John 14:18-21

"I will not leave you orphaned; I am coming to you.... On that day you will know that I am in my Father, and you in me, and I in you."

We live in a God-saturated world. As Christians we affirm that we cannot go anywhere God is not. There is no circumstance where God is not present, no relationship where God is not active, no silence or privacy where God is absent. God's loving, forgiving, caring presence surrounds us constantly. This is love's gift. Herein rests the hopeful, liberating meaning of the Holy Spirit—the post-Easter power.

John 14 points to a mystical triple relationship: two persons of the Trinity and us. Mystery does not set easily with many of us, but Jesus does not invite debate. He declares a certainty. Notice his word choice: "I will not" (v. 18); "you will see me" (v. 19); "you will know" (v. 20); "will be loved by my Father" (v. 21); "I will...reveal myself" (v. 21).

God is actively present with us even when we are unaware of it. Wesley called this prevenient grace. Our spiritual hunger, our urge to search for God, to grope in the hope of finding God, is itself the action of God's Spirit within us. Is this presence burdensome? Only when we seek to escape God's call. It is a great relief to know that even our searching for God is really God's searching for us. God's love will not let us go.

PRAYER: O God of such wonderful love, even if I flee from you, you will not let me go. You keep me alive and will not let my feet slip. You constantly invite me but do not force me against my will, for you believe in me. With joy I praise your name. Amen.

SATURDAY, MAY 8 • Read 1 Peter 3:13-14

"Do not fear what they fear, and do not be intimidated."

To avail ourselves of this scripture's meaning, we must identify with the ancient ones. Because we may not explore fear in the abstract, allow me to mention some personal struggles. I have spent several months pondering the question: "Of what am I afraid?" I urge you to do the same.

1. *Am I afraid of failure?* I used to be, but my imperfect nature guarantees that I will fail often. Am I to live an anxious life, fearing failure; or am I to embrace God's grace and accept my failure as God accepts it?

2. *Am I afraid of facing my death?* Friends around this world regularly risk death as church leaders. Their confidence in the Resurrection has undermined my fear of death.

3. *Am I intimidated by the success and strength of others? Must they falter so I can look good?* No, I am to thank God and celebrate with them.

4. *Am I fearful for the well-being of my loved ones and friends?* Oh, yes, here it is. If any circumstance threatens to bring them harm or pain, I feel a knot of fear and a rush of anger or anxiety. My concern in this area severely tests my confidence in God's care.

Then these questions have come: Can you trust enough to release this special fear into God's care? Can you focus the energy this fear creates into creative action? Can you participate in creating a circle of shalom around those you love? around all others?

PRAYER: **With your help, O God, I will try to identify and face my fears. Use my fears to teach me. Prepare me to trust, for I am weak. Amen.**

SUNDAY, MAY 9 • Read 1 Peter 3:9-10

"Do not repay evil for evil or abuse for abuse; but, on the contrary, repay with a blessing. It is for this that you were called—that you might inherit a blessing."

Each of us has a vocation of blessing-giving. Every congregation is to be a center of blessing. Christ intends that persons receive blessing through their association with us. We are blessing carriers.

To give a blessing is to extend a gentle benediction to others. With compassion we pray for others even when their behavior is abusive. Said another way, we carry the "light of the moon." We are not the sun. We bear the healing warmth of the sun into the life of others. Post-Resurrection power energizes the followers of Christ to fulfill this role.

Jesus' instruction richly reflects this calling: Love even your enemies. Openness to God's forgiveness depends upon our ability to forgive others. We inherit God's blessing by carrying blessing to others. When we or our congregations forsake our calling as blessing carriers and focus only on ourselves, we turn away from God.

If someone asks, "Has God called you?" your answer is simple. "Oh, yes, God has smiled on me and made me a blessing carrier."

PRAYER: God and giver of blessing, teach me to repay with blessing. May I do this with a tender heart and humble mind. I freely confess that I can bless others only because you have blessed me. In Christ's name. Amen.

God's Reign, Our Hope

May 10–16, 1999 • Elizabeth Canham*

MONDAY, MAY 10 • Read Psalm 68:32-35

A former Archbishop of Canterbury once said, "When we act wisely, God reigns; when we act foolishly—God reigns!" The lectionary readings this week invite us to become more fully conscious of the powerful reign of God and to find our hope for faithful Christian discipleship in the assurance that God encompasses us with the undefeatable strength of love. Our own unwise decisions, the foolishness of warmongering nations, power-hungry oppressors, or abusive policy makers does not change this ultimate conviction—*God reigns*!

The psalmist calls upon all the nations to sing God's praises, ascribing power to the One whose majesty is over Israel and visible in the heavens. By implication, the chosen people evidence God's reign through the power and strength given them by the Creator. David, Esther, Jeremiah, Judith, John the Baptist, and the women who remained at the cross bear witness to that power and strength. And for countless others, their conviction that God reigns nerved them to stand firm for truth.

As you reflect on this psalm, I invite you to ponder a question: Where do I see evidence of God's reign today, and how may I make it visible through my words and actions? Most of us receive a call not to spectacular public proclamation but to living in such a way at work, in community, and with our families that we make God's reign known through our commitment to truth, justice, and compassion.

PRAYER: Be known, almighty God, in the wonder of creation and through the power of truth spoken by your people. Amen.

---

*Episcopal priest; founder and director of Stillpoint Ministries; author, teacher, and retreat leader; living in Black Mountain, North Carolina.

TUESDAY, MAY 11 • Read 1 Peter 4:12-13; 5:6-11

Writing to Christians experiencing persecution and hardship the author of First Peter offers a wonderful, reassuring promise that God will restore, support, strengthen, and establish them. Then he ascribes power to God, the One who reigns even in those times when believers experience the hostility of the world unleashed against them. Those who hand over their cares to God, knowing the embrace of divine compassion, have no grounds for anxiety.

The English mystic Julian of Norwich (c. 1342–c. 1416) lived in a period of darkness. Many came to her for the encouragement that the church did not provide. She spoke to them of God's love like a great cloak enfolding each one. "All shall be well," she counseled because God reigns. God holds the world, which owes its being and protection to endless creative love, like a hazelnut resting in the hand. Julian also spoke of Jesus as a tender mother, who feeds us from his own life energy, and assures that we will not be overcome.

Like Julian we are asked to wake up and see the reign of God in a power-hungry world that tries to deny it. Perhaps pondering something small like a hazelnut or remembering God's grace in the past will move us from anxious fear to hopeful trust. God waits to restore our faith; God promises to support us on our journey; God is ever ready to strengthen us for service; and God will establish us in the commonwealth of truth and love. God reigns!

SUGGESTION FOR MEDITATION: Pick up a leaf, rock, pinecone, blade of grass, or some other natural object. Meditate upon it, asking yourself, *How does this speak to me of God's reign?*

WEDNESDAY, MAY 12 • Read Acts 1:6-8

Questions fill the disciples of Jesus. After traveling with him, listening to him, watching him heal the sick and embrace outcasts, his death and the apparent triumph of human power devastate them. Then they begin to encounter Christ in Resurrection power. Two of them have met him on the road; twice the gathered disciples have experienced his presence as they met behind closed doors; and for forty days following the crucifixion they have come to an awareness that his word lives on. Now they want to know if he is about to restore the kingdom to Israel, and perhaps receiving no answer disappoints them. Instead of an answer, Jesus tells them to remain in Jerusalem until they receive the power of the Holy Spirit and then to go out as witnesses throughout the world.

All too often our questions seem to go unanswered while we wait for God to act. Many psalms express a human longing for answers: "How long, O Lord?" (13:1) "My God, my God, why have you forsaken me?" (22:1) We find it hard to be in the place of not knowing and to accept with patience the waiting time that precedes a new phase on our faith journey. At the beginning of a thirty-day retreat my director handed me a piece of advice offered by Teilhard De Chardin: "Trust in the slow work of God." I needed that advice as the retreat time unfolded and my initial enthusiasm began to wane. I have needed it often since: every time my demand for answers meets the invitation to be present trustfully in the waiting, no matter how uncomfortable it makes me. Believing in the gift of Spirit power to come fills the waiting time with hope.

PRAYER: God of grace, bless my waiting as I live with questions that slowly unfold into your time of empowerment and calling forth. Amen.

THURSDAY, MAY 13 • Read Acts 1:9-14
ASCENSION DAY

Only Luke records Jesus' ascension, mentioning it briefly at the end of his Gospel and again, with little fanfare, in today's assigned reading. The Gospel writer focuses less on the amazing event and more on its meaning for the church's future. The historical Jesus, crucified and buried, has become the risen Christ who now takes his place of authority where God reigns. Two men in white robes admonish his earthly followers not to stand gazing up toward heaven but to become the worshiping, witnessing community that continues to proclaim good news to all. At Pentecost the power of God's Spirit infuses them, banishing fear, uncertainty, and tentativeness. The church is born.

Back in Jerusalem the disciples and a number of women, including Mary the mother of Jesus, gather together in community as they await the day of Pentecost. This is a time of prayer, expectancy, and a reshaping of ideas and experience. During this transition time many things lack clarity, but great hope is growing.

We look back through twenty centuries of Christian teaching to these first believers and have difficulty imagining how unformed their theological ideas were. However, we draw encouragement from their commitment to one another as our experiences of Christ's risen power in the contemporary community of faith shape our own response to Christ.

Transition times plunge us into chaos and can be fear filled. Yet as we recall these stories of Christian beginnings and remind ourselves that God reigns and empowers us through the gift of the Spirit, our fear can become faith.

SUGGESTION FOR PRAYER: **Consider the transitions of your experience at this time and notice where God can turn your fear to faith through the power of prayer.**

FRIDAY, MAY 14 • Read Psalm 68:1-10

The theme of God's powerful, creative presence revealed through nature permeates scripture and is present in today's assigned reading. God "rides upon the clouds" and marches before the covenant people causing the earth to quake and the heavens to pour down rain to restore the land. We may see evidence of the all-powerful Creator by observing the marvels of the universe, but God is also intimately present among us as One who parents the orphan, protects the widow, gives a home to the desolate, and sets prisoners free.

When Saint Antony responded to God's call to embrace solitude and prayer, he climbed to a cave high up a mountainside in the Sinai desert. Asked how he would worship without the scriptures, he pointed to the landscape around him and said that this book would tell him all he needed to know of the presence and power of God. We all know that we are restored as we spend time by the ocean, in the mountains, by waterfalls, or where open spaces and the night sky fill us with wonder.

How does God show compassionate care for those who are poor and unprotected? Primarily this happens through the hearts and hands of those who have become the community of faith and respond to others out of gratitude. Saint Athanasius described Antony as "a physician given by God to Egypt" because those who met him grieving left rejoicing, the angry found kindness, the doubtful found peace of mind. Where might we respond to God's grace by reaching out to others who will come to know their belovedness through our caring?

PRAYER: **Loving Creator, open my eyes to see your hand at work in the world around me, and open my heart to embrace those who need your touch of healing, acceptance, and dignity. Amen.**

SATURDAY, MAY 15 • Read John 17:1-5

John's Gospel presents eternal life as a current reality for those who believe that Jesus is the Christ sent by God. Knowledge of God and of Jesus as the Christ inaugurates the new era in which fullness of life is given and God's reign made manifest. Those who receive Christ the Word are given power to become children of God (John 1:12). For them life is transformed as they become participants in eternal life, the *now* of God's reign.

Chapter 13 of this Gospel tells of Jesus' washing his disciples' feet, thereby teaching them that servant ministry and not domination must characterize their mission. Then, in the rabbinic style, he gives his final instructions and assurances to the disciples to prepare them for his death and to empower them to continue his ministry (chapters 14–16). In chapter 17 we listen in on Jesus' prayer to the Father, in which he hands over his work and asks protection for those who will continue the ministry. In this prayer of letting go, Jesus teaches that clinging to the past can hinder God's work as he models for us the importance of trusting others with what he has begun.

What is this the moment for? Be aware of your response to this question not only in life's big decisions but in the mundaneness of every day. Jesus lived in awareness of his "hour," the moment to act, the *kairos* time. He now says to his Father, "The hour has come." He is ready to relinquish his earthly ministry and enter into the glory that was his from the beginning of time. What is this the moment for in your life?

SUGGESTION FOR MEDITATION: **Take some time to reflect on the tasks and responsibilities you carry, and prayerfully consider what God is asking you to release.**

SUNDAY, MAY 16 • Read John 17:6-11

Some scholars have suggested that the author of John's Gospel has designed his account like a Jewish trial. The author gathers witnesses, tells stories, gives teaching, and presents evidence. He then calls upon us for our own, personal response to Jesus the Christ. Again and again, the narrative draws us in and invites us to participate in the reign of Christ which, as Jesus tells Pilate, is not of this world (18:36). As we believe, we become witnesses to Christ's power to transform human experience.

Today's passage tells of Jesus' praying for the disciples who will continue his ministry. He asks that God protect them and make them one with himself and the Father. Their source of strength comes from this intimate union; they are not alone in their proclamation of God's reign. A later verse particularly encourages those of us who continue to share our faith in Christ twenty centuries later: "I ask not only on behalf of these, but also on behalf of those who will believe in me through their word" (v. 20). Jesus prays for you and me, people who have believed through the word spoken by generations of Christians, and we too are gathered into that strong union with Father and Son.

Sometimes we may be tempted to think that if only we had been there, had seen and heard Jesus in the flesh, our faith might be stronger. Jesus revealed himself to honest, questioning Thomas and banished doubt from the apostle's mind. In his believing, Thomas received blessing, which made Christ think about us—those who have not seen yet believe. We are those for whom Christ prayed and to us belong all the blessings of the reign of God.

PRAYER: Father, I thank you for the strong union I share with you and your Son in the power of the Holy Spirit. Make me a living, faithful witness in the world that others may come to believe through my words and actions and, with me, share in your reign of love. Amen.

The Spirit of God

May 17–23, 1999 • Lamar Williamson*

MONDAY, MAY 17 • Read Numbers 11:24-30

Generous and free

The people's grumbling has worn out both God and Moses. In answer to Moses' complaint about them, God tells Moses to gather seventy of the elders of Israel and bring them to the tent of meeting. There God will "take some of the spirit that is on you and put it on them" (Num. 11:17) so they can share the burden of leadership with Moses. Eldad and Medad decide not to go out to the tent of meeting with the rest of the chosen elders, but God's Spirit comes upon them anyway. There they are, prophesying in the camp in the absence of Moses and the other elders—without permission. The people might well think that the mantle of leadership has passed to these two while the others are off at some meeting, indifferent to their plight! Isn't Joshua right to ask Moses to stop them? But Moses replies to his concern, "Would that all the Lord's people were prophets, and that the Lord would put his spirit on them!"

Joshua jealously guards Moses' position. Moses' generous reply underscores his genuine humility (Num. 12:3) as well as his true greatness—the greatest of Israel's prophets. More than revealing anything about Moses, this incident reveals something about God, whose Spirit "blows where it chooses" (John 3:8), choosing sometimes the most unexpected persons, times, and places.

SUGGESTION FOR MEDITATION: How do you feel when people point to evidences of God's Spirit at work in other denominations, networks, or parties?

---

*Ordained minister, Presbyterian Church, USA; Professor Emeritus of Biblical Studies at the Presbyterian School of Christian Education, Princeton, New Jersey; mission volunteer in theological education in Zaire, Africa.

TUESDAY, MAY 18 • Read Psalm 104:24-30

Creator Spiritus

Psalm 104 is a majestic hymn to God the creator and provider. Verses 24, 29, and 30 celebrate the Spirit of God as the divine agent in creating and sustaining the life of all creatures great and small, including human beings. "In wisdom you have made them all," "when you take away their breath, they die," and "when you send forth your spirit, they are created." These verses echo the opening verses of Hebrew Scriptures where we read that "a wind from God swept over the face of the waters. Then God said, 'Let there be light'" (Gen. 1:2-3).

One of the most durable hymns of the Western church is the prayer, *Veni Creator Spiritus*, "Come, Creator Spirit." Attributed to Rhabanus Maurus (776–856), deacon, teacher, abbot, and finally archbishop of Mainz, this hymn has served as a vehicle of grateful praise and prayer to the Holy Spirit for more than a thousand years.

The wind/breath/Spirit of God (three ways of translating into English the same Hebrew word) breathed and blew in the first moment of Creation. That same Spirit breathes the breath of life into every animate creature. When that breath/Spirit is withdrawn, they and we die, for it is in God that "we live and move and have our being" (Acts 17:28).

Christians did not invent the Spirit of God. At Pentecost, we join all creation to praise the Creator and to pray for ever new infusions of the Spirit's creative power.

SUGGESTION FOR MEDITATION: Spend at least five minutes in silence, listening for and breathing in the breath of God.

WEDNESDAY, MAY 19 • Read Psalm 104:29-34, 35*b*

Lord and giver of life

Bless the Lord, O my soul" is a cry of joyful gratitude that opens and closes Psalms 103 and 104. Psalm 103 celebrates the God who forgives sins. Psalm 104 praises the God who creates and sustains life.

But why is Psalm 104 the lectionary psalm for Pentecost, as it has been since early in church history? A phrase in the Nicene Creed provides the answer. In this creed we Christians affirm our belief in the Holy Spirit as "the Lord, the giver of life." This language applies not only to the Spirit's work as primordial giver of life at the Creation but also in giving the new life of the age to come to a diverse group of people on the day of the church's birth. The creators of the early lectionary saw a connection between God's gift of physical life at Creation and the gift of spiritual life at Pentecost. When liturgists read Psalm 104 at the celebration of Pentecost, the refrain chanted by the people was, "Lord, send out your Spirit and renew the face of the earth."

James L. Mays, to whom I am indebted, has expressed this connection well: "The Spirit of God is the source of life in every sense that the word 'life' can have" (*Interpretation Commentary, Psalms*, 337).

PRAYER: Lord, make your glory known now by pouring out your Spirit on the church and on me. Touch my life and make it glow. For all the times when I have felt the breath of your Spirit, praise the Lord! Amen.

THURSDAY, MAY 20 • Read Acts 2:1-13

Spirit of power

"**W**hat does this mean?" The astonished crowd in Jerusalem raises this question just fifty days after the Passover at which Jesus had been crucified. Certain noisy phenomena have erupted among a small community of believers in Jesus who are waiting in Jerusalem as Jesus had commanded them. The risen Lord had told his disciples to wait for "the promise of the Father...the Holy Spirit...power" (Acts 1:4-5, 8). Now, in the spine-tingling phenomena of rushing wind, fiery tongues, and the miraculous ability to speak about God in languages they had not learned, they recognize the presence and power of the Holy Spirit at work among them.

These phenomena amaze the devout Jews who have gathered in Jerusalem from all over the Roman Empire to celebrate the "feast of weeks" (Exod. 34:22). The bystanders don't know what to make of it, but they are curious and want to find out more. Others in the crowd, however, even in the presence of these powerful evidences of the presence of God, cannot discern the Holy Spirit. Their preconceptions readily provide another explanation for the evidence: "They are filled with new wine." Confronted with behavior that does not conform to traditional norms for the occasion, they can only scoff at these excited believers in Jesus. They go home that day unaware that anything special has happened.

God's Holy Spirit is one of power, but it does not fall equally on all. On that first Pentecost, the ones God's power transformed were those who were expecting something, though they didn't know just what form it would take.

PRAYER: Lord, sustain your church today by the same Spirit of power that gave it birth. Rouse us from our enslavement to routine, and give us eyes to see your Spirit's work in others even when their behavior seems inappropriate or bizarre. Amen.

FRIDAY, MAY 21 • Read Acts 2:14-21

Spirit of prophecy

"These are not drunk....No, this is what was spoken through the prophet Joel." With these words Peter begins the first apostolic sermon in Acts. The Spirit that empowered uneducated Galileans to speak foreign languages empowers this disciple who denied his Lord to proclaim to the entire house of Israel at the end of this sermon that "God has made him both Lord and Messiah, this Jesus whom you crucified" (Acts 2:36). The powerful Spirit of God is also the Spirit of prophecy: The Spirit moves people to proclaim the word of the Lord.

Peter takes his text from the prophet Joel (2:28-32). What Joel predicted for the distant future, Peter announces as present reality in an event that signals the inbreaking of the last days, the end-time fulfillment in the kingdom of God. God pours out God's Spirit on all flesh—old and young, men and women, slave and free, Jews and proselytes from all over the known world, and even Gentiles—on everyone who calls on the name of the Lord!

Pentecost marks the beginning of a mighty movement in which Christians take the good news of what God has done and is doing through Jesus Christ to the ends of the earth. This text invites its readers to believe the gospel and, inspired by the inclusive Spirit of prophecy, to proclaim it by word and deed to every living creature.

PRAYER: Lord, raise up Spirit-filled preachers in your church. Let me also by my eager hearing, glad obedience, and willing testimony be a faithful witness to your word. Amen.

SATURDAY, MAY 22 • Read John 20:19-23

Breath of the risen Christ

The account in John's Gospel of how the Spirit came upon gathered believers differs greatly from Luke's account in Acts 2. The writer of Luke separates the gift of the Spirit from the resurrection of Jesus by forty days, the time line enshrined in the church's liturgical tradition of Easter and Pentecost. John's Gospel never mentions the Feast of Pentecost at all. Instead, the writer tells how Jesus breathes his Spirit into the community of fearful disciples the evening of the day he was raised from the dead.

In Luke's account, the Spirit erupts in visible, noisy phenomena, while in John the imparting of the Spirit is as silent as a breath. Luke tells of the launching of a Spirit-driven movement based on the apostles; John tells of the creation of a new community based on the indwelling of the spirit of Christ. Both convey important truths about God's intention for the church.

In John's Gospel, the Holy Spirit is the breath of the risen, living Christ by which Christ lives in us and we in him. Here, Christ's gifts in and by the Spirit are peace and joy; the forgiveness of sins becomes the work of the entire community. The Spirit-filled community is to be Christ's presence in the world, a presence which is like light. To turn from Jesus and a Spirit-filled, loving community constitutes what the writer of John calls sin. Coming to the light of Christ in a Spirit-filled community brings peace, joy, and the forgiveness of sins. (Thanks to Gail O'Day, *The New Interpreter's Bible*, 9, 847.)

SUGGESTION FOR PRAYER: **That the living Christ will breathe upon the church and make of it his Spirit-filled community of love. That I, with all believers, may know the joy and peace of participating in Christ's presence in the world.**

Living water

In both Acts 2 and John 20, the Spirit comes upon a gathered Christian community. We may read these passages as addressed to the church as a whole. However, in today's text Jesus offers a sweeping invitation to individuals: "Let anyone who is thirsty come to me, and let the one who believes in me drink." Jesus here addresses a personal word to you and me, though not to us exclusively. The living Christ invites us to come to him for living water.

Jesus issues the invitation at the Feast of Tabernacles or Booths (John 7:2). At the Feast of Tabernacles, persons brought water from the pool of Siloam to pour on the altar as a reminder of God's provision for Israel during the time in the wilderness. Jesus uses the metaphor of water to speak of the Holy Spirit, which believers would receive later. The Spirit that the risen Christ gives to those who live in intimate fellowship with him is like water in a dry and thirsty land.

To this invitation Jesus adds a wonderful promise: "Out of the believer's heart shall flow rivers of living water." These words quoted as scripture in verse 38 do not appear in any single text from Hebrew Scriptures. They seem to be a composite of several texts that refer to life-giving water or wisdom or the Spirit. Elsewhere in John's Gospel the writer uses water to symbolize the life that Jesus gives (4:10, 14; 6:35), but only here does Jesus promise that the water he gives will also flow from those who believe in him!

PRAYER: O Holy Spirit of the risen Lord, come slake my thirst for God. Give me eternal life, and let it overflow from me into the lives of others. Amen.

Faithfulness to God, Creator and Redeemer
May 24–30, 1999 • *Walter Harrelson**

MONDAY, MAY 24 • **Read Genesis 1:31–2:4**

"God saw everything…[created], and indeed, it was very good."

Sometimes we overlook the fact that God's creation remains very good despite human failure and sin. Not even the terrible story of human failure and corruption that brings on the Flood (see Genesis 6) changes that great assertion. God's world gets bent and twisted, but it remains God's good world.

Much follows from this biblical truth. We may come close to despairing over a world that seems bent on violence. We may long for a return to earlier times when public and community life seemed safer. But God's word from Genesis reminds us that we live in a creation that God declares to be "very good."

Though we may not realize it, new kinds of failures as well as remarkable gains and successes mark our world. Even when older persons long for the good old days, they also recognize that life on the planet demonstrates movement toward what God intends for the world. Evil abounds, but good makes gains over evil throughout the world.

Our progress enables us to see just how bad things still are. Advances sharpen our vision of human failure and sin. But the progress exists—in race relations, in gender relations, in our readiness to share life and goods with our neighbors worldwide, and in our care of the creation.

PRAYER: Help me, O God, to watch for signs of the goodness of life in your world. And help me do my part to honor and cherish your good creation. Amen.

---

*Adjunct professor, Wake Forest University Divinity School; member of Southport Baptist Church, Southport, North Carolina.

TUESDAY, MAY 25 • Read Genesis 1:27

"God...created them; male and female."

God did not create some human beings inferior to others. What a marvelous truth from the Bible's first chapter! God creates male and female together. Even Genesis 2, which seems to place the male at the center of things with the female as his helper affirms the same truth. Both man and woman emerge in their completed form from the deep sleep that God brings. Both have responsibility for the garden. God walks with both in the cool of the evening.

God's first direct command is given to the first human pair: Be fruitful, multiply, and fill the earth. Human beings, male and female, are to nourish and cherish life on earth. They serve as companions, enjoying life with each other, ensuring that there is a next generation. In fact, every couple has responsibility for the next generation, whether they have children of their own or not. This responsibility for the next generation extends to all persons— couples or singles.

"Be fruitful!" Human life bears fruit in many ways through acts of love, thoughtfulness, and tenderness. The Gospel of John calls all followers of Jesus to bear much fruit (John 15). Companionship with a loved one makes life fruitful, and companionship with our Creator and Redeemer enables us to fulfill this first biblical command.

Small wonder that David can cry out, "I love you, O Lord, my strength" (Ps. 18:1). God created human beings for love and for sharing life to ensure a future.

PRAYER: I thank you, loving God, for the companionship of loved ones that enriches my life so deeply. And I praise you that you have entered my life with such power and blessedness in Jesus Christ. Amen.

WEDNESDAY, MAY 26 • Read Genesis 1:27-28

"Subdue [the earth]."

What a remarkable command God makes here! God creates human beings in God's image and likeness. These human beings share life with God and are God's special companions. However, their creative power differs from that of God the Creator, even though God commands them to subdue the earth. Human beings enhance the creation, not redo it. That difference is immensely important.

Sometimes today we see only the damage that human civilization wreaks on the creation: the alarming destruction of the rain forests, the pollution of streams and air and earth, the disfigurement of landscape, and the clearing of forests. We forget that God "commands" human beings to enhance the creation, making it even more productive of human life than it has been. Human beings discover cures for diseases, learn about possible life on other planets, break the genetic code. All the passions of human beings to know, to understand, and to see more deeply stem from our Creator's having created us with the urge and the ability to subdue the earth. We not only damage the creation; we also enhance it, enabling creation to serve more fully God's intended purposes.

Why can't we commit ourselves to enriching life rather than exploiting and damaging life? This question haunts every generation. Perhaps we underestimate the value of our lives as God's creation. We fail to recall or understand that God counts on human beings to care for the earth and for one another. We might begin each day with the question, "What will I do today to make God's world safer, more productive of good, and more beautiful?" Responsible life in community is not just a good thing; it is what God commands of every human being in creation.

PRAYER: Teach me, O God, to love your creation as you love it and to care for it as you have called me to care for it. Amen.

"Out of the mouths of babes and infants"

We often use this line from Psalm 8 to comment on remarkably wise or clever things that children say. The quotation means much more. Psalm 8 presents human beings as charged by God to exercise rule over the whole of God's creation, just as Genesis 1 does. And the psalm suggests that the power of human beings to do so comes from one special divine gift: human speech.

Human beings can speak. Even babies babble before they can speak, and their babbling reminds us of what lies ahead for them. One day they will be able to express love, say clever things, share their thoughts and ideas. And one day, of course, they will be able to lie, to hide their feelings, to mislead, to hurt and destroy—also through the gift of speech.

Speaking is the bulwark against one's foes to which the psalm alludes. Speaking can bring order, beauty, insight, and judgment into the world, for speech embodies our very world. But polluted, unfaithful, or self-serving speech can bring disorder, foulness, and shame to God's universe. The speech of babes and infants reminds us that God intended the gift of speech to help human beings rule over God's creation. Babies don't yet lie or deceive or curse or wound others; they only experiment until speech begins to take orderly shape. But the day will come!

PRAYER: O blessed God, I thank you for the gift of speech and for thought, feeling, and judgment. Help me use my gift of speaking to bring hope, help, and healing to your world. Amen.

FRIDAY, MAY 28 • Read Psalm 8

"How majestic is your name!"

Psalm 8 praises God, not human beings, though it marvels that God has made us but a little lower than divine beings. Actually the psalmist praises God's name. Why single out God's name for praise? Surely because human beings can name God's name, can call the deity by a personal name, and in that intimate way enter deeply into the very life of God.

Psalm 8 lifts up the mystery of human speaking. The most marvelous use of the human voice is to name God's name, to praise and adore God, to pray. We can and do talk with God, hear and feel God's responses to our speaking, and continue the conversation in prayer. Our ability to name God's personal name makes that speaking ever so personal and intimate. Who disclosed this personal name to Moses? God did on the sacred mountain, first in the encounter at the burning bush (Exod. 3:14-15) and then atop the mountain in intimate conversation with Moses (Exod. 33:17-23; Exod. 34:5-7). The Christian's most intimate name for God is Jesus.

Worship of God, then, offers us the best possible way to exercise dominion over the whole of God's creation. We care for earth, seek out earth's mysteries, pass on our learning to the next generation. We also name God's sovereign name in prayer and praise and thereby claim the whole of the universe for its Creator and Redeemer. Prayer is, by its very nature, evangelism.

PRAYER: How I thank you, God, that you hear my prayers, honor my labors, and let me share the depths of my life with you in Jesus Christ. Amen.

SATURDAY, MAY 29 • Read Matthew 28:16-20

The closing lines of Matthew's Gospel have rung in the ears of countless Christian missionaries who have carried the good news literally to the ends of the earth. The risen Jesus reminds his disciples that the authority God conferred on human beings at Creation has now been claimed and exercised in his own life, teaching, suffering, death, and resurrection. Jesus now entrusts this authority over heaven and earth to his disciples. They are to teach the people of the nations what it means to be children of God, what it means to live as God's people in God's world. They are to baptize, lay out God's demands and God's promises, and offer confident hope in God to all who will hear and heed.

Making disciples of the nations means much more than warning them of the consequences of sin and urging them to come to God in repentance. Disciples of Jesus share fully in God's authority entrusted to Jesus and intended for every human being. We claim our place in God's good creation, acknowledge what it means to be a human being created in God's image, and tell our neighbors and all we meet of our joy in sharing life with our Creator and Redeemer.

This good news has no place for the crippling fear of a stern Judge. The text invites the entire human community to share in God's rich gifts, prepared from Creation for all. God's purpose from the beginning is clear: renewal of individual life in God's love and forgiveness, responsible citizenship in God's world, a community of believers who support and care for one another, and living out together the life God purposes for all human beings.

PRAYER: Help me, God, to share the good news with my neighbors and strangers alike. Amen.

SUNDAY, MAY 30 • Read 2 Corinthians 13:11-13
TRINITY SUNDAY

Paul closes this second letter to the Corinthian church with a trinitarian blessing, speaking of the grace of Jesus Christ, of God's love, and of communion in the Holy Spirit—a good text for Trinity Sunday. In time, the early church will develop a specific doctrine of God as Triune, a doctrine affirmed in worship and word on Trinity Sunday.

The doctrine of the Holy Trinity, like all central Christian teachings, seeks to express the actual beliefs and experiences of the Christian community. Is not our experience of God wonderfully well captured by reference to Creator, Word, and Spirit or Father, Son, and Holy Spirit? We know God as the Creator and the Sovereign of history and nature. We know God as intimately present in the life of human beings created in God's image and as powerfully and uniquely present in the incarnate Jesus of Nazareth. And we also know God as present in the community of believers through the ages, present as Person and as Spirit and Life-giver. Ancient Israel knew much of this reality as well, even as it affirmed the oneness of God.

While Christians acknowledge our understanding of God's relationship to us in three ways, we also affirm God's oneness as strongly as do Jews and Muslims. This One God is sovereign over the entire creation; and wherever people worship God, it is the One God we worship—whatever names we may use. How the assurance of divine love, known through Jesus' cross and resurrection, blesses us! And what a delight to share life in the Spirit, individually and as a community, day by day, acknowledging our unity as a people in the One God!

PRAYER: I worship and adore you, Creator, Savior, Spirit, for in you I find my life, my purpose, and my most sublime joy. Amen.

Conversations with God

May 31–June 6, 1999 • *Benoni Silva-Netto* *

MONDAY, MAY 31 • **Read Genesis 12:1-9**

Abraham has an interesting conversation with God and receives both a problem and a promise. The problem: How can he leave the place that has become so much a part of him for about seventy-five years and go to a strange land where uncertainty and anxiety shrouds the future? God asks him to leave his family, abandon the comfort of the familiar, and free himself from dependency upon the secure and stable so he can follow God's call.

The promise: God will make him a great nation; Abraham will be blessed; and through Abraham God's blessings will reach all the people on earth. While being chosen for a special purpose is always a privilege, awesome responsibility accompanies privilege.

I have never ceased to be amazed at the many fascinating ways God talks to us. Our worship experience on Sunday morning and on other occasions can become a place of conversation with God. When we share openly and listen attentively, offer generously and receive gratefully, any aspect of our lives can become a genuine conversation with God. We hear the invitation and respond with enthusiasm.

My most meaningful worship experiences come at those times when my conversation with God reaches the level of genuine intimacy. Then my spirit is open to hear the problem of God's call to me as well as the promise of God's blessings for me.

PRAYER: May I find joy in my intimate conversation with you, O God, so that my ears may listen to the soft whisper of your calling to some special purpose in life. Amen.

---

*Pastor of Grace United Methodist Church, Stockton, California; Professor of Pastoral Care and Counseling at American Baptist Seminary of the West and Graduate Theological Union in Berkeley, California.

TUESDAY, JUNE 1 • Read Psalm 33:1-3

The Book of Psalms is a compilation of songs and hymns used in worship at the Temple. David, to whom many of the psalms are attributed, had some rough times in his relationship with God. The Book of Psalms reflects those rough times, acknowledging profound human passion as well as an understanding of who God is and how God deals with us. Essentially, we might consider Psalms the individual's conversation with the Divine. The conversation is genuine, candid, sincere, and honest.

The psalmist suggests that one way we commune with God is through song. Persons often refer to music as the language of the soul, a channel through which we express our emotions and passions, our joys and our pains, our laughter and our tears, our hope and our despair, our fears and our faith.

I suspect that the different cultures in the world have unique ways of singing love songs. If we could count all the love songs written and sung through the years, we could affirm the fact that God has set within the heart of every human being a need to love, to be loved, and to articulate that love through music.

The psalmist encourages us to sing a new song to God. People of a particular culture or community of faith generate songs that express their experience. And songs emerge from our personal experiences and the unique circumstances of our individual lives. Our songs can reflect both the tradition of the past and the vision of tomorrow.

Our songs for God in our worship may open for us the ancient pages of history, recalling what God has done; they may also empower our journey toward the future as they remind us of what God continues to do.

PRAYER: **May I sing your praises, O God, from the depth of my soul, from the inner chamber of my heart, from the sacred corridors of my spirit, from the cloistered spaces of my consciousness. Amen.**

WEDNESDAY, JUNE 2 • Read Psalm 33:4-12

The stretch of highway that connects the city of Stockton to the San Francisco Bay area offers fascinating scenery. By now the farmers have finished plowing the fields and planting their crops; the brown tapestry has given way to the verdant colors of asparagus, tomatoes, onions.

The one-hundred miles of delta river slithers through the farms like a restless snake; fisherfolk, boaters, swimmers, and campers return as the warm summer wind thaws the cold of winter. Various birds take sanctuary in the delta marshes and cavort above the vast carpets of green.

As I drive this highway every week, a magnificent work of art unfolds before my eyes, as though a giant painter has taken the skies for her canvas and is painting a picture that constantly changes from dawn to dusk. With the sun as her brush, the artist paints changing shapes and colors of the clouds in the sky that portray an awesome and magnificent masterpiece no human artist could rival. The scene calls to mind the psalmist's words about God's creation of the sky, and God's breathing into being the stars. One can picture the Creator embracing the waters of the deep and gathering them "into a heap." Surely all the earth should worship the Lord!

I first discovered worship through nature in my youth as part of our youth fellowship activities. We would gather by the hillsides or along the beach or within the woods and spend the first portion of the worship service in silence listening to sounds of nature. We assumed that God would speak to us through the created world. It took me awhile to understand this concept, but now I cherish my time alone with God in the midst of nature.

PRAYER: Listen, Lord, the birds sing their praises and the gentle breeze whispers its prayer to you. May my heart fill to overflowing with the sounds of laughter, and may my spirit cry out with shouts of joy with the thunder and the rain. Amen.

THURSDAY, JUNE 3 • **Read Romans 4:13-25**

Nature offers many fascinating and awesome miracles. A small seed planted in the ground dies. After a number of days, a seedling pokes up. It sprouts leaves and branches and eventually becomes a tree.

Although the leaves of the trees of the Midwest explode with awesome colors during the fall, they all dry up and fall to the ground in winter. The trees seem to die. A friend pointed out a black oak tree whose dead leaves clung tenaciously to its branches even through the harshest winters, through the coldest of blizzards or ice storms. He told me to observe the black oak through the coming of the spring: New leaves shot out from deep inside the tree and pushed out the dead leaves that winter had failed to remove. Spring provided the stage for the unfolding drama of the renewal of nature.

When Paul talks about Jesus' being given to die for our sins and being raised from the dead to make us right, I remember those dead leaves of the black oak tree. Even nature declares God's promise of new life for us. Using this metaphor, we may consider Abraham at one hundred to be in the winter of his life. We see no hope for him and Sarah to have children. But God keeps God's promise to Abraham through the birth of their sons.

Through the death and resurrection of Jesus we realize that God has broken through the dark night of human history and has given us a sure sign of God's faith in and high purpose for our humanity. Although we experience many tragedies and misfortunes, we have the assurance of God's promise that the dawn of a new morning surely will break upon our lives. We can renew our excited and faith-filled anticipation of the coming of God's kingdom.

PRAYER: May I, like Abraham, grow stronger in my faith and give you praise, O God, as I continue to trust that you are able to do what you have promised. Amen.

FRIDAY, JUNE 4 • **Read Matthew 9:9-13**

Throughout the Gospel stories, Jesus calls people to follow him. Those who do experience a radical transformation of their lives. The blind receive sight; the hungry are fed; the leper finds cleansing; the demoniac discovers peace; the Samaritan woman receives living water; the woman caught in adultery accepts forgiveness; and the lost, the last, and the least find abundant life. All inherit eternal life while gaining a sense that their lives have profound meaning in the here and now.

Matthew, an ordinary man engaged in the ordinary business of making a living, has a serious conversation with Jesus. The Lord makes him an offer, and he accepts. His life is transformed.

An organist of a huge cathedral in Germany was practicing alone in the sanctuary when a stranger came in, waited for a while in the aisle, and then moved toward the organist. He asked if he could play the organ. The organist, quite protective of his precious instrument, ignored the request. At intervals the stranger repeated his request. Reluctantly, the organist gave in. The stranger sat on the stool and began to play. Immediately, music greater than had ever yielded before burst forth. It shook the foundation of the building. It awakened sleeping choirs of angels. The stone pillars shouted aloud their praises. The sweet notes of the music filled the cathedral and dwelt in every hollow of the branching roof. And as the melody died away, the organist who was profoundly touched seized the shoulder of the stranger and asked, "Who are you?" The stranger replied, "I am Mendelssohn." "And to think," said the organist, "that I nearly refused to allow you to play my humble instrument."

Accept God's opportunities and open yourself to new possibilities.

PRAYER: **Enter my life, Lord Jesus, and play your music that the grieving may hear it and find comfort; the restless may experience peace; the bitter and the angry may know love, compassion, and forgiveness. Amen.**

SATURDAY, JUNE 5 • Read Matthew 9:20-22

Her illness has chained her to a life of pain and discomfort. She has been sick for twelve years, and none of the physicians in her community can make her well. What a profound sense of powerlessness! Some of us can empathize, knowing what it means to be powerless in the face of illness or death or other misfortunes. Depression sets in, and some of us become miserable enough to consider desperate measures.

Out of her genuine faith the woman decides, "If I only touch his cloak, I will be made well" (Matt. 9:21). Jesus sees the woman, perceives her faith, makes her whole. Her brief conversation with Jesus changes her life.

Notice the interrelationship between the physical and the spiritual dimensions of life in achieving healing and wholeness. Often we find the source of physical illness in the realm of the spirit, the place in our life where we struggle with the issues of meaning and values, ultimate and significant concerns, and our relationship with God and other human beings. At the same time, the spiritual dimension of our life can provide the resources for dealing with our brokenness and disease.

The practice of counseling has been referred to as healing conversation. Many of us long to be heard, and we seek people and places for expression of our thoughts and feelings, of our profound emotions that normally lie below our surface presentations to others. In my experience, when persons realize that they have been truly and genuinely heard, they weep for joy; they sense their release from the prison of loneliness; they experience wholeness. May our conversations with God bring us such joy, release, and wholeness.

PRAYER: Touch me, O Lord, at the points of my deepest need that I may experience the power of your presence and the gentle embrace of your grace. Amen.

SUNDAY, JUNE 6 • Read Matthew 9:18-19, 23-26

The words of the synagogue leader reveal both the pain of grief and the hope for life. He says to Jesus, "My daughter has just died; but come and lay your hand on her, and she will live (Matt. 9:18). When death enters the house of this man, he comes face to face with the reality of his own powerlessness and the depth of his sorrow. When Jesus enters his house, the synagogue leader experiences the power that vanquishes death.

We know death as a present reality that hovers over us like a sword. It can come upon us as gently and silently as the whisper of an evening breeze or as loudly and frantically as the sound of galloping horses from the distant plain. And when it comes, death shocks us, shakes us, shatters us.

To his disciples, Jesus' death on the cross must have been God's broken promise, a horrible end to a failed mission. They could do nothing but pick up their lives and shattered dreams and walk back into endless despair and shadowed loneliness. And they did that until the risen Lord came back into their lives.

Persons have different experiences of death: misfortunes and failures, broken relationships and emotional pains. These "death" experiences may convince us of God's abandonment. But God wants the conversation to continue—even as we walk through the valley of the shadow of death.

A tour of the Holy Land some years ago led me to meaningful places in Jesus' life and ministry. The meaning of Jesus' journey to Calvary touched me deeply. Death remains an inevitable reality for us, but God assures us that no evil is powerful enough and no hate bitter enough to separate us from God's love.

PRAYER: **You walk the dusty roads of our lives, risen Lord. I know you have the power to open my eyes to a world of wonder and to heal the hurts of my life. Amen.**

Prayers, Promises, and Action

June 7–13, 1999 • *Harriett Jane Olson**

MONDAY, JUNE 7 • **Read Genesis 18:1-15**

Abraham and Sarah have trusted God long and often in the many decisions of their lives. They have moved from the land in which Terah settled, dealt generously with Lot, and followed God's instructions regarding worship. Abraham has also heard the word of the Lord: He will be the father of a great nation. Since Sarah does not conceive, Abraham makes various arrangements to ensure the promise's fulfillment.

In today's text, Abraham extends lavish hospitality to three men who give no account of themselves at all. They appear to have neither baggage nor retinue, but Abraham treats them with great courtesy all the same. In so doing, Abraham extends the hospitality practices of this nomadic people. He also opens himself to hear God's word spoken by these visitors. By taking the servant role (in this passage he refers to himself as such, and in the next section he actually serves them), Abraham accords his visitors the sort of respect that allows him to hear their later confirmation of God's promise to Abraham.

The text alternates between "three persons" and the use of the singular ("Lord") in reference to the visitors. At some point in the conversation, Abraham appears to recognize this event as a divine visitation. Perhaps we too might experience insights into the divine will if we learn to respect one another and listen deeply enough.

SUGGESTION FOR MEDITATION: **Think of times in your life when listening to a stranger (or perhaps a marginalized person) allowed you to hear God's promise.**

---

*Vice President, Editorial Director, and UMC Book Editor of The United Methodist Publishing House; associate member of McKendree United Methodist Church, Nashville, Tennessee.

TUESDAY, JUNE 8 • Read Matthew 9:35–10:8

This Gospel lesson pictures Jesus going about, teaching and healing. The disciples accompany him, watching the work and hearing the word. We glimpse Jesus' response to what he saw—"he had compassion." He mourns the "harassed and helpless" state of the people who crowd around him seeking the good news and healing. In the face of this need, Jesus calls the disciples to himself and instructs them to pray for additional workers.

How often have you lifted someone up in prayer, only to find that through some action of your own, you became part of the answer to your own petition? This is the disciples' experience in this story. Jesus commissions them to minister in the same style of service they have observed in his life among them: proclaiming the gospel and healing. Then he sends them out.

Jesus gives the disciples authority to take up the work of healing and instructs them to go to their own people and to the outcasts— the sick, the lepers, the demon-possessed. From stories of Jesus' healing we know that this activity often involved touching the sick person in some way, thereby violating all sorts of taboos and religious and cultural boundaries. This work of healing is not a quiet and uncritical exercise of the healing arts. This work pronounces judgment on the society that has produced the amalgam of disease and isolation and involves a degree of political and cultural risk that might give one pause. We also are called by name, through the sacrament of baptism, to be engaged with God in God's gracious work.

SUGGESTION FOR MEDITATION: **Think about the persons for whom you are praying. In what way do you sense a call to be part of the answer to prayer? What taboos are holding you back?**

WEDNESDAY, JUNE 9 • Read Matthew 10:9-23

Warnings, comfort, and direction. Just what you would expect from a family member or friend if you were to set off on a dangerous errand. This instruction is what Jesus provides in these verses to the newly called and commissioned disciples—and to us. As the warnings in this text indicate, the Gospel writer had in mind at least two time frames—the pre-Easter setting of the story itself and the post-Easter response to the Great Commission. As our post-Easter work on the Great Commission continues, this sobering depiction of the demands of discipleship is equally instructive to all of us who are called (by our baptism) and sent.

By telling the disciples not to take extra provisions Jesus reinforces their need to depend on God's power and care. He sounds the same note in verses 19-20 when he assures them that "the Spirit of your Father" will provide their words of defense. We might consider what things make us feel strong and "in control." Are they things like salary, health insurance, pension, or perhaps owning a home or a car or having a certain amount in savings? Is it possible that these things keep us from realizing our utter dependence on God and therefore limit our growth? Perhaps freedom from all possessions is not required to convince us at the deepest level of God's faithfulness and our dependence, but we may need to dismantle the illusion of control.

SUGGESTION FOR MEDITATION: To whom might God be sending you? Are they among the "least of these" or those who are outcast by our society for one reason or another? Can you see ways in which you have been or are being prepared for this work?

THURSDAY, JUNE 10 • Read Romans 5:1-8

We can tell the story of our suffering, the suffering that does not embarrass or demean us but actually produces fruit in our lives. Through repeated experiences of God's abiding care in our suffering of various kinds, we accumulate memories that give us confidence that God is at work in our own lives as well as in the lives of our forebears in faith. This confidence confirms our faith and helps us persevere.

I am not a consistent journaler, but I turn to this discipline in times of struggle or searching. These written reflections chronicle my wrestling in God's presence and God's gracious response. Rereading my journal entries from time to time I see the deepening of my love for God as God's deep and consistent care unfolds in every interlude of struggle along the journey.

Paul says that suffering produces character. Perhaps it is this Christian character that enables us to continue in the practices and observances that form the context of our lives of faith and keep us on the journey of fellowship with God.

Finally, this persistence produces hope. Verse 1 describes this hope, founded on our experiences of confirming that God's promises are true, as is "our hope of sharing the glory of God." This verse may refer to an eschatological hope in the coming fulfillment of God's victory over evil, but it seems also to refer to the present work of the Holy Spirit in our lives. Through this process of suffering, learning, and confirmation of God's grace, we find ourselves increasingly free to experience the joy of God's presence in our hearts.

PRAYER: Hope of my present and Hope of my future, I give you thanks for my experiences of your presence and care in the deepest struggles of my life. May these experiences produce in me the deepening of my spirit that enables me to share in your glory. Amen.

Friday, June 11 • Read Romans 5:1-8

In this passage Paul sets up an interesting progression. We move not from hope to faith but rather from faith to hope. We gain a settled confidence in the activity of God in our lives and in the world. The experience of enduring suffering shapes us and forms our character. However, this endurance does not seem principally to be the gritting our teeth and toughing it out variety; this endurance does not lead to isolation and independence. Rather it leads toward the humility we need to acknowledge our dependence—dependence on God— and to move in that spirit to confidence in God's presence in us.

This confidence does not derive from our own actions or the depth of our suffering or the quality of our faith. Its source is the Holy Spirit that we have received. According to Paul, the Holy Spirit is at work, pouring God's love into our hearts. This image of pouring—not a careful, measured, don't-spill-any approach—is wonderfully provocative. Imagine God's love gushing over our hearts—more than we can take in at any one time but available in such boundless, unending supply that we need not worry about capturing and preserving every drop. What an image for the parched soul!

This overwhelming, grace-filled self-giving of God is like the self-giving of the Incarnation: without reserve, independent of our ability to receive or comprehend, and demonstrative of God's nature. God entrusts this gift to us, knowing that each of us is fragile and limited in his or her ability to receive this love. God engages us in a process of transformation that deepens both our capacity to receive and our thirst for this outpouring.

PRAYER: Spirit of the living God, fall afresh on me! Drench my soul in the outpouring of your love and draw me ever more deeply into the hope that does not disappoint. Amen.

SATURDAY, JUNE 12 • Read Psalm 116:1-2, 12-19

The first verse of this psalm points out that God's love and God's loving action precede our love for God and evoke our response. God's response to the psalmist's anguished prayers sets the context for this paean of thanksgiving. The psalmist claims, perhaps boldly, that God responded directly to his or her prayers. We sometimes reluctantly assert that a particular event or outcome shows the working of God's hand, although we may willingly affirm God's care for us and God's activity in the world. Although we rightly fear a return to superstition, perhaps we could garner some deep spiritual lessons by learning to see and to name God's work in our lives and in the world around us.

It seems entirely fitting that this psalm is one of several psalms read during the seder meal in the celebration of Passover. Like the psalmist's individual story, the Passover commemorates a time of suffering, prayer, and God's gracious and mighty acts in liberating the people of Israel from slavery in Egypt.

Telling and retelling stories of deliverance (personal and corporate) remind us that God desires to remain in relationship with us, even in the midst of suffering and that we can have confidence in God's presence with us despite our feelings of isolation caused by suffering. Even when we have no sense of God's enfolding care due to emotional and spiritual drain, we can rely on what we know about God's past actions and depend on God's faithfulness.

SUGGESTION FOR MEDITATION: **Think of experiences that have demonstrated God's presence in your life or in the life of someone close to you. Reflect on what these experiences tell you about God's nature and your ability to trust that God is active in your life.**

SUNDAY, JUNE 13 • **Read Psalm 116:1-2, 12-19**

Once we have identified God's gracious acts of redemption and deliverance in our lives, how might we respond? The psalmist responds in a variety of ways. First, the psalmist promises renewed faithfulness: *God has heard me this time; therefore I will continue to call on God's gracious response in the future.* This trust in God's gracious action in our lives may affect the writer's willingness to call on God and to acknowledge dependence in this way.

Worship is another response. The "cup of salvation," the payment of vows, and the "thanksgiving sacrifice" probably all refer to the tabernacle offerings that were part of the people's worship life (see Lev. 7). In public and private worship, we also offer thanksgivings in our prayers, hymns, and readings. Members of Korean churches commonly make an offering (of money) to the church as a sign of thanksgiving (on the birth of a child, relief from sickness, or other answers to prayer).

Another response might be humility. The psalmist's claim to be the Lord's servant—like Mary's response to the Annunciation—humbly acknowledges that this great blessing is the Lord's work rather than the result of the speaker's own actions.

Finally the psalmist publicly witnesses to the work of God. The psalmist tells the story in the psalm and at the time of the thank offering "in the presence of all [God's] people." We too have opportunities to testify to God's work in our lives by sharing our stories with people who are praying for us or with our Sunday school class, Bible and lectionary study group, or covenant group.

PRAYER: Gracious Lord, help me see your hand at work in my life, and may I respond to your gracious acts in a way that marks them for myself and for others. Amen.

Dead and Alive

June 14–20, 1999 • Thomas R. Albin*

MONDAY, JUNE 14 • Read Romans 6:5-11

Dead and alive in Christ

Spiritual insight and richness of theological truth fill the epistle to the Romans. Today's text addresses the central issues of life and death. Paul clearly states that the life, death, and resurrection of Jesus Christ are "the power of God for salvation" for those who have faith (Rom. 1:1-17; 3:21-31). God's freely given grace makes the miracle of saving faith possible. We are to be "united with him in a death like his" so that we might "certainly be united with him in a resurrection like his." Paul implies that his readers have also been crucified, having died to sin and thus freed from sin. Yet our living with Christ resides in the future: "We will also live with him."

Dead and alive. The now and the not yet. How can we consider ourselves dead to sin and alive to God in Christ? For Paul, to become truly Christian one must be united with Christ in his death and live into a future of resurrection with Christ. What things diminish your life? From what thoughts, feelings, attitudes and actions do you need to be freed?

Irenaeus, an early Christian leader, said that we best see the glory of God in persons who are truly alive! What a powerful spiritual concept—to live as though truly alive in Christ!

SUGGESTION FOR MEDITATION: Verse 11 contains the climax of all the readings for this week: "You also must consider yourselves dead to sin and alive to God in Christ Jesus." Ask the Holy Spirit to guide your spiritual imagination so that you might see and feel what it would to be like to be united with God in Christ.

---

*Director of Contextual Education and Instructor in Christian Spiritual Formation, University of Dubuque Theological Seminary, Dubuque, Iowa.

TUESDAY, JUNE 15 • Read Romans 6:1*b*-6

Dead and alive in baptism

Growing up on a farm in rural western Kansas and attending a small Methodist church in a three-point charge gave me a wonderful theological education and ample time to reflect on the meaning of those things I learned. As I have reflected biblically and spiritually on what it means to be "baptized into Christ Jesus," I remembered the time of testing that Jesus experienced in the wilderness immediately after his baptism (Luke 3:15–4:13).

Jesus was tempted to compromise his standards to meet his physical needs. Have you been so tempted? I have.

Jesus was tempted to compromise the teaching of the Bible in order to meet his social needs. And Jesus was tempted to put God to the test inappropriately. Have you? I have.

Romans makes it clear: God's grace is free, but it is not cheap—and those who follow Jesus cannot escape his suffering and death. Too often we have undervalued the cost of discipleship. We want "newness of life" without the crucifying experiences. In the Christian faith, death precedes life: "*If* we have been united with him in a death like his, [*then*] we will certainly be united with him in a resurrection like his" (emphasis added).

The New Testament term translated in the New Revised Standard Version as "united with him" implies a deep organic union with Jesus. The term applies to plants that derive their life from another, like mistletoe upon the oak tree.

The good news for Christians is that "we have been buried with him by baptism into death, so that, just as Christ was raised from the dead by the glory of the Father, so we too might walk in newness of life."

PRAYER: Ever-living Christ, lead me to share in the baptism of your death, that I might share in a deeper union with you. Fill me with new life so that I might live and speak your praise. Amen.

WEDNESDAY, JUNE 16 • Read Matthew 10:24-31

Dead to false fear and alive to fear God

At the beginning of this chapter Jesus gives the disciples "authority over unclean spirits" and the power "to cure every disease and every sickness" (v. 1). As they go, they are to "proclaim the good news.... Cure the sick, raise the dead, cleanse the lepers, [and] cast out demons" (vv. 7-8).

What an exciting commission! With this clear message and this miraculous power without doubt the whole world will be impressed and the church will prosper, right? Wrong! Jesus' words of caution still ring true: "A disciple is not above the teacher, nor a slave above the master....If they have called the master of the house Beelzebul [the worst of the evil spirits], how much more will they malign those of his household!" In these verses Jesus clearly lays out the cost of discipleship. It should not surprise us when those outside the church refuse to understand, and we can expect opposition.

A few years ago while in Indonesia, I saw firsthand the struggle of our Christian brothers and sisters in a country where Christians are a small minority of the population. When Indonesians become Christian, they know they will face opposition and persecution—both overt and covert. Why is it that they are not afraid? In the face of such opposition, why are their churches gaining members?

I believe this passage answers those questions. They do not fear those who "kill the body but cannot kill the soul" (v. 28a). They have died to false fear and are alive to a godly fear. Their love, awe, and respect of God are so great that fear has no power over them.

PRAYER: **O Divine Master, help me die to fear that keeps me from you. Make me alive to the true awe, wonder, fear, and love of what you did for me on the cross. Give me a double portion of your Holy Spirit, I pray, in Jesus' name. Amen.**

THURSDAY, JUNE 17 • Read Matthew 10:32-39

Dead to silence and alive in witness

"Everyone therefore who acknowledges me before others, I also will acknowledge before my Father in heaven; but whoever denies me before others, I also will deny before my Father in heaven." The unapologetic demand that Jesus makes of his disciples in verse 32 sounds harsh to modern ears in North America.

Where did we get the idea that Christian living is enough? It certainly did not come from Jesus or the first disciples. It did not come from the early Christians who accepted persecution, torture, and even death before those who had both seen and heard the believers' public testimony of faith in Jesus Christ. For centuries the disciples of Jesus Christ understood faithful witness to include both word and deed. The Protestant Reformation spread across Europe because John Huss, Martin Luther, John Calvin, and others refused to be silenced. Eighteenth-century Christians like John and Charles Wesley confessed their faith in Jesus Christ despite opposition in England, Ireland, Scotland, and Wales.

Students have influenced my life profoundly. One Chinese woman spoke of the suffering Christians endure when they acknowledge Christ. As a little girl during the Cultural Revolution, she saw her mother severely beaten because of her witness to Jesus Christ. Instead of becoming fearful, her mother became stronger.

Even though faith in Jesus Christ has continued to create physical and social hardship for our brothers and sisters around the world, they grow stronger because they embody in both word and deed the truth and power of Jesus' words: "Whoever does not take up the cross and follow me is not worthy of me. Those who find their life will lose it, and those who lose their life for my sake will find it."

PRAYER: O God, let me die to selfishness, fear, and silence that I might live and speak your praise. Amen.

Waiting for deliverance

This psalm teaches a powerful lesson about waiting. The writer indicates just how desperate he is in the verses that precede today's reading. He feels the panic and fear of one sinking in deep mire where there is no foothold, and the water is up to his neck (vv. 1-2). Try to imagine yourself sinking in the mire, and read the passage again beginning at verse one.

A spiritual reading of Psalm 69 touches some of the deepest human emotions: desperate fear (vv. 1-2, 14-15, 21), overwhelming guilt and shame (vv. 5, 10-12, 19-20), the experience of being hated and abused by others (vv. 4, 7-8, 17-21, 29), the desire for revenge (vv. 22-28), and the demand that God act now (vv. 1, 6, 13, 16-18, 29).

I believe the courage to express our deepest feelings to God is an essential path to genuine faith. Deep faith grounds itself in an understanding of the nature of God as the one who knows us fully and intimately.

The God of the Bible is a God of deep, steadfast love. The Hebrew word translated as "steadfast love" is *hesed*, which expresses a deep, committed love in a covenant relationship. This relationship involves the pledge and exchange of life and all that is needed to sustain life. As a Hebrew, David understood the steadfast covenant love of God, which served as the foundation for his faith. He knew that the unfaithfulness of failing human beings could not invalidate the mercy and faithfulness of Israel's covenant God. Therefore, fear of his enemies, of persecution, pain, and death—all lost their power in comparison to the abundance of God's steadfast love.

SUGGESTION FOR MEDITATION: **Meditate on the unconditional covenant love of your God.**

SATURDAY, JUNE 19 • Read Genesis 21:8-16

The death of a child and a hope

Abraham's barren wife, Sarah, selects Hagar, a trusted and valued slave, to be a surrogate mother. Hagar gives birth to a son named Ishmael. After some initial domestic trouble (Gen. 16), everything is fine until God's promise to Sarah is fulfilled; and she conceives a child of her own at ninety years of age (chapter 17:15ff.). Abraham is 100 at Isaac's birth. Then Hagar's world begins to fall apart.

Imagine Hagar's feelings when Abraham sends her away from the camp with nothing but Ishmael, some bread, and a skin of water. Soon the homeless mother and child run out of water; Hagar places the child beneath a bush and sits down to await his imminent death.

Then and now the world does not make sense at times; injustice, pain, and misery abound. This passage focuses on death—the death of a vision, the destruction of hope, the terrible inexplicable circumstances of life. Hagar's only hope rests on God's promise that Ishmael will one day be the head of a nation. But now she weeps alone over her child of promise and asks God only for the mercy of not having to watch him die.

How many mothers in the world today know the same pain and tears of Hagar, having to watch their children suffer because their meager resources have run out and having no reason to hope? How grateful I am for every person who works with God to make a difference in our world—particularly in the lives of children. The United Methodist Bishops' initiative on "Children and Poverty," begun in 1996, is one of many opportunities for Christians to reach out to those like Hagar and Ishmael.

PRAYER: **O God, have mercy on those in poverty and pain this day. Give me eyes to see, a heart to feel, and hands to serve. Amen.**

Dead to fear and alive to God

Once Hagar had been confident that her son would inherit Abraham's wealth and provide for her future. Now the boy's father has cast them out, and they have nothing. Surely this experience justifies her pain and despair. What kind of God would allow this to happen?

To cry out to God in anger, pain, and frustration reflects genuine biblical spirituality. To ask God for relief in the midst of suffering is also an authentic response. Yesterday's reading ended with a desperate mother's asking God for the small mercy of not having to watch her only son die.

Today's lesson serves as an eternal reminder that God can and does act in the fullness of time, if we continue to focus our attention in the right direction. "The angel of God called to Hagar… 'What troubles you, Hagar? Do not be afraid.…Come, lift up the boy and hold him fast with your hand, for I will make a great nation of him.'" Often our vision must die before our eyes open to God's vision. In the midst of desperate circumstances Hagar remained open enough to listen to God and obedient enough to respond. She let go of her vision for life in Abraham's camp; she let go of her fears; she got up, lifted her son, and moved on to where God could provide for their needs.

As you worship this Sabbath day, focus your attention on God.

SUGGESTION FOR MEDITATION: **What fears are blinding your eyes and stopping your ears? What keeps you from obeying when God speaks?**

PRAYER: **O God of Abraham and Hagar and Sarah, God of Ishmael and Isaac, come to me and to all your children. Speak, Lord. I long to die to fear and be made alive in faith. Free me for joyful obedience, through Jesus Christ, our Lord. Amen.**

Keep on Walking

June 21–27, 1999 • Cecil Murphey*

MONDAY, JUNE 21 • Read Genesis 22:1-14

How could Abraham believe that God wanted him to sacrifice his son? If a voice told me to make a burnt offering of my child, I'd run to a therapist. God doesn't speak like that to me.

For us, human sacrifice is abhorrent. Yet God speaks through culture and circumstances to help Abraham understand that nothing must come between him and his God. The text seems to imply that Isaac has become Abraham's idol.

What message would God give us through our culture? The intent of the command remains, "You shall have no other gods before me" (Exod 20:3).

God's message to each of us would differ: "Leave that relationship." "Quit work and go to college." "Your children are gifts for you to enjoy, not gods for you to serve."

Yet what God asks isn't as important as the fact that God's finger touches our idols. When anything blocks our commitment, God speaks, "Take your son, your only son, Isaac, whom you love....Sacrifice him" (NIV). The reason for the command lies in the words *whom you love*. As we read these words, we can fill in the blanks for ourselves: "Take your [job, family, drive for success], ...whom [or which] you love....Sacrifice [it]."

The purpose for us—like Abraham—is to put God above all else.

PRAYER: Holy God, rid me of anything that blocks my relationship with you. Amen.

---

*Former missionary and Presbyterian pastor; author of seventy books including biographies of Ben Carson and Franklin Graham.

TUESDAY, JUNE 22 • Read Genesis 22:1-8

What must it have been like for the father and son to walk up to the place of sacrifice? The Bible says twice, "The two of them walked on together." Abraham had awaited his son's birth for twenty-five years. Now God demands the boy's life. Sadness and pain beyond words must fill his thoughts as they walk.

Despite his pain and sadness, Abraham responds in faith. He tells his two servants that he and the boy will go and worship "and then we will come back to you." When Isaac asks about the sacrifice, Abraham replies, "God...will provide."

As Isaac walks up the mountain, he asks his father about the sacrifice, but otherwise we know nothing of his thoughts. Maybe this day is one to spend special time with his father. Two figures walk up a mountain: one with thoughts of death, the other with thoughts of joy.

We often get caught in that tension between joyful expectancy and fearful reality. We're moving on to new adventure, but we know the experience will cost us. Moving on means leaving something behind. If we're going to walk forward with God, we may have to face death—literally or symbolically. Life may take away what seems the most precious.

As the story unfolds, Abraham doesn't have to kill his son; but by walking together with him to the mountain, he shows his willingness to obey. His actions say, "I hold back nothing from you, God."

One lesson we learn from the story—and it may be our biggest challenge—is to keep walking when our hearts are breaking and the pain seems more than we can bear.

PRAYER: God, make me willing to walk wherever you choose to lead me. Amen.

WEDNESDAY, JUNE 23 • **Read Matthew 10:40-42**

"I'm a nurse. Call if there's anything I can do,"she said after Dan told her about his older sister who lived with his family due to her poor health. Then Dan's sister's condition worsened. Physically unable to care for her himself, he phoned the nurse who had offered assistance. "I need help tonight. We have a private-duty nurse coming in tomorrow night," Dan said. "The hospital can't take her for a week."

The nurse offered to cook a meal. When Dan stated plainly, "I need someone to stay with my sister tonight," she gave him telephone numbers of various agencies.

"I wept after I hung up," Dan said. "Like others who had volunteered, she wanted to help—as long as it didn't inconvenience her."

Helping others is a spiritual responsibility. Jesus extolled the virtue of giving only a cup of cold water. His words may sound easy, but what if Jesus really meant, "Be inconvenienced for others and you won't lose your reward"?

In places without modern plumbing, providing a cup of water could demand that one run to the nearest river or draw water from a nearly dry well in an arid region. Today "a cup of cold water" might mean sitting by the bedside of the dying, helping a stranded motorist, cleaning someone's house, driving miles out of the way to take someone to church.

Life gives us daily opportunities to offer a cup of cold water. We often miss those opportunities because, like the nurse, we don't want to be inconvenienced. May we remember that each opportunity seized moves us closer to God's presence: "Whoever welcomes you welcomes me, and whoever welcomes me welcomes the one who sent me."

PRAYER: God of compassion, teach me to help despite the inconvenience. Amen.

What a strange psalm. For the first four verses, the writer cries out to God, "Stop hiding from me! Come to me!" The psalmist feels forgotten and is hurting. Unexpectedly, the last verse turns in a new direction. The psalmist praises God for bountiful blessings. How can a heavyhearted person say so abruptly, "But I'm going to rejoice in God's blessings"?

As I pondered those verses, I thought, *That's the way our lives operate.* Some days our spirits sag. The unfairness of life overwhelms us, and we focus only on problems, roadblocks, and failures. The more we think about them, the more they overpower us and depress us.

Sometimes it helps to remember that we examine our lives subjectively—those are our feelings, and they *are* real. Yes, very real, but also subjective—limited by our emotions. By contrast, we also can look objectively at our world: We need a new car and haven't paid off the old one. Our office is going to be downsized, and we need alternate employment quickly. Our doctor tells us we have a serious illness.

If we surrender to our emotions, we'll walk the road of despair. However, if we look at life more objectively, we can say, "Yes, I've got problems; but God has always provided for me in the past. I'm going to rejoice in what God has done, knowing that divine grace is at work. I trusted in your steadfast love. I can choose to rejoice and sing. I don't know how long bad things will happen—this time." Even when all is well, I know bad times will come again. The one constant factor in my life is God's steadfast love. In that I can rejoice.

PRAYER: Loving God, sometimes I cry out, "How long?" and wonder when the light will shine again. Yes, I wonder, but I know that it will shine again. Amen.

FRIDAY, JUNE 25 • Read Psalm 13

For eighteen months God's face was hidden from me. I never doubted God's existence or love; I simply had no sense of God's presence. "How long will you hide your face from me?"

I believe God never forsakes us. I've moved past asking, "Why, God?" when confusing experiences bring pain into my life. But I wasn't prepared to live in a world where I had no sense of God's face shining on me, no sense of God's whispering in my ear, or gently laying a guiding hand on my shoulder. I had a sense of being "out there" on my own.

In some ways, those eighteen months were the hardest test of my faith. I searched my heart and cried out for God to show me if sin or disobedience had brought about the darkness. Others' careers zoomed forward; I felt stuck, going nowhere.

Life wasn't bad, but I felt as if I were walking through a dark tunnel with no light to guide me. I did the only thing I knew to do: I kept walking forward. In the darkness of divine absence, my emotions felt frozen; and my life seemed spiritually empty. But I kept on.

Then one spring morning, a sliver of light penetrated the darkness. That morning I awakened to discover—and I can't explain how—God's presence again. No longer did I have to ask how long God's face would be hidden from me because I knew the divine face smiled on me. The waiting had come to an end.

PRAYER: God, I don't know why you choose to hide your face from me. I do know that you won't keep me in darkness forever. For this, I thank you. Amen.

SATURDAY, JUNE 26 • Read Romans 6:12-14

I lied. Then I felt bad about it all day. That same week, another writer got an assignment that I wanted—and had made it known that I wanted it. When the publisher chose her, jealousy tugged at me.

Guilt. Jealousy. Normal feelings? Of course. But that's also the problem. Doesn't being a Christian mean anything? I asked. Doesn't trying to live a consistent, faithful life make me different? To make matters worse, I encountered verses in the Bible that piled on the guilt, such as Romans 6:14: "For sin will have no dominion over…"

Okay, I can figure out that dominion means that I won't allow sin to control my life. I'm not being *controlled* by sin—I just fail from time to time. Paul writes, "Do not let sin exercise dominion in your mortal bodies, to make you obey their passions." Sin tugs, strikes, and tempts. Sin hits our vulnerable spots and knocks us down where we're weak. I don't have problems with stealing. I don't want to kill anyone. But I do have areas of weakness, and that's where I struggle to stay free from sin's control.

Perhaps the apostle is suggesting that our sensitivity to sin and awareness of its power keeps us free. I know that before my conversion to Jesus Christ lies were no big deal, and what was wrong with a little jealousy? Now that I've been a Christian for several years, I'm leaving that dominion farther and farther behind because I know the "benefit you reap leads to holiness" (v. 22, NIV).

PRAYER: God of all power and grace, you assure me that sin won't control my life. Help me give myself fully to you so that I live in holiness. Amen.

Sunday, June 27 • **Read Romans 6:14-23**

"Nobody asked me how I was doing when my wife went through serious surgery. I felt helpless and alone," Ken said. Ken and his wife had two preschool children. Ken spoke those words at a men's retreat designed to help those in attendance develop an awareness of persons' needs—especially when the needs go unspoken.

As one of a group of men who repented of our indifference to others in need, I committed myself to remember the needs of the spouses of those in pain. A small thing in some ways, but it reminds me that when I pray faithfully I choose to be a "[slave] of righteousness." I wouldn't ordinarily use the word *slave*. After all, who chooses slavery today? The term suggests imperialism, loss of dignity and rights.

However, as slaves of righteousness we strive to live so that we give ourselves unreservedly to the will of God. Paul exhorts us to choose to become God's slaves. We may find it easier to think about *voluntary* slavery rather than *involuntary*. Paul points out that before we turned to Jesus Christ we were involuntary slaves of sin. That was our nature, our way of life. To put it less theologically, our concerns centered only on ourselves: *our* needs, *our* desires, *our* feelings.

Choosing to serve God doesn't remove us from slavery, but we become a distinct kind of slave—one who serves God, not out of a sense of duty but out of love. And the real proof of our slavery to God shows itself when we touch the hurting people around us with God's love.

Prayer: O God, allow me to be your slave of righteousness. May I desire to please and honor you in everything. Amen.

Transformed and Transforming Learners

June 28–July 4, 1999 • Roy I. Sano *

MONDAY, JUNE 28 • Matthew 11:29*a*; Romans 12:1-2

Disciples as learners

In our changing world, "doing business as usual" will no longer suffice. Christians around the globe are learning this lesson. If we specialize in intensifying what we have always done, and even improving it, we isolate ourselves from our children and from our changing neighbors in a shrinking world.

Thanks be to God for congregations that interact in new ways with the hurts and hopes of a variety of people in a turbulent world. These congregations "reinvent" their ministries, spreading the transforming life of the risen Christ to a wider range of people.

Other sectors of society around the globe find themselves involved in similar developments. Because "doing business as usual" makes industries, health-care systems, and educational institutions obsolete, these systems are reinventing themselves. As organizations attempt to extend their services in a changing world, they learn to do new things in better ways. These organizations refer to themselves as "learning organizations." The organization expects everyone, regardless of role, to become a "learner."

Interestingly enough, this concept of becoming a learner is fundamental to Jesus' understanding of his ministry. Making disciples was a central task during Jesus' life on earth. The root meaning of *disciple* is "learner." We will focus this week on learners who are transformed and who are transforming their world.

PRAYER: In all that I do, help me focus on becoming a learner who knows Jesus personally and is learning new ways to share the risen Christ with a hurting world. Amen.

---

*Resident bishop, Los Angeles Area, The United Methodist Church.

TUESDAY, JUNE 29 • Read Matthew 11:16-19, 25

Open to learning

Disciples who express openness to new ideas remain learners. The learned, in contrast to learners, bask in their knowledge and resist learning more.

The most prominent opponents to Jesus were the learned. In Matthew's Gospel, Jesus exposes their fickle and frivolous views of judgment, using the image of children. On the one hand, opponents complain of John the Baptist's threatening and ascetic lifestyle: He does not participate in their festivities. On the other hand, to their way of thinking, Jesus is a glutton and a drunkard because he does not fast with them. Neither John nor Jesus suits their expectations; neither offers anything the learned choose to embrace. Opponents complain about surface differences they have with John and Jesus but fail to learn of "weightier matters"; namely, justice, mercy, and faith, which John and Jesus teach. The "children" strain out gnats and swallow camels (Matt. 23:23-24).

Jesus lifts up the image of infants as a counterpoint to that of the complaining children in verses 16-19. The infants are ready and eager to learn something new and different. After all, a vastly different world, in all of its richness and possibilities, awaits disclosure to them.

Like Jesus' and John's opponents, we can close ourselves to those who raise troubling issues of justice, mercy, and faith in the ways we treat the poor, the diseased, the alien in our midst, and the prisoners. Jesus calls us to be like infants, open to exciting and demanding discoveries about the richness of the world and its people.

PRAYER: **Help me, dear God, to grow in openness to the troubling issues I so easily avoid. May I learn from caring, courageous, and creative people who pave new ways to serve those who differ from me. Amen.**

WEDNESDAY, JUNE 30 • Read Matthew 11:25-30

Open to revelation

Jesus thanks God for those who accept Jesus' mission and message. Once again Jesus contrasts the qualities of "the wise and intelligent" with the image of "infants" as learners. Our acceptance of Jesus as a divine messenger does not hinge on our abilities or religious interests; it comes as a revelation—a gift—from God. Only grace enables our religious and spiritual perceptions.

In verse 27, Jesus pictures himself as the recipient of direct knowledge from God based on relationship. Jesus' religious and spiritual understanding stems from the intimate relationship between God as Father and him as Son.

We may marvel at the inability of many in Jesus' time to perceive Jesus as God in the flesh: the carping "children" who play games by their own rules, disallowing the witness of both Jesus and John; the learned and the wise who simply miss the whole point as they look for revelation in all the wrong places.

So we come as learners—open and eager—to receive God's revelation. We come open and eager to be in relationship with God. And to those who are open and eager to learn, Jesus issues an invitation: "Come to me,…and I will give you rest. Take my yoke upon you, and learn from me." Jesus' yoke is one of servitude and obedience. In our day of conflicting religious claims and offers of superior knowledge, Jesus invites us to set aside those claims and reclaim our empowering relationship with God the Father.

PRAYER: **God, I come eager and open, ready and waiting to receive your revelation. May I see the world and my place in it with fresh eyes. Amen.**

THURSDAY, JULY 1 • Read Genesis 24:34-38, 42-49, 58-67

Discover a caring God

To fulfill his fatherly role before he dies, Abraham sends his servant to find a wife for Isaac among their kindred in the north. The servant asks God to guide him to a hospitable woman. When he arrives at his destination, the servant sees Rebekah leaving a spring carrying a jar of water and asks her for a sip of water. Rebekah not only provides enough to quench his thirst but waters his camels as well.

The servant bows his head to worship and blesses the God who helps him fulfill his task. As you read the servant's story, notice how often he seeks God's guidance, how often he acknowledges God's work in his life. In his public testimony before Rebekah's family, the servant mentions all the blessings from God that Abraham has received. Abraham called this God the Lord "of heaven and earth" (Gen. 24:3), who provides helpers to guide us on our way as we fulfill our responsibilities (Gen. 24:7, 40, 48). Abraham's servant confirms this providential care and affirms Abraham's God as a God of steadfast love and faithfulness (Gen. 24:12, 27).

The church believes that Jesus Christ is this Lord. Jesus states that he is one with God, whom he called Father (Matt. 11:27), and who manifests steadfast love by knowing us intimately and seeking to meet our needs.

Each of us has a role to play if we, with others, are to experience the reality of this actively caring Sovereign. Abraham obeys God's command, and the servant ventures forth to do his part. Rebekah decides to go with the servant, and her mother and brother give their blessing. And in this relationship where God has been the active, unseen partner, Isaac receives Rebekah and loves her.

PRAYER: **Caring God, who never abandons me but works to fulfill your best intentions for me, help me do my part in fulfilling your care for me and others. Amen.**

FRIDAY, JULY 2 • **Read Romans 7:15-25a**

Discover a saving God

Jesus says, "Come to me, all you that are weary and are carrying heavy burdens, and I will give you rest" (Matt. 11:28). The apostle Paul vividly depicts the reason for our weariness and offers a solution for rest.

Paul suffers an internal conflict. While he agrees that the law of God is good and even delights in it, Paul cannot do what is good and right. In point of fact, Paul does the evil that he hates.

Paul tells us that sin operates like a powerful force within him, nudging him to do what is sinful and evil. This nudging and Paul's choices agree so consistently that he describes the sequence as a "law of sin" that dwells in him.

What begins as a puzzlement becomes a desperate cry: "Wretched man that I am! Who will rescue me from this body of death?" Rather than falling into despair or a blame game by saying, "See what evil forces make me do," Paul moves quickly to a grateful confession of faith: "Thanks be to God through Jesus Christ our Lord!" In this setting, we discover that the Lord who is sovereign, lovingly caring for creation, is also savior.

In Romans 5:1-2, Paul summarizes salvation through faith in God's grace. He describes the widely ranging transformations in and among us, as well as creation itself. Salvation promises resolution, and, therefore, rest from our turmoil.

PRAYER: Come, Lord Jesus, and become my Savior amidst the sin and evil I know. Lead me to share your saving grace with others in their struggles. Amen.

SATURDAY, JULY 3 • Read Psalm 45:10-17

Sovereign Savior

Moses knew the God who prevailed over Pharaoh and delivered the Hebrews from slavery. For Moses and the Hebrew people, the Lord was both Sovereign and Savior, liberating them from social, economic, and political domination. Psalm 45 also reflects this understanding.

Although Psalm 45 originally celebrated the marriage of a princess to a king, Christians read this psalm primarily as the promised union between believers with their God who is king or sovereign. However closely they may have experienced the presence of the Lord Jesus Christ, members of the early church recognized the church's status as comparable to a bride who is engaged and not married, awaiting the consummate union. Jesus Christ as Lord was the groom who was yet to come and be united fully with the bride (Rev. 19:6-8).

Verses 1-9 describe the actions of the Sovereign and what those united with this Sovereign can do. If Jesus is this Sovereign, Jesus is worthy of praise because he hates wickedness and loves righteousness. As the Lord, Jesus supports the cause of truth and defends what is right. Others who join him will decisively overcome those who obstruct these ends. They join Jesus Christ in the process of rectification. Being united with Jesus Christ as Sovereign who is Savior means we are saved from our personal sins. It also means we accompany him in overcoming sin and evil in society.

PRAYER: Thank you, O God, for the measure of union I experience with you through Jesus Christ and for inviting me to join you in spreading your reign. Amen.

The cost and joy of discipleship

Even if we join the Sovereign Savior in spreading God's reign, sin and evil continue to damage, defile, and destroy the order and beauty in God's creation. We witnessed the fierce responses of sin and evil with the beheading of John the Baptist and the crucifixion of Jesus. Those who accompany Jesus Christ in creating God's realm may experience similar opposition, which is part of the broader meaning of discipleship.

Disciples are learners who accompany Jesus in his ministry and mission. They answer his call, "Follow me." Following Jesus means we will deny ourselves and take up his cross as our own.

Following Jesus hardly sounds like an easy yoke and light burden. Yet unlike the learned who make demands, Jesus asks only one thing of us: our personal allegiance to himself. The long lists of shoulds and oughts pale in comparison to this single request.

We learn from Jesus who struggled before he humbly surrendered to God (Matt. 26:39-42). This surrender made him courageous and gentle before his enemies and obedient to death. When we humbly surrender ourselves to God, we too can be gentle in the face of opposition. We experience a new surge of life coursing through us, making the yoke lighter and the burdens easier to carry.

PRAYER: Dear Christ, as I follow you by denying myself and bearing your cross, grant that I too will be raised to newness in witness and service that shares your love and life with others. Amen.

God's Purpose in Our Lives

July 5–11, 1999 • Anne Crumpler*

MONDAY, JULY 5 • Read Genesis 25:19-28

"These are the descendants of Isaac, Abraham's son." From the first verse, we expect a long list of begats. Instead, the scripture tells us these facts: Isaac is forty when he marries Rebekah. Rebekah, barren for twenty years, finally conceives and gives birth to two sons: Jacob and Esau. Esau grows up to be a hunter. Jacob grows up to be a mother's boy. Isaac loves Esau; Rebekah loves Jacob. The scripture relays the facts and sets the stage.

If we look more carefully, the scripture tells a deeper story. Isaac, like Abraham, has children when he's older. Rebekah, like Sarah, is barren. God tells Rebekah who her children will become: two nations, one stronger than the other. With a few simple statements, the scripture reminds us of God's covenant with Abraham (see Gen. 12:1-9), which comes to fruition in the lives of Abraham's children. The clues—barrenness, old age, nations—let us know that God is at work fulfilling God's purposes.

Genesis 25 is about the birth of Jacob and Esau. It's also about God and a promise and a people. God's covenant with Abraham will be fulfilled in the lives of his descendants. God will be their God, and they will be God's people.

More, the God we worship is the God of Abraham, Isaac, and Jacob. We live our lives, generation after generation, in the context of God's promise. What clues indicate that God is at work in our lives?

PRAYER: Be my God and teach me to be your child. Fulfill your purposes in my life as you did in the lives of Abraham, Isaac, and Jacob. Amen.

---

*Writer, editor; Presbyterian layperson living in Nashville, Tennessee.

Jacob is cooking when Esau arrives hungry. "Gimme some of the red stuff," demands Esau. "I'm half-starved."

"Only if you give me your birthright," replies Jacob.

"Anything! Just give me something to eat."

We recognize the plot: two kids squabbling over dinner and power. Jacob is savvy; Esau is gullible. Jacob makes a better deal; frankly, Esau is hungry. We might miss the point by judging Jacob and Esau or by turning the story into a psychological case study.

What does the story mean? Its context is God's covenant with Abraham; God is the central character in the story. God's promise is the central theme. We already know that God will keep the covenant through Jacob (see Gen. 25:23). Before birth, God chooses Jacob. So the story is not really about Jacob's acquiring God's favor at Esau's expense. We know that decision is made already. The story relates how God works out God's purposes in the lives of Jacob and Esau, who may or may not realize what's going on.

God fulfills God's purposes in the ordinary, day-to-day stuff of human life. God uses sibling rivalry; struggles for power; hunger; bartering; the quirks of culture, occupation, and character to bring about God's purposes. God works through individuals and through nations. Jacob and Esau represent Israel and Edom; or at least, they have taken on the stereotypical characteristics of two nations.

God's involvement extends far beyond miracles and acts of kindness. God works in smoke-filled rooms; in bitter rivalries; among politicians, con artists, and the intelligentsia. God is working out God's purposes in our lives. And much of the time, we don't notice.

PRAYER: God, fulfill your promises in our world. Amen.

WEDNESDAY, JULY 7 • Read Psalm 119:105-112

Psalm 119 is like the game of categories. The theme is God's law; each section begins with a letter of the Hebrew alphabet and makes a statement about the law. In the interest of ABC form, the psalm sometimes gets garbled. Still it beautifully expresses our love of God's word and our reliance on God's law.

Verses 105-112 state that when oppressed or afflicted, we turn to God's word. "I hold my life in my hand continually," says the psalmist, "but I do not forget your law." Life is up for grabs; we turn to God and to God's word.

Though the psalm refers to God's word as law, precept, ordinance, statute, it does not see the scripture as a book of rules. Understanding the law means living in God's care, following God's direction, and trusting in God's promises. "Give me life, O Lord," cries the psalmist, "according to your word." God's word is life.

"Your word is a lamp to my feet." Picture a circle of light in the darkness, like the light of a streetlight pooled on the sidewalk. We live in the safety of the light, resting in God's loving care.

But God's word is also "a light to my path"—less the soft glow of a streetlight and more like the high beams of a car. It lights up the darkness and shows us what's ahead. We know God's plan for our future: God's word promises a land and a kingdom to come. We know what's ahead. So we can drive straight into the darkness, where "the wicked have laid a snare" for us, because God lights our way.

PRAYER: Light of my soul, when life seems tenuous, give me hope in your promises. Light my way through the darkness. Make your word a joy to my heart and a guide for my life. Amen.

THURSDAY, JULY 8 • Read Matthew 13:18-23

In Matthew's Gospel, Jesus' parable of the sower indicates persons' differing responses to the good news of the kingdom. The seed is the word of God. Some people hear the word but do not understand. Others receive God's word with joy, but their enthusiasm wanes when they see the dangers of discipleship. Others hear the word and grow in faith, but the concerns of this world strangle faith. Sometimes the word falls on fertile soil. People hear the word, understand, and bear the fruit of faith.

Preachers tell us to prepare ourselves to receive the word, and we do. We'd like to think that we are the good soil, people of faith. Not only do we receive God's word, but we understand. We do good works and proclaim the word, scattering God's seed.

Maybe. Let's look again.

We hear God's word, but too often the words of faith confuse us. What exactly does it mean to seek God's kingdom or to accept the lordship of Jesus Christ? Perhaps we don't understand.

We hear God's word, but do we believe in Jesus? Put to the test, would we be willing to stake our lives on him? Perhaps the initial fervor of young faith has become more mature apathy.

We have heard God's word, and we have grown in faith. But faith seems to get lost when we're overworked and underpaid. We go to work, come home, watch a little television, and fall into bed exhausted. What happened to faith? Why do our lives feel so empty?

The good news is that despite our failures, God is faithful. Our faith is weak, but God is strong. God plows under the seedlings, pulls up the thorns, works the soil, sends out the word. And God reaps an abundant harvest of faith and understanding.

PRAYER: God, when I fail to hear and understand, give me faith. Amen.

FRIDAY, JULY 9 • Read Matthew 13:1-9

Jesus tells a parable about the ways people receive the word of God's kingdom and the results of that receptivity: "A sower went out to sow." Some of the seeds fall on the path, and the birds eat them. Some fall on rocky soil. They sprout quickly, but the seedlings wither in the sun. Some fall among thorns. The plants grow, but the thorns choke them. Other seeds fall on good soil and bring forth grain.

When we hear the beginning of the parable, we know what to expect. Sowing reaps a harvest. But Jesus tells about a sower who scattered the seed and nothing grew. The seeds fell on bad soil. The plants died.

The parable of the sower relates to God's coming kingdom, something we all wonder a little about. Jesus said the kingdom was near, but we can't see it. God seems conspicuously absent in a world where sin and death are commonplace. Jesus taught us to pray, "Thy kingdom come"; but nothing happens—no heavenly city, no miraculous changes, no evidence of the seeds of the kingdom.

The parable tells the good news: "Other seeds fell on good soil and brought forth grain, some a hundredfold, some sixty, some thirty." Have faith, the scripture says. The kingdom of God will come with a sure and abundant harvest.

Read the parable again. Verse 8 sounds more like a continuation of the story than an unexpected miracle. And the seeds' bringing forth grain thirty, sixty, a hundredfold is an average crop, nothing spectacular.

Consider: If God does not bring in the kingdom with unexpected extravagance, perhaps God's kingdom comes through average days and even failures, as well as through miracles.

PRAYER: God, make yourself known. In failures and miracles, bring in your kingdom. Amen.

SATURDAY, JULY 10 • Read Romans 8:1-11

Spirit and flesh. We often think of ourselves as isolated individuals; and we tend to divide our lives and ourselves into physical, intellectual, and emotional sections. Christians are apt to think of flesh (physical) as sinful and to condemn the things of the flesh: eating, drinking, sex. Spirit (intellectual, emotional) is somehow closer to God. Paul seems to support our understanding when he says in effect: "Those who are in the flesh cannot please God."

In recent years, we have begun to long for more spiritual lives. We want to get away from the stress of everyday life, to spend quiet time alone with God. Again, Paul seems to support us: "To set the mind on the Spirit is life and peace."

However, Paul doesn't divide people into spirit and flesh; he writes about two ways of ordering life's priorities. And Paul doesn't condemn the physical world, God's good creation, nor does he advocate escaping the world for snatches of personal communion with God. Paul's letters, like most books of the Bible, are pretty down-to-earth. So what is Paul's point in Romans 8?

Paul expects the Messiah to usher in a new social order, defined by God's purposes. He knows the scriptures' hope for peace, harmony, abundance, life.

Paul believes that Jesus is the Messiah and that in Jesus' life, death, and resurrection, the new social order has begun. The Holy Spirit, given to the community of faith, evidences God's reign.

To live "according to the Spirit" or to set our minds on "the things of the Spirit" means that we allow God's purposes to define our lives. We live for the new social order. When we live "according to the flesh," we allow the old social order where sin and death reign to define us. Every day's living presents choices. If we set our mind on the Spirit, we find life and peace.

PRAYER: **God, give me your Spirit and teach me your purposes. Amen.**

SUNDAY, JULY 11 • Read Romans 8:1-11

Paul explores the conflict of faith expressed in Romans 7:18-19, "I can will what is right, but I cannot do it. For I do not do the good I want, but the evil I do not want is what I do." As Christians, we're supposed to be good—we want to be good, but we're not.

Romans 8 begins with an announcement: There is "no condemnation for those who are in Christ Jesus. For the law of the Spirit of life in Christ Jesus has set you free from the law of sin and of death."

Jesus Christ's life, death, and resurrection forgive us and transform us to become citizens of God's new social order. That citizenship frees us from the values; the thinking; the social, economic, and political constraints of the human world, where sin and death rule. Because God dwells among us, we live according to the Spirit, adjusting our lives and changing our minds so that we keep God's purposes before us. In Christ, communities of faith conform to the character of God's new world.

Of course, we are human beings living in a human world. Though we may pretend to transcend the "things of the flesh," we cannot easily separate sacred and secular in ourselves or in our communities. We live "according to the flesh" in a transient world dominated by sin and corrupted by death. We are sinners, plain and simple.

Being redeemed means living in between the sacred and the secular. Christian faith is a struggle. We live in the world according to the laws and customs of the world. But we have glimpsed in Christ a vision of God's new world, a world of "life and peace." Further, we know that as God raised Jesus from death, God will raise us and our communities to new life, ordered "according to the Spirit" of Christ.

PRAYER: **God, set my mind on your new creation so that I live according to the spirit of Jesus Christ, our Lord and Savior. Amen.**

The Irresistible God

July 12–18, 1999 • Brett Webb-Mitchell*

MONDAY, JULY 12 • Read Genesis 28:10-19a

Theophany. Biblical theologians use this word to describe an event in which God or God's messengers are revealed to human beings. A commentary writer explains that such theophanic images usually take place at night, especially in dreams. Moses' hearing the Lord's voice coming from the burning bush would be a theophany. It also describes Jacob's experience as he lay down his tired head on a hard stone pillow.

Some would explain the story of Jacob's dream away rationally, historically, or psychologically; none of which robs us of the sheer awe and hopeful wonder that this wild dream elicits. Yet we can interpret this story of Jacob's wild dream in another way: Jacob receives the gift of God's brilliant imagination. God thrills Jacob—and us—with the extravagant gesture of the heavens filled with angels ascending and descending enormous ladders that extend between this world and the heavens above. Jacob realizes the momentousness of this occasion and is justifiably frightened. He awakens and finds himself captive to the holiness of the place where he has envisioned this dreamscape: "This is none other than the house of God, and this is the gate of heaven." And none other than the irresistible God of Israel promises Jacob faithfulness to all the generations of Jacob's children to follow.

PRAYER: God of Jacob and Leah, may your angels fill my dreams. Like Father Jacob, I always need to remember that you, O Lord, watch over me carefully. You tend to my well-being, whether in the rush of midday madness or in soulful slumber. Amen.

---

*Assistant Professor of Christian Nurture, Duke Divinity School; ordained clergy in the Presbyterian Church, USA; author and lecturer.

TUESDAY, JULY 13 • Read Psalm 139:1-12

The founder of the Catholic Workers' Movement, Dorothy Day, and the psalmist who wrote Psalm 139 had something in common: They were reluctant believers. In *The Long Loneliness*, Day writes of the first evening she heard Francis Thompson's poem, "The Hound of Heaven." The idea of God as the Hound of Heaven fascinates yet terrifies her, as she realizes that the God who created us pursues us relentlessly. Dorothy Day only gives in to God because submission finally brings her some relief. She surmises that we can depend upon people to fail us: "Even those most loved show their frailty and their weaknesses and no matter how we may *will* to see only the best in others, their strength rather than their weakness, we are all too conscious of our own failings and recognize them in others." Putting herself into a church, into the atmosphere of prayer, she prays to God, explaining her decision in this way: "It was an act of the will."

In Psalm 139, God, that "Hound of Heaven," leaves the psalmist astonished at God's total involvement in life. The omniscient God of Creation, who knows our fragile loyalty and wavering trust and fleeting admiration, this God of heaven hounds us into willing submission as we fall to the love of the Creator for us, his creatures. God knows when we sit down, rise up, walk on the path of life, speak a word, flee quickly from God, taking the "wings of the morning and settl[ing] at the farthest limits of the sea." But even there God's hand leads us, and God's right hand holds us fast; in light of day or the dark cover of night, God sees us. "For darkness is as light to you," utters the psalmist. The Hound of Heaven loves us into the hope that was born in creation's dawning.

PRAYER: O God, great Hound of Heaven, I surrender my life to you. It is too exhausting to hide from you, for you know my hiding places. It is futile to run, climb, or sprint from your gaze, for you who created me and the earth I live upon are well acquainted with this quaint domicile. Such love is too marvelous for me. In my emptiness of heart, fill me with your wonder. Amen.

WEDNESDAY, JULY 14 • Read Psalm 139:23-24

"Search me, O God, and know my heart; test me and know my thoughts. See if there is any wicked way in me, and lead me in the way everlasting."

With the "mask" we wear for others, we try in vain to repeat the psalmist's words in safety. Or we try to look good in our best "humble-pie" suit before the eyes of the world. *Search me* are brave words—not to be taken either lightly or with overly simplistic pietistic fervor, for God may answer our prayer. And we will never be the same. Ever. Never again.

For when we pray, "Search me, God, and know my heart," the search will not be a quiet one. The God who created us will search us. The search will be thorough: The one who cradles us in love will also seek out and remove those things that lead us away from God. Knowing the contorted and conflicted desires of our heart and mind is one thing. But praying, "See if there is any wicked way in me, and lead me in the way everlasting," is another. We pray to be cleansed of all that is wicked, dark, evil, and unholy in our lives. Perhaps the words *kyrie eleison* should be on our lips as well: "Lord, have mercy." For who knows what God's power will do to us in God's searching, knowing, and changing us, and whether or not we will have time to say, "Have mercy."

PRAYER: Search me, O God, and know my heart; test me and know my thoughts. See if there is any wicked way in me, and lead me in the way everlasting. It is in the name of the Father, the Son, and the Holy Spirit that I, as part of Christ's body, pray this prayer. Amen.

THURSDAY, JULY 15 • **Read Romans 8:12-17**

Adoption—a good word to explain best the way our lives as Christians are saved: by adoption.

Amid all the clamor for and idolatry of being a biological, nuclear family in this modern age, we Christians forget far too easily that our being one of God's children is not a result of biological birth. One is not a Christian simply because of one's biological pedigree or social status. Rather, God makes us God's children through our adoption by God in Christ. We may use the name "Christian" because the Holy Spirit has drawn us into the household of God. Paul writes, "You have received a spirit of adoption." This alone is why we Christians can proclaim that God is "Abba! Father!" This undeserved gift is deserving of praise.

Who has adopted us? That is a fair question for any child who is swept up unexpectedly into the broad swath of eternity's fabric. The Spirit of God adopted us. And the Spirit of God in us as God's adopted children makes us heirs of God. We are joint heirs with Christ, the "heir supreme."

Why has God adopted us? Clearly not because of our own actions or for all our misplaced good intentions, which make us much more the debtors. Nor is it out of our willful desire, for we do not have the commitment of character like Jesus. Rather, God has adopted us solely because of God's love for us, which alone can pay the deep cost incurred by our sins. While we were yet sinners, resisting God's call to follow, Christ suffered for us so that we may be glorified with him. It is Christ's sacrifice that changes our relationship with God for all eternity. Such is the nature of God's love. Such is our hope.

PRAYER: "Abba! Father!" I pray this as my prayer because of your gift of adoption, O God. At my baptism in Christ, through the Holy Spirit, I became a child of the Most High God. To you, O Lord, do I give my thanks and praise. Amen.

FRIDAY, JULY 16 • Read Romans 8:18-25

For an actor, there is nothing in life like the adrenaline rush that surges through every part of the body in those few minutes before striding onto the stage to take position or to execute the crucial denouement of a playwright's well-crafted words. The butterflies of nervous energy that usually rest quietly within us suddenly form a "V" formation and soar to destinations unknown. As the butterflies take flight, they leave our hearts beating faster and our minds racing wildly through the script to fathom our next line or our next move. Unexpectedly, all is a blur, leaving the actor with only a simple "Oh" on the lips. The audience waits, hoping the actor will remember what's next.

So it is with creation. Creation is the actor, whose time is not yet fulfilled. Like the actor, creation is waiting in the wings of the cosmic stage to reveal itself totally in glory as we welcome the new heaven and new earth (Rev. 21:1). Paul writes that creation, along with God's children, waits with "eager longing for the revealing of the children of God." While God is in creation, creation first finds itself in God. Yet such truth is left stuttering as decay holds creation itself in bondage. All of creation, caught in bondage due to Adam's sin, is groaning, filled with unmet expectation, writhing in pain. The radical hope that creation awaits emancipation will come in time. Without anxiety, but in the sureness of hope born of God, "we wait for it with patience."

PRAYER: O Christ, I pray that you will place me in and among those who are well acquainted with the practice of patience's virtue. I pray that you will keep me in the company of strangers who may have mercy upon me and teach me to wait with you and the communion of saints. Amen.

SATURDAY, JULY 17 • Read Matthew 13:24-30

Christians do not find it surprising that evil exists in the world. In explaining both evil's origin and its demise, Jesus offers his followers the parable of the weeds among the wheat. Jesus tells us that amid the bounty of good seed planted in the wheat fields of the world, the enemy also sows weeds. The slaves (or disciples) in this parable get upset when they discover the weeds: "Master, did you not sow good seed in your field? Where, then, did these weeds come from?" In citing "the enemy" as the sower of the weeds, the householder, who is Jesus, does something surprising. Rather than gathering the weeds, which would also uproot the wheat, he lets them grow together until harvest. At harvest time the weeds will be separated from the wheat.

This is not a naive response from the householder. It is a response of a person of great faith who understands only too well the magnanimous power of God's grace to vanquish evil, even in the devil's playground. Perhaps Flannery O'Connor says it best in *Mystery and Manners,* explaining what makes her stories work: "An action that is totally unexpected, yet totally believable…is always an action which indicates that grace has been offered. And frequently it is an action in which the devil has been the unwilling instrument of grace." O'Connor goes on to say that oftentimes a character in the "territory held largely by the devil" practices the action of grace. The householder in this parable from Matthew's Gospel practices a gesture of amazing grace.

PRAYER: O Christ, for the gift of the parables, I give you thanks. In these timeless parables you make real for me the ways of heaven in my life on earth. Spirit, give me the wisdom to know the difference between wheat and weeds, both in this life and the life to come. Amen.

Jesus exhorts the crowd: "Let anyone with ears listen!" at the end of his explanation of the parable of the wheat and weeds. Why does Jesus close with such a point? Maybe because Jesus' original audience did not "get the point" of the parable. This is not a new experience for Jesus. Throughout Matthew 13, we read of Jesus' awareness that many will hear his words with their ears but still miss the message of the small story with the big point. To this day and days to come, people will hear or receive this very parable but miss the point.

Why? Because we do not practice listening for the message. And Jesus himself embodies the message in the parable told. Developing an ability to hear Jesus, the living Word of God, the One who embodies God's story of love for this world, requires practice. The children of God in the many-layered, tradition-bound rituals of a church's life learn the practice.

We must hone our listening skills to hear the point Jesus is trying to convey in a parable. And in the practice of living our shared life together as Christians in the discipline of faithful living, slowly but surely we begin to hear the "old chestnuts" of parables anew.

By the irresistible grace of God, which gives us the desire to practice listening to Jesus' parables, the Spirit reaches out to all God's people. The Spirit invites us to live the good news embodied in a story of wheat, weeds, and a wise farmer who knows that one day "the righteous will shine like the sun in the kingdom of their Father."

PRAYER: To you whose reign shines like the sun, I give you praise. Continue to teach me the gestures that make possible my hearing, seeing, and receiving of the good news as embodied in our Lord and Savior, Jesus Christ. Guide me evermore in the practice of the gestures that make way for the coming of God's irresistible reign. Amen.

The Unfolding Mystery of the Kingdom

July 19–25, 1999 • *Lynne Mobberley Deming**

MONDAY, JULY 19 • **Read Matthew 13:31-33, 44-52**

According to Mark 1:15, Jesus inaugurated his public ministry with the statement, "The kingdom of God has come near; repent, and believe in the good news." Think about it. If you had heard that statement, wouldn't you have wondered what Jesus meant? We can imagine that his statement intrigued many people. Perhaps they asked him to elaborate.

Jesus often used parables to offer further explanation of his statements. This week's Gospel reading contains six such parables; each one illumines a different aspect of the kingdom of God. At the end of the week, we will know a little more about the nature of God's kingdom, but its mystery will not (and cannot) be fully revealed.

The well-known parable of the mustard seed illustrates the idea of potential and its relationship to the kingdom of God. When we read the parable of the leaven we "see" a kingdom of God that is not always visible but nevertheless real. The parable of the treasure in the field reveals that the kingdom of God can be irresistible. It is also of great value, as the parable of the pearl of great price illustrates. As a net cast into the sea gathers in everything it can, the kingdom of God includes everyone and everything. The last parable illustrates the importance of valuing the past as well as the present.

PRAYER: O God of mystery and surprise, may I always seek to discover something new in the midst of the familiar. As I read these well-known passages, may they reveal new mysteries about your presence in my life. Amen.

---

*Publisher, United Church Press and Pilgrim Press, United Church of Christ, Cleveland, Ohio.

TUESDAY, JULY 20 • Read Matthew 13:31-32; Romans 8:28-36

We have all heard the parable of the mustard seed many times. What new insight might the parable have for us today?

This parable and the parable of the leaven (tomorrow's passage) speak of growth and transformation—of humble beginnings, great expectations, and amazing results. The end looks very different from the beginning. The tiny mustard seed grows into a tree so large that birds can nest in its branches. Amazing! What inherent potential within this tiny seed!

When I was young I remember my parents' telling me that when I grew up I could be anything I wanted to be. As a young adult looking back on my childhood, I concluded that my parents were just trying to bolster my sense of self-confidence by telling me that my abilities had no limits. In young adulthood, my awareness of my limitations began to develop.

But now I'm not so sure. Now as a parent, I have heard (and still hear) myself saying the same thing to my own children that my parents said to me—and meaning it. For children are like seeds: They can grow and transform in amazing ways. And yes, they can be anything they want to be. At least I believe that about my own children.

Paul offers this same message to his followers in Rome. With the presence of God and the intercession of Christ Jesus, we can do anything. Hardship, distress, persecution, or other evils will not deter us. According to Paul, in God's reign we have great potential to transform from small seeds into lush, beautiful foliage.

PRAYER: Loving and transforming God, with your ever-present help I can achieve my greatest potential. May I live up to the challenge you offer. Amen.

WEDNESDAY, JULY 21 • **Read Matthew 13:33; Romans 8:26-27**

What might the kingdom of heaven have to do with yeast? Those who bake bread know something of the quality of yeast. Yeast has the ability to change the look and feel of bread in a way that seems very mysterious. We can smell the yeast and sometimes even taste it, but we cannot see it. Bread just would not be the same without it.

You may have seen a television commercial that advertises its product by saying something like, "We don't make the shoes; we make them better." In a recent staff meeting, one of our editors described his work by saying that he could identify with that company's slogan. He doesn't write the manuscripts; he makes them better in almost invisible ways. We see beautiful prose without seeing the editor's hand in the process.

In today's passage from Romans, Paul describes the presence of the Holy Spirit in our lives in such a way that it reminds us of the presence of yeast in a loaf of bread or the presence of an editorial hand in the making of a book or the small act of kindness that produces amazing results. The Spirit intercedes in our weakness and changes us in such subtle ways that we do not recognize the presence of the Spirit in our lives. That presence is real nevertheless. The Spirit doesn't create us; the Spirit makes us better by bringing us into the presence of the holy.

PRAYER: O invisible and mysterious God, I am grateful for your presence in my life, even when that presence is not visible to me. I know you are there, and that is enough. Amen.

THURSDAY, JULY 22 • Read Matthew 13:44; Genesis 29:15-20

In this parable, Jesus describes a man who comes unexpectedly upon a treasure. Unlike the man in the parable about the pearl of great price, this man does not spend a lifetime looking for the treasure. We can imagine his simply stumbling upon it lying in a field. Remember the line from the old television show, "Candid Camera": "Sometime, somewhere, when you least expect it…"? That is what happened to the man in Jesus' parable. When has something like that happened to you?

A long-lost friend calls from out of the blue. You find money in the pocket of a jacket that you haven't worn for a long time. Your baby son utters his first sentence. These are treasures hidden in a field. Some years ago I got a letter in the mail with a large check inside. My mother's cousin had died. In her will she left sizable amounts of her estate to me and my brother because my mother had kept in touch with her for many years. That check was truly a treasure hidden in a field that I stumbled upon unexpectedly.

In Jesus' parable, the fact that the man isn't particularly looking for the treasure he finds doesn't matter. It is a treasure nonetheless.

The story in Genesis is like that too. Nothing indicates that Jacob is looking for the love of his life that day at the well in the desert. But imagine what goes through his mind when he sees Rebekah for the first time. She becomes his unexpected treasure in a field. And that is what the kingdom of heaven is like sometimes— unexpected, of great value, beautiful in its own way. A treasure to be cherished.

PRAYER: Generous and giving God, I am grateful for the treasures you send me when I least expect them. Amen.

FRIDAY, JULY 23 • Read Matthew 13:45-46; Genesis 29:21-28

Unlike the person in yesterday's passage who comes upon a treasure rather unexpectedly, today's merchant goes in search of fine pearls and eventually finds one of great value. Its value is so great, in fact, that this merchant sells everything in order to get the money to buy the pearl. Although we can all identify with this merchant's desire to own this one valuable pearl after his lengthy search, would we actually sell everything we have in order to get it? Probably not. But this merchant was willing to sacrifice everything to get the pearl.

Jacob would have understood that kind of sacrifice. In order to marry Rachel, he works a total of fourteen years for his uncle. Jacob's determination reminds us of the merchant whose desire for the pearl made him willing to sell all that he had. Verse 20 says that Jacob loved Rachel so much that seven years of servanthood seemed like just a few days.

And that feeling is, at least in part, what the kingdom of heaven is like. Some years ago a man named Peter Jenkins walked across America from coast to coast, encountering many different kinds of landscapes. At his adventure's end, he found the perfect spot to settle in a rather unlikely place: The rolling hills of middle Tennessee. Spring Hill, Tennessee, became his pearl of great price; and he settled there.

PRAYER: Loving God, persons enter your presence in many ways. Some of us search long and hard for you; others find you in unexpected ways and places. I give thanks for those encounters, however they happen. Amen.

SATURDAY, JULY 24 • Read Matthew 13:47-50; Romans 8:37-39

"The kingdom of heaven is like a net that was thrown into the sea and caught fish of every kind." What is Jesus trying to tell us here about the kingdom of heaven? For one thing, the kingdom of heaven includes everyone. When we throw a net out into the sea, the net catches everything within its reach, regardless of what it is. Imagine what might have been caught in such a net—fish of various kinds, wood from shipwrecks, shells, pieces of clothing. In the same way, the kingdom of heaven will include everything available when the net is cast. What kinds of persons might have been caught? Who might be caught today?

In verses 47-48, we see that at some point we have to make choices. In our everyday language, we often call this process separating the wheat from the chaff. How do you suppose Jesus intends that the choices be made? What reasons would or should be used to include or exclude persons from entering the kingdom of heaven? What factors would we use today to make these choices?

SUGGESTION FOR MEDITATION: Reread Romans 8:37-39. Verse 39 summarizes Paul's message: Nothing can separate us from the love of God in Christ Jesus. Think for a moment about the factors in your life that tend to separate you from the love of God. What gets in your way—physical or emotional pain, job anxieties, worries about family members, other factors? List these one by one. Then pray for the wisdom and strength to overcome these obstacles.

SUNDAY, JULY 25 • Read Matthew 13:51-52; Psalm 105:1-11, 45*b*

Today's passages speak of the virtue and value associated with the past, and the necessary balance between the past and current existence. In Matthew 13:52, Jesus speaks of the scribe who treasures what is old and what is new—that is, a person well schooled in Mosaic law (the past) and a disciple of Jesus (the present). We might characterize this kind of person as "eclectic," having an interest in both antiques and contemporary art. In faith terms, this kind of person might value traditional liturgy while at the same time appreciating inclusive language.

Psalm 105 praises God's great deeds on behalf of the chosen people. We can imagine this psalm being read aloud at one of Israel's major annual festivals. How comforting is the reassurance of God's presence, now as in the past. Notice the shifts in tense in this psalm. God "made" a covenant with Abraham; God "is mindful" of the covenant forever. This psalm balances its consideration of God's past deeds on Israel's behalf with praise of God for honoring this covenant even to the present.

So balance is the key—balance between the past and the present. We often hear the lament that our churches are aging; we don't have enough young people. While young people may bring vitality and energy into the church, balance is the key here as well— a balance between the importance of the past and the importance of the present. We need always to remember and value the stability and wisdom of our older church members, even as we gain new ideas, energy, and vitality from the young.

PRAYER: **Loving and gracious God, I thank you for your presence with me, both in the past and in the present. May I never take that presence for granted. Amen.**

The Grace of God

July 26–August 1, 1999 • *William W. Morris**

Whenever persons discuss Paul's writings, all agree that Paul wrote Romans. Romans differs from the other epistles because it does not stem from a particular problem or congregational crisis.

Paul sets forth his message in a systematic way that consequently sheds light on Paul's theology. Paul is on his way to Spain, and he wants to preach in the Roman church. Uncertain of the Roman church's reception of him, Paul clearly states in verses 1-5 his credentials for drafting the letter and for visiting Rome.

Paul addresses a thorny subject, the salvation of the Jews—or Israel. There is the feeling that Israel has been the recipient of a marvelous spiritual legacy. The Jews have been part of the legacy from the beginning. Although Israel has been chosen, her elect status does not reside in ethnicity or in being better than others. Israel's election comes through her obedience, accountability, and responsiveness to God. Paul's sadness arises with his concern about the people's receiving Christ. If not, what will happen? Paul's answer is the only one to make— God will make the decision. Is this unjust? No, for Paul reminds us of God's response to Moses, "'I will have mercy on whom I have mercy, and I will have compassion on whom I have compassion' So, it depends...on God who shows mercy" (vv.15-16). That's it! God wants no one to perish and makes God's mercy available to everyone regardless of ethnic group.

PRAYER: Eternal God, may I too come to understand that when I am chosen, I am to serve you more faithfully and more nearly day by day. In Jesus' name. Amen.

---

*Resident bishop, Alabama-West Florida Episcopal Area, The United Methodist Church.

TUESDAY, JULY 27 • Read Psalm 17:1-7, 15

The Psalms throughout the generations continue to serve as an oasis in life's dryness, a comfort in times of distress. The Psalms cover a variety of experiences: confession, penitence, thanksgiving, liturgy, and celebration. The psalmist speaks clearly and directly to the issues at hand, yet never doubts who is in charge. The tie between experiences of the past and the present free the Psalms from time and culture.

In Psalm 17, the psalmist deals with the reality of his situation in a direct way. Verse 7 makes it clear that the psalmist has enemies, personal enemies, for he declares,

Wondrously show thy steadfast love,
O savior of those who seek refuge
from their adversaries at thy right hand (RSV).

But the psalmist also believes that God is just and that God hears and responds to prayers. In verses 3-4, the author builds his case for asking for God's help: He is neither a wicked nor a violent man, and he has followed God's mandates.

The psalmist does not hesitate to request deliverance from his enemies:

Keep me as the apple of the eye;
Hide me in the shadow of thy wings,
from the wicked who despoil me,
my deadly enemies who surround me (vv. 8-9, RSV).

Without question we, like the psalmist, must see God as having the power to make a difference in life's events. The steadfast love of God will deliver from their enemies those who trust and live for God.

PRAYER: O Lord, may I have the confidence and assurance of the psalmist to believe that you reward the faithful in this life as well as the next. In the Master's name. Amen.

WEDNESDAY, JULY 28 • Read Genesis 32:22-31

Genesis is the book of beginnings, the book that details God's entry into human history. It shares with us God's creative activity and desire that all creation knows and serves the Creator. Although our sin thwarts God's intentions, God's love never wavers.

Abraham represents God's promise and covenant with Israel. God's promise continues through the family of Abraham and Sarah, coming to rest with the two sons, Esau and Jacob. Jacob's wresting of the birthright from his brother sends him off to live with relatives. Years go by; the brothers exchange no words. We can understand some of Jacob's distress at the thought of returning home

Jacob's life will change substantially at the river Jabbok. After sending his family across the Jabbok, Jacob remains alone to face the future and to think about his destiny. Jacob wrestles with a man all night long until the breaking of day. This wrestling match changes Jacob from what he is to what he can become, and he receives the new name of Israel. Hence the birthright is fulfilled; Jacob is now Israel, the continued life of Abraham and carrier of the covenant.

Wrestling with God is serious business, and it may leave us bent out of shape for our own desires but put in shape for God's desires. Wrestling with God heightens our awareness of our relationship with God and of God's expectations of us. We may take an inventory of our behavior as Christians, intentionally assessing whether we have experienced life-changing moments in Christ or whether we are just drifting away.

To struggle with God's demands is challenging, and it frequently takes us where we would not choose to go. The joy comes in knowing that we never go alone, for God has gone before us and goes with us.

PRAYER: **Eternal God and heavenly Father, give me courage to do what I know I ought to do and to believe that I never walk alone. In Jesus' name. Amen.**

THURSDAY, JULY 29 • **Read Genesis 32:26-31**

Jacob does not want to go home, even though his situation with Laban is not the best of all possible worlds either. But the word has come from God to go home. Jacob, an individual determined to succeed at any cost, is a risk-taker, a trickster. He always seems to be thinking ahead.

Jacob meets his match in Laban. After working seven years to get Rebekah as his bride, Jacob is reminded by Laban of the cultural custom of the elder daughter's marrying before the younger. So Jacob gets Rebekah as a wife on the installment plan—and seven years more work.

When it comes time to leave, Jacob has a huge herd, a large family, and a lot of wealth. Once again, he outsmarts his adversary. As Jacob heads toward home, we do not see a decidedly changed man. He is still conniving and devious, and he has the birthright.

For Jacob to change, God will have to act, and God does. God changes Jacob's physical being, giving him a limp. More importantly, God changes Jacob's name—a new name for a new man, God's man.

We rarely welcome change. Change means shedding the familiar and learning that which is new. To serve in God's world is to allow ourselves to be changed by God. Only as God changes and sustains our lives are we equipped for living.

> Have thine own way Lord! Have thine own way!
> Thou art the potter; I am the clay.
> Mold me and make me after thy will,
> while I am waiting, yielded and still.

PRAYER: God, make me a captive of love and grace and then I shall truly be free. Strip me of pride, greed, and all else that stands in the way of serving you. Make me yours, truly yours. In Jesus' name. Amen.

FRIDAY, JULY 30 • Read Matthew 14:13-14

Matthew's Gospel is the first book of the New Testament because it serves as a good teaching document. The Gospel writer seeks to present every detail of Jesus' ministry. In Matthew we learn of Jesus as a teacher, preacher, and healer. Matthew 14 offers the opportunity to see the disposition of our Savior. John the Baptist has been Jesus' forerunner, clearly stating that his role is to prepare the way. In Luke's Gospel, John and Jesus are kinsmen.

John's directness in his proclamation about the coming of the Christ and the inevitable results get him into trouble. Herod imprisons John because of John's challenge of Herod's right to marry his brother's wife, Herodias. Herodias's daughter dances before Herod, and he promises her anything she likes. She asks for John the Baptist's head on a platter. The deed is done.

Jesus hears about John's death. He withdraws until the crowd catches up with him. Despite his loss, the crowd follows him, and he responds by coming to shore. He sets aside his personal grief and has compassion on them. Matthew's Gospel shows us Jesus' humanity. He endures a death in his personal circle. Yet he sets aside his sorrow in order to heal those who are hurting, remaining conscious of others' experiences.

Compassion in the purest form requires a high degree of concern and understanding of others' pain. This concern drives our response to the pain. We feel compelled to make a difference. Christ's compassion continues to vibrate in hospitals, in Habitat for Humanity programs, in soup kitchens, in substance abuse programs, in parents' day out ministries, and in hundreds of other ways.

PRAYER: Gracious Master, never let me be satisfied as long as there is suffering in the world. Help me reach out and touch the lives of others, making the world a better place in which to live. In Jesus' name. Amen.

SATURDAY, JULY 31 • Read Matthew 14:15-20

All four Gospels record this story. Each gospel mentions the fact that five thousand men are fed, but only Matthew recognizes the entire family with these words: "besides women and children" (v. 21).

The rest of the story pictures the environment as a lonely place. This sense of loneliness affects the disciples to the degree that they want to send the crowd into the villages to buy dinner. But Jesus tells the disciples to feed the masses, they who have only five loaves and two fish. The disciples serve the fish and the loaves, and everyone is fed.

The text offers no clue as to how Jesus feeds so many with so little. He blesses the food and breaks it and gives it to the disciples. The twentieth-century mind, ruled by cause and effect, finds this feat incomprehensible. Our advanced technology no longer allows us to take miracles seriously or to believe that miracles happen. Yet how often do situations that defy rational explanation present themselves?

When one thinks about the feeding of the five thousand, it might register that Jesus, functioning as the Son of God, has only to ask and those around him will receive. God supersedes all scientific theory simply because God is Creator, Redeemer, and Sustainer of the universe.

We are kindred spirits with our spiritual ancestors, the disciples, for they too often forgot who Jesus was; they failed to realize that God's ways are mysterious and only God can interpret them and make them plain to us. It's a miracle!

PRAYER: Heavenly Father, thank you for those moments that help me realize that this is your universe. Make me sensitive to the miracles that still surround us. Help me truly worship you in thought as well as in deed. In Jesus' name. Amen.

Today's text reminds us that even after everyone has eaten (all five thousand men plus women and children), they collect leftovers—twelve baskets full. The feeding of the five thousand helps us see the humanity and the divinity of our Lord and Savior. Death strikes and does not spare even the Son of God from grief and sorrow, but he doesn't lose touch with the human need that surrounds him. While saddened by John's death, Jesus still has compassion for those who seek his presence for help, for healing, for instruction, and for direction.

Despite the circumstances, Jesus places the crowd in groups of fifty to lessen the chaos. (See Luke 9:10-17.) He takes a boy's lunch and feeds thousands of people. Jesus' actions demonstrate God's concern for the total person. It further demonstrates that, by example, the least of these must also be a concern of ours. Jesus' actions declare that to deal actively with the physical, whatever the need, opens one to think about the spiritual.

The reciting of this story can help us see that we all are subject to the seen and unforeseen changes in life. While these changes can devastate us, Jesus shows us that life goes on; and we have to continue moving with the flow of events. The feeding of the five thousand attempts to call us to believe once again that while miracles are not ancient history, they are beyond our control. They come to life at God's command with no explanation. The challenge comes in our receptivity to them.

Finally, Jesus can carry out his ministry because God is with him. This is our hope too—that God is with us.

PRAYER: Gracious Master, life is like a river, filled with many bends and turns. Sometimes I fall out of the boat, but I thank you for rescuing me time and time again. Continue to have mercy upon me and keep me in your loving care. In the Savior's name. Amen.

The Presence Ahead of Us

*August 2–8, 1999 • Ron Mills**

MONDAY, AUGUST 2 • **Read Genesis 37:1-4**

"**T**his is the story of the family of Jacob." God weaves again the saving plan in an inconspicuous place—a family. When we think of divine actions in human affairs, we picture spectacular intrusions—earthquake, wind, and fire. Yet God's movements at times so assume our ordinary and natural rhythms that we live oblivious to the heavenly current running beneath existence.

Jacob gives an extravagant tunic to the child of his old age: the dreaming one. The father's gift introduces discord into the family that soon will pierce the old man's heart. Still, Jacob and Joseph move into a landscape fashioned by God. Neither man sees. Both participate. The unfurling dream belongs to God.

That God would unfold salvation through the tedious, vulnerable, and seemingly unpredictable pilgrimage of a human family baffles us. Time and again though, the Almighty chooses the way of weakness. God leans, listening to the laughter of Abraham and Sarah. God watches a mother tentatively place her three-month-old son into a papyrus basket at the river's edge. The eternal One sways to the rhythm of Hannah's song. The Holy One remains just behind the curtain of Joseph and Mary's wonder.

God works in sea-splitting, mountain-shaking ways, to be sure. However, the escapades of the family of Jacob teach us that the divine way flows behind the scenes of ordinary family life too. As surely as Jacob and Joseph participate in God's design without awareness, so do we. We all take part in a dream of God, a saving presence ahead of us, unfolding a journey to an abundant place.

PRAYER: God, I trust my meandering soul to your unseen presence ahead of me. Amen.

---

*Pastor of Ridgeway United Methodist Church, living in Martinsville, Virginia.

TUESDAY, AUGUST 3 • Read Genesis 37:12-28

Joseph saw, without understanding, the drama of God's purpose unfold. He spoke the dream into his brothers' ears, ears already hot with hatred at the tunic he wore. The tunic was hard enough to bear; now Joseph offers arrogant fantasies. Neither Joseph nor his brothers understand the reality spoken forth in the dream. His brothers feel threatened by the mystery though—threatened enough to make plans to silence it. So Joseph, the dreamer, strolls innocently toward the hatred watching him from a distance.

Whenever we enter God's drama, we become, in some ways, the disturbers of the peace of the human family. Society and culture desire to order human life a certain way. The emerging dream/drama of God threatens that way. Though we may be unaware of the impact of our faith on the world around us, the very name *Christian* drapes our lives like an eye-catching tunic. The world sees but does not understand the garments of salvation. Joseph is not the only threatened God-bearer. You and I are too because the divine dream threatens the status quo of any age.

Despite all threats, God weaves and protects the holy purpose guiding us toward the promise. Traveling ahead of us, God's strength awaits us before we need it. Holy comfort awaits us at the precise location of our collapse. God measures provision against our lack. Our brother Joseph calls us to understand our lives as part of a vast dream, the dream of God that has the power to keep us—even in a hostile environment.

PRAYER: Lord, I trust your presence with me, though I do not understand how I have ended up in this place. Amen.

WEDNESDAY, AUGUST 4 • **Read Psalm 105:1-6, 16-22, 45**

The psalmist looks back in grateful recollection over the events shaping Israel's history. Characteristic of human vision, we do not read very well, if at all, the way of God in our dailyness. When chaos threatens to engulf us, we feel abandoned to our circumstance even as God weaves a way for us behind the scenes. In looking back, we uncover a sequence of divine movements that enable us to say, "Surely the presence of the Lord was in this place and I did not know it" (Gen. 28:16). God was at work, even in the painful events of Joseph's life, to make a way for the covenant people. Joseph bore in his body and experiences the way of deliverance for God's community. He suffered too for the bearing.

Only in retrospect can one fathom this pain. The psalmist, looking back with his people's eyes, urges them to give thanks to God. Joseph's pain now carries the name, "wonderful works." The psalmist's praise enables the hearts of all who seek God to rejoice in the One working behind the scenes of our earthly existence— though pain-filled—to accomplish the holy purpose.

Joseph moves as the grace of God—preveniently. Enslaved, hurt, collared, and imprisoned, grace awaits its moment. In the shadow of deliverance of a whole people, Joseph understands his private pain. God's purpose and presence with us transform suffering into faithful service. In our faithfulness others come to know life.

PRAYER: Looking behind me I see your faithfulness, O God. Let the memory of your presence with me yesterday provide a confident assurance of your presence with me today. Amen.

We follow Joseph's trail of faithfulness. His life hints at the tribulation that comes to those who live with God. We listen to Moses and what he tells us about this journey. With God we touch and handle the right things. We halt our hand when it reaches for the wrong thing. We keep to the honorable paths and hurry past the questionable ones. We do what is good, and avoid what is evil.

God offers a different way through this earth. Human beings do not travel haphazardly toward the holy. Moses tells us the truth: Those who approach God require skill in right living because God revealed that to us on the thundering, shaking mountain.

It is a journey for the strong. We know that now from our exhaustion. The burden of "good-enough" has been too much to carry to God's altar. We tried. It seems like such an impossible journey now, with our shoulders already drooping.

Then Paul, one of Jesus' men, travels our way. "Stop wondering how you will get to God," he says. "You already are too tired to travel toward glory. It is a journey of faith. Jesus is Lord. Believe that!" The apostle vanishes down the road.

*Faith...Jesus is Lord...*the words linger in the air. Paul talks as if the journey is no longer tentative and precarious but assured. Only in God can that happen. We know the strength is not in us. A curious message the apostle leaves us. The way to God and the life we seek comes not by hands and feet but lips and heart.

PRAYER: Give me this faith, O God. I thought I would last longer. I have worn myself out reaching for you. Now...reach for me. Amen.

FRIDAY, AUGUST 6 • **Read Romans 10:9-15**

Eternity moves dream-like beneath our lives. Christ, the incarnate interpreter, comes. Jesus enters our landscape, littered as it is with broken, discarded attempts to reach God. He journeys alongside us weary pilgrims, exhausted now by the burden of a goodness we cannot possibly carry. He offers rest: eternal, soul-satisfying, joyful rest.

Jesus travels with us unrecognized at times because he suffers. He hides the generosity of his companionship beneath his suffering. We keep our distance from weakness. The journey Godward demands strength, so we think; or so we have been told. We distrust a suffering messenger. What God would construct a sacred journey through weakness?

No one noticed what Jesus had accomplished until it was over. Those who long for God understand. The weary and the broken stare at this suffering Emmanuel and see salvation's silhouette. One by one, we pilgrims toward God recognize him by our heart's release. We know him by our soul's mending. Walking here by his side we feel the yoke shared, and the way eased. We sense the journey's end given to us, not earned.

We thought it to be a journey of the hands and feet: proper steps taken; proper things handled. Instead, in Jesus, we discover it to be a pilgrimage of the heart, a word spoken. All of the riches of the kingdom lodge in the name rising to our lips—Jesus. Like Joseph's family, receiving at his hands a wondrous benevolence enabling their survival, we receive more of life than we can imagine in the way of Jesus. He is generous to all who call on him. His word is near us.

PRAYER: Lord Jesus Christ, in gratitude I receive your generous gift, weary traveler toward God that I am. Amen.

Jesus makes the disciples get into a boat and go ahead of him to the other side of the Sea of Galilee. He dismisses the crowd and finds a place to be alone. He withdraws from the heart of his mission— proclaiming the kingdom of God and forming the twelve disciples—in order to be by himself to pray. Quite a message for hands-on people like us. We convince ourselves that life's major accomplishments succeed only when borne by our relentless effort and ceaseless activity.

What will happen if we stop pushing this hope-mingled mass of clock and schedule, debt and investment, family and career, heaven and hell on the road ahead of us? Surely it will roll back on us and crush us if we don't keep pushing. Or will it?

Jesus' times alone for prayer bid us think about the unseen forces (*grace* may be a better word) that assist our lives along the way. Pressing projects, bathed in prayer, move with heaven's help. Persons dear to us, entrusted to the One who hears our supplications, live under the shadow of God's wings.

The solitary journey to a place of prayer brings us to a listening place. We hear the beating of our heart, literally and spiritually. We remove ourselves from the noise, the pressure, and even the pleasures of the outer world to be instructed by the silence. From that deep central region within us we hear the Creator's voice. We empty; we fill. We mend; we renew. We leave the solitude as a partner with the silent workings of grace. With Jesus, we move back toward the world. We find ourselves replenished with the quiet trust of God's prevenient grace.

PRAYER: O Renewer of all weariness, Replenisher of all emptiness, in the silence of this moment I entrust my life to you. Amen.

SUNDAY, AUGUST 8 • Read Matthew 14:26-33

When Jesus sends his disciples ahead of him, not only is Jesus alone, his disciples find themselves without the master's presence. These who have walked with Jesus, listened to Jesus, and depended on Jesus, now find themselves in a storm, flailing helplessly about and at the point of perishing. After a time of prayer Jesus returns to the disciples, walking on the water. Ghostlike, he frightens the beloved crew.

All who would be disciples find themselves in the same "boat" over and over again. We live with Jesus. We enter the storm. Eventually, the One who intercedes on our behalf in heavenly places comes to us in the darkness. Another divine irony occurs when the God with whom we travel on land becomes unrecognizable to us in the eye of the storm.

Perhaps it is easier to trust in God's benevolence and the certainty of tomorrow when solid earth lies beneath our feet and warm sunlight illumines our way. Discipleship appeals to us when God is a comfortable arm's reach in a familiar location, and perishing is not an issue. When perishing is the issue, however, Jesus does not abandon us. He comes to us, the same life-holding presence. At times we resist his approach. We do not recognize his storm-obscured face until he speaks out of the darkness. From pulpit, from book, from friend, from silence, his word comes and then we know it is our Lord. "Take heart," he says. He offers us what we have the least of when our lives are threatened: heart in the eye of the storm, peace when adrift in violent forces.

PRAYER: Lord Jesus, let me hear your offer of peace in the midst of this storm. Amen.

God's Family: Marked by Mercy

August 9–15, 1999 • Carmen Lile-Henley*

MONDAY, AUGUST 9 • **Read Genesis 45:1-3**

The readings for this week underline the depth of God's mercy and give us insights about what it means to be members of God's family. In the well-known Joseph story, Joseph serves as a metaphor for God and knows firsthand of God's mercy in his life. In today's reading, Joseph reveals himself to his brothers, who have treated him with brutality, hatred, and betrayal.

The depth of Joseph's continued love for his family reveals itself in his loud weeping—so loud that the Egyptians and the entire household of Pharaoh can hear it. Joseph's brothers are so dismayed by this revelation, that the one they betrayed is now in a position of power, that they cannot speak. Joseph holds their lives and their survival in his hands, and he expresses concern for those family members left behind in a place of famine and scarcity.

Our human nature often leads us to greed, sibling rivalry, jealousy, and acts of betrayal. We have every reason to feel dismayed in God's presence, for God has every reason to punish and avenge. But this is not God's way or Joseph's way. God's way is that of mercy and concern for the human family.

God is always moving toward self-revelation despite our efforts to rid ourselves of God's presence. God's purposes of love and reconciliation enfold our acts of betrayal and greed.

SUGGESTION FOR MEDITATION: **Reflect on those places where you feel dismay, and ask forgiveness from God, who offers mercy.**

---

*Associate pastor, Belmont United Methodist Church, Nashville, Tennessee; bereavement specialist and HIV ministry advocate.

233

TUESDAY, AUGUST 10 • **Read Genesis 45:4-8**

In today's reading, Joseph urges his dismayed brothers to come closer as he comforts them. They might have expected revenge, but Joseph relieves their fears. He asks that they not be angry with themselves for selling him into slavery. Joseph can discern God's purpose within human decisions, even those of hatred and deceit.

Joseph sees the blessing that emerges from tragedy and acknowledges God's action in his life. He sees God's grace moving within human acts of destruction and darkness. With this theological and spiritual awareness, Joseph can act as God acts: with compassion, reconciliation, and mercy.

The story of Joseph goes beyond immediate family to illustrate God's deep concern for the entire human family. God works through Joseph to save the covenant people of Israel and the world from starvation. God uses individuals to make a difference for the whole family of God.

The God of Joseph is a God who preserves life, reconciles the estranged, forgives the sinner, and creates community. This God chooses to work for the good of all people within the limits of human freedom and our capacity for making choices that yield brokenness and suffering. This God can turn a curse into blessing and can bring life out of death.

SUGGESTION FOR MEDITATION: **Think of places in your life where God has been working to bring good out of evil. Think of ways you can help God create blessing out of cursed situations. Where do you discern God's purposes being acted out in your life?**

WEDNESDAY, AUGUST 11 • Read Genesis 45:9-15

Today's reading from the Joseph story shows God's purposes of reconciliation among the human family. After revealing himself to his brothers, Joseph moves decisively toward the future. Joseph, like God, provides a future marked by reconciliation, peace, plenty, protection, and security for the human family. God's purposeful action on behalf of humankind is grounded in mercy.

As we look back over the Joseph readings for the past two days, we see God's presence with Joseph in times of suffering. God works behind and through tragedy to create a new humanity and a new family. No matter what the past struggles, no matter how many wrongs, God responds with mercy.

Like Joseph, God acts in unexpected ways. Instead of disowning us, God claims us as family. Instead of retaliating, God provides for our needs. Instead of turning away and giving up on us, God continues to reveal Godself to us in mercy with the purpose of reconciling all people to God and to one another.

Joseph's dismayed and speechless brothers can speak to him only after receiving mercy. Only after kissing and weeping does their reconciliation with Joseph become verbal. A powerful emotional reconciliation precedes any attempts at words. God's work of reconciliation goes beyond human language and results in restored communication among formerly estranged family members.

SUGGESTION FOR MEDITATION: **Do you trust that God's future of reconciliation will be one of peace and plenty? In what situations do you refuse to be reconciled to others and to God? How are you helping God create a new human family?**

THURSDAY, AUGUST 12 • **Read Psalm 133**

This psalm echoes the themes of mercy and family found in the Joseph story. God intends harmony for the extended human family, a unity made possible by God's love and mercy showed to all humankind. This divine love serves as our model for all relationships: family, organizations, workplace, neighborhoods, communities, denominations, the church universal, and all creation.

The possible unity is precious, like the oil used extravagantly on tribal pilgrimages to the Temple. To "waste" the oil symbolized well-being, security, festivity, and prosperity among the tribal family. The psalmist also likens family harmony to the mountain dew of the arid desert—the precious moisture gives cause for joy in its pleasant, refreshing, life-giving presence for the community.

God intends such blessing for the whole community—not for isolated, solitary individuals. Community itself is a blessing, over-flowing with joy, delight, and generosity. The community God intends and desires for the human family is carefree and extravagant in its self-giving and without hostility, quarreling, or vengeance.

Just as family unity is one of the greatest joys, so estrangement, strife, and conflict among kindred engenders one of the worst kinds of human pain. How tragic it is when the family God created for nurture, support, security, and happiness becomes a place of silence, violence, or absence. God created us for harmony and community, for peace and joy. May God give us grace to live in the unity for which God formed us.

SUGGESTION FOR MEDITATION: **What barriers prevent you from living in unity in all relationships? How can you help God create harmony and community?**

FRIDAY, AUGUST 13 • **Read Romans 11:1-2***a***, 29-32**

In today's reading, Paul emphasizes the inclusiveness of God's family and the universal reach of God's mercy. Paul assures his readers that God has not rejected the covenant with Israel. God issues an irrevocable calling; God's election and promise is everlasting. This merciful God uses human limitations and even our disobedience to bring all people to salvation and wholeness.

Paul wants the church to know that God's steadfast loving-kindness extends to all, not just to one group. But the family chosen to convey the blessing—Abraham and Sarah and their descendants—was and is chosen and blessed in order to be a blessing. Family becomes the means by which God shows the world God's purposes of hospitality, inclusiveness, forgiveness, mercy, and love.

In the family of God, we experience mutuality despite our many differences. We all play a role in God's saving work. Each member and each group contributes to the salvation of the whole. None of us enters the family of God by way of our own accomplishment. Only by God's mercy are we grafted and regrafted into one community, one family. All of us—Jews and Gentiles, male and female—participate in the fullness of God's blessings begun in Jesus Christ.

SUGGESTION FOR MEDITATION: **In what ways can you discern God's bringing diverse peoples together? How can you and your group(s) contribute to the wholeness of God's family? In what ways can you show God's purposes of inclusiveness and mercy?**

SATURDAY, AUGUST 14 • **Read Matthew 15:10-20**

Today's Gospel reading shows our strong tendency to become legalistic rule keepers, tallying up our own merits and the offenses of others. Neatly categorizing and defining our relationship with God and one another makes us feel more secure. However, such attitudes usually serve only to separate us from one another, moving from mercy and a sense of family to "us-them" categories.

Jesus knows that focusing on the external to the exclusion of the inner life leads to barriers and separation. That focus can blind us to God's grace so that we cannot perceive God's presence in others. The Pharisees' focus on religious food laws kept them from seeing the true meaning of holiness. What keeps us from being holy is not the kind of food we put into our mouths but the kind of actions that flow from our inner being, which our words reflect. The language of love in action truly marks holiness.

In the household of God, our acts of inclusiveness and mercy make love and holiness visible. What God offers us, we are to offer the world: gathering, belonging, and generosity—no barriers, no separations, no categorizing, no judging. God's family does not spend time and energy tallying up merits and offenses but reaches out to embrace the whole world. The distinguishing characteristic of God's family is not external appearance but love given to the world in word and deed.

SUGGESTION FOR MEDITATION: What "us-them" categories prevent you from loving others more fully? How can your words and actions reflect more love and mercy?

SUNDAY, AUGUST 15 • Read Matthew 15:21-28

The continued Gospel reading underscores the irony of Jesus' actions toward an "outsider." In yesterday's reading, Jesus stated that "what comes out of the mouth proceeds from the heart"; language becomes a mark of holiness that issues from the inner being. In today's text, Jesus speaks harshly to the Canaanite woman who comes for healing on behalf of her child.

Recall the early church's struggle to become ecumenical, to break visible and invisible barriers, to overcome distinctions between "us" and "them." The first Jewish Christians were learning that the covenant of the Jews did not exclude Gentiles. In the continuing story of God's mercy, outsiders become insiders and insiders become outsiders. The true insiders are those who act as God acts, with inclusive, broad hospitality. The true outsiders are those who run counter to God's love through exclusive, narrow, inhospitable actions and words.

We may have difficulty accepting the fact that the foreign woman shapes and influences the human Jesus. Yet God sends an "outsider" to help redefine and reshape the understanding and definition of God's "children." The foreigner broadens Jesus' understanding of mercy and inclusiveness. The stranger widens the church's concept of what it means to be a member of God's family and God's covenant.

This remarkable encounter between Jesus and the woman shows us the reciprocity of God's grace: God sends the woman to bring new depth to Jesus' understanding, and then Jesus heals the woman's daughter. The encounter enhances the wholeness of all three—the woman, her child, and Jesus. May God give us grace to be open to the "outsiders" who come to reveal God's love to us.

SUGGESTION FOR MEDITATION: How is God sending strangers to you to broaden your understandings of inclusiveness? In what ways is God redefining "family" for you?

Challenge and Change

August 16–22, 1999 • *Justo González**

MONDAY, AUGUST 16 • **Read Exodus 1:8-14**

We are approaching the end of summer and the beginning of fall. It is a time of transition for many of us: those who attend school or who teach, those who have children or spouses who attend school or who teach, those who work on seasonal jobs. It is also a time of new beginnings in our churches: People return from vacations; students move to new classes in Sunday school; youth programs get geared up for school; college students get ready to leave. Many of our churches even have new pastors.

New times bring new changes, which may appear overwhelming at first. The old is tried and comfortable. The new is unknown and sometimes even menacing. Furthermore, the new is not always better than the old!

This uncertainty becomes clear as we read the story of the children of Israel in Egypt. They have made their home there—although Egypt is not their home. They have risen in society, becoming powerful and numerous. And now everything changes!

But the Israelites are not alone. God will use their new challenge for even greater blessing. God stands with them in their future. God also stands with us, no matter what uncertainties we face.

PRAYER: God of Israel, God of the church, God of ages past, God of all futures to come, give me confidence in your presence both as I face present challenges and as I face the end. In the name of Jesus, the Beginning and the End. Amen.

---

*Retired member of the Rio Grande Conference of The United Methodist Church; Director of the Hispanic Summer Program and Executive Director of the Hispanic Theological Initiative.

TUESDAY, AUGUST 17 • Read Exodus 1:15–2:10

We all know the story: When Israel is sorely oppressed in Egypt, God raises up Moses to lead the Israelites to freedom.

What we often miss is the importance of some characters whom we might consider to be "secondary" but who are nevertheless central. In today's story—even before the birth of Moses and during his infancy—a number of women play a crucial role. First are the midwives. Their valor saves Israel even before Moses is born. Then Moses' mother hides him for three months at great risk to her own life. She then thinks up and executes a plan to see that her child lives, even against the wishes of the mightiest ruler of the times. Moses' sister becomes part of the plot as she watches to see what will become of her baby brother and makes suggestions that eventually bring Moses back to his home and his mother's bosom. And finally, even unwittingly, Pharaoh's daughter plays a role. She is supposed to do nothing more than enjoy herself and lead a lazy, useless life. But God uses her to greater ends.

As we face today's challenges, we tend to find answers in obvious places—experts, powerful friends, or resources. But let us not forget that God also provides answers where we least expect them. And let us remember that we too, even in the midst of our own uncertainties and difficulties, may well be part of God's answer.

SUGGESTION FOR MEDITATION: Choose a particular challenge you face—perhaps even one you fear. List the obvious resources you have, such as friends, experts, money, etc. Now list other people around you who may share the same challenge with you. Might they be resources God is offering you? Could you be a resource for them?

WEDNESDAY, AUGUST 18 • Read Psalm 124

This psalm recounts and celebrates the outcome of the Exodus story, the story whose beginning we have read during the past two days. However, for the psalmist those events are already in the past. Israel is no longer in Egypt. The Exodus has taken place. This psalm of thanksgiving proclaims that Israel's deliverance from Egypt occurred only because of the Lord's action.

Such thanksgiving serves a further function. Israel sings this psalm in order to remember, when new difficulties arise, that the God who delivered them from Egypt is still the Lord. So while the body of the psalm deals with past events, the last verse brings all of those events to bear on the present: "Our help is in the name of the Lord, who made heaven and earth."

New challenges often overwhelm us because all we see in them is the "new." Obviously, without the newness the challenges might seem inconsequential. Our daily routine hardly challenges us. We do it without thinking, because we already know the proper action at each particular time of the day. The newness is the aspect that makes events a challenge. The newness also makes them interesting and exciting.

When any challenge threatens to overwhelm us, we need to remember that the God who has seen us "through many dangers, toils, and snares" is the same God whose grace has brought us safe thus far and whose grace will lead us home.

SUGGESTION FOR MEDITATION: Read slowly, or sing, the hymn "Amazing Grace." As you do so, think not only of all that God has done for you thus far but also of your present challenges. Place them all before God's grace.

THURSDAY, AUGUST 19 • Read Romans 12:1-2

Throughout this week we have considered challenges: challenges brought about by changing times or seasonal challenges that come with the end of summer and the beginning of fall. Today's passage, deals with a much deeper sort of challenge: the challenge not to "be conformed to this world."

When we speak of "challenges," we might distinguish between two kinds of challenge. The first is a challenge common to all of us who live in this world and this society: We have to make a living and provide for our basic needs as well as the basic needs of those for whom we care. The second is the more specific challenge of being a Christian in a secular society. Paul sets that challenge before us in this passage: "Do not be conformed to this world."

In what ways do we easily conform to this world? Perhaps the most common way comes when we judge our success in life by the standards of society around us. Our society measures success in terms of income—sometimes even in terms of expenditures, so that whoever buys more is more successful—of fame, of power. The Bible measures success in terms of love and obedience. The most successful person loves God and neighbor and in so doing obeys God. Jesus, who had nowhere to lay his head and who was executed as a criminal, is the epitome of Christian success!

SUGGESTION FOR MEDITATION: **Think back to your earlier reflections this week. As you thought about the challenges confronting you and sought God's help, were these challenges specifically Christian? Did you perceive yourself challenged primarily to love or to succeed?**

FRIDAY, AUGUST 20 • **Read Romans 12:3-8**

Yesterday we acknowledged that the greatest challenge before us, and the most specifically Christian, is to love. Not to "be conformed to this world" but rather transformed by the renewing of our minds requires us to practice love in a world that seems to function with other purposes in mind.

We must emphasize an important characteristic of love: One cannot love by oneself. Love requires at least one other to love—and when genuine, love immediately spills out to a wider circle. In the prologue to one of the early Methodist hymnals, Wesley declared that "there is no holiness but social holiness." If to be holy is to love, then one person cannot be holy by himself or herself.

In these verses from Romans, Paul moves from the challenge not to "be conformed to this world" to the further challenge that we live in and build a community of love. No one is to think too highly of himself or herself. When we do, we destroy the mutuality that love requires. On the contrary, when we think of ourselves as individual members of a body, we come to realize that each is important for the rest, and that no one of us can dispense with the rest.

Thus, the challenge to love becomes the challenge to love in community, which becomes a challenge to the community of the church. Paul advocates the transformation of the individual as well as of the community.

PRAYER: O maker of heaven and earth, whose power to transform turned chaos into creation, transform me and my church so we may be faithful to you and not be conformed to this world. Amen.

SATURDAY, AUGUST 21 • Read Matthew 16:13-20

We know the story well. On the road to Caesarea Philippi, Jesus asks his disciples what people think of him. They have various answers. Then Jesus asks his disciples the same question, "But who do you say that I am?" And Simon responds, "You are the Messiah [or the Christ], the Son of the living God." Jesus replies with words of commendation and gives Simon a new name: "You are Peter [that is, Rock]."

This week we have been dealing with challenges. We now come to the greatest challenge of all: confessing Jesus as Christ and Lord.

To understand the challenge of this confession, we have to place ourselves in Peter's sandals. If he declares that Jesus is a great teacher or a prophet or even Elijah who has come back, Peter will have to learn from Jesus—but Peter will not have to change his entire life. If, on the other hand, Peter declares that Jesus is the expected Christ, the Son of God, then everything will have to change.

So as soon as Simon declares that Jesus is the Christ, Jesus gives him a new name. He will no longer be simply Simon the fisherman; now he will be Peter the Rock.

In our day when so many call themselves Christian, we have lost the sense of the radical challenge of faith in Christ. If Jesus is Lord, then all other pursuits either become secondary or have to be abandoned altogether. Are we willing to declare that Jesus is the Christ and, in turn, have him give us a new name, a new being?

SUGGESTION FOR MEDITATION: **Consider the aspect of your life that most needs to be brought under Jesus' lordship. Imagine a name that Jesus would give you if you were obedient in that aspect of your life—for instance, "Loving," "Generous," "Forgiving." Put that name on a card and carry it in your wallet.**

SUNDAY, AUGUST 22 • Read Matthew 16:13-20

On the road to Caesarea Philippi, Simon puts himself at Jesus' disposal. By declaring Jesus the Christ, the Son of God, he also declares himself willing to obey Jesus as Lord. Jesus responds, not only by giving him a new name but also by putting himself and his power at the disposal of Peter and the church built upon him and upon all others who make a similar confession. Jesus does not simply accept Simon's obedience as an autocratic potentate would; rather, he immediately offers himself back to Peter by declaring that the gates of Hades will not prevail against the church and that all that Peter and the other disciples tie on earth will also be tied in heaven.

This passage has generated a good deal of theological controversy. Did Jesus give Peter and his successors special authority? Is the power to bind and unbind the power to forgive sins? In our controversy, we have missed the central point: When Christians surrender their power at the feet of Christ, he in turn puts himself at their disposal, so that his power becomes theirs.

In a way, this brings us back to the psalm we studied on Wednesday, where the psalmist acknowledges God's power and then concludes with the words of confident assurance: "Our help is in the name of the Lord, who made heaven and earth."

PRAYER: Lord, my God, who brought Israel out of Egypt, who turned Simon the fisherman into Peter the Rock, I now declare myself totally and unreservedly yours. Lead me out of my sin. Do not let me be conformed to this world but transform me by your Spirit. Make me wholly yours and become wholly and truly my God and my strength. Amen.

Finding God in Unlikely Places

August 23–29, 1999 • *Steve Christopher**

MONDAY, AUGUST 23 • **Read Exodus 3:1-6**

In this famous story of Moses' calling, Moses is confronted by the mysterious presence of God revealed through a bush that burns but is not consumed. Moses does not know why God would choose revelation through a burning bush; he only knows that he somehow finds himself in the presence of the God worshiped by his ancestors, and he is compelled to respond.

At this point, neither Moses nor the reader knows what God will require. But if God continues to behave in the same manner as in Genesis, God's requirement is sure to be as exciting and terrifying as Abraham's journeying to a strange land or Joseph's being taken into slavery and ending up second in command to Pharaoh.

Today God continues to call us in ways as mysterious and terrifying as a bush that is not consumed by fire. Like Moses, we do not know why God has chosen to take an interest in us, yet we acknowledge the call is authentic. We know that the God revealed to us is the same God who was revealed to our ancestors—those persons who have handed down the faith generation after generation to us. Like our ancestors, we feel compelled to respond.

We who worship the God who was revealed to Moses do not choose to respond to God's call because we believe in our usefulness to God. We respond because when we stand in the presence of God; everything else that promises to bring salvation—money, success, prestige, things—pales in comparison to the presence of the One who speaks out of the burning bush.

SUGGESTION FOR MEDITATION: Reflect upon times when God has been revealed to you in mysterious ways.

---

*Associate minister, Madison Street United Methodist Church, Clarksville, Tennessee.

TUESDAY, AUGUST 24 • Read Exodus 3:7-12

The call to free the Israelites from captivity represents a major turning point in Moses' life. The most surprising thing about Moses' call is that it forces him to return to the place he had fled. The one who had fled Egypt and settled into a comfortable life of shepherding must now return to the very place he has been avoiding at all costs.

The calling of Moses suggests several things about the divine-human encounter. Most importantly, it implies that the decision to enter into relationship with God does not provide a ticket to emotional or material security. It may require that we, like Moses, go to places we do not wish to go. We might have to relinquish all claims to affluence, success, and prestige to accomplish what God has called us to accomplish. The decision to embrace a life of discipleship may even require us to sacrifice life itself, the price paid by a certain Jewish itinerant preacher from Nazareth.

The calling of Moses also implies risk for those whom Moses is sent to represent. Obeying the voice of God spoken through a stranger named Moses requires the Israelites to enter a new and unfamiliar world in the desert. Despite the oppression of Pharaoh, life in Egypt provided stability and security.

But the call of Moses also reveals that as God sends us into strange and unfamiliar places, God promises to be with us. The ordinary people God calls can match wits with magicians who turn staffs into snakes and with pharaohs who turn wilderness into cities. These ordinary people draw strength and guidance for the journey from the One who stands beside them.

PRAYER: Almighty and everlasting God, give me the insight to discern your will and give me the courage to follow it, even if it takes me to places that I do not wish to go. Through Christ I pray. Amen.

WEDNESDAY, AUGUST 25 • Read Exodus 3:13-15

On the surface, the confrontation between Moses and Pharaoh would seem to be a mismatch: an unknown ex-shepherd versus all the might and majesty of Egypt. And without the One who stood beside Moses, this confrontation would have been a mismatch. Moses would have been only a minor irritation for Pharaoh, someone considered to be a god in human form and shielded by all the political and military power of Egypt. What evens the scales is that the One who stands beside Moses has been revealed to be the Creator and Sustainer of all that is.

This balance of power is surprising. Logically Pharaoh, the one with more earthly power, would have the more powerful god supporting him. Logically the God who chooses sides with a nobody like Moses would be a lesser deity than the god of Pharaoh. Certainly the more powerful god would not be disgraced by associating with anyone besides the most powerful human beings. But instead God turns the tables. The One who stands beside Moses is not only more powerful than Pharaoh but is the One who brought even Pharaoh himself into being.

Moses' encounter with God exemplifies another great mystery of faith: The Creator and Sustainer of all that is chooses to enter into a relationship with human beings. If that were not surprising enough, God has a peculiar habit of entering into particularly deep relationships with the lowly and despised: nobodies like Moses, Amos the gardener, and David the shepherd.

SUGGESTION FOR MEDITATION: **Consider places in the world where persons are in bondage. How might God be calling you to respond to this bondage with liberation and healing?**

THURSDAY, AUGUST 26 • Read Psalm 105:1-7, 23-26, 45c

While the psalmist's message reflects and records history, it is history with a significant twist. The psalmist interprets history through the theological claim of God's activity in history. Viewing history through this interpretive lens dramatically alters the way we perceive our past and radically impacts the way we understand ourselves and the world around us in the present moment.

The message of the psalmist is also thoroughly eschatological in the sense that it moves from recounting God's activity in Israel's past toward a vision of what God will do in the future. The psalmist looks toward the future not with morbidity but with joy and expectation, anticipating the full realization of God's purposes for the world. The optimism of this historical vision resides in the psalmist's envisioning the future as God's future.

Many consider this way of understanding history to be strange and alien. Today we find it commonplace to interpret history with no sense of divine direction or purpose. History becomes nothing more than the disconnected, random events that happen in our world. Human beings exist as the result of cosmic chance and the random collision of particles.

The imperative for people of faith today is to proclaim the psalmist's message: History recounts the mighty and glorious acts of God in our world. Another imperative demands that we look forward with the psalmist to the full realization of God's purposes here on earth, a world of shalom and the fruition of the "reign of God." The Jewish tradition has given us a way of understanding history. May we continue to embrace and affirm our heritage.

PRAYER: Loving God, may I see your guiding hand at work in my life, and may I look forward to the day when your purposes for me and for the world become fully realized. Through Christ I pray. Amen.

FRIDAY, AUGUST 27 • **Read Romans 12:9-21**

Central to Jesus' message about his vision of the "reign of God" is the exaltation of servanthood. This strange paradox overturns our way of understanding earthly power and authority. Jesus' Mediterranean listeners, accustomed to a rigidly hierarchical social order, associated servanthood with powerlessness and shame.

Three decades after Jesus proclaimed this message, Paul and the early church are still trying to understand what it means to live as "servant" people. How does the church live as authentic disciples within a society that associates servanthood with the bottom of the economic, social, and political ladder? The metaphor of the disciple as servant held great power for Paul's community; it reminded them of the radical nature of their calling. Paul's community needed to gather regularly to strengthen and encourage one another in order to remain faithful to this difficult calling.

Two thousand years later, Paul's struggle remains our struggle. It remains a struggle for us today because our world lives and breathes the same model of power that was operative in Paul's day. Disciples today live and work in a social setting that measures success in terms of the automobile we drive, the clothes we wear, and the opulence of our office space. The ethos of our surrounding social order does not lend itself well to those who would accept the mantle of servanthood. Accepting and remaining faithful to the call to be servant people will require the same wisdom, diligence, and courage that Paul's community exhibited.

SUGGESTION FOR MEDITATION: **Reflect upon the association of discipleship with servanthood. What might it mean for you and your community of faith to live as servant people?**

SATURDAY, AUGUST 28 • Read Matthew 16:21-23

This, the first of the passion predictions, comes immediately after Peter's confession of Jesus as the Christ (the rough Greek translation of "the Messiah" or "the Anointed One"). Perhaps Matthew deliberately placed these two key texts back-to-back to emphasize Jesus' overturning of the traditional Jewish expectations of messiahship. Jesus' contention that the Messiah must suffer dispels any notion that as the Christ, Jesus will be the One to stand in the line of David, drive out the Gentiles, and reestablish the kingdom of Israel. Later, after the Resurrection, the disciples realize that Jesus had come as the Messiah and had delivered them. Jesus brought a deliverance from their own sins rather than from their political enemies.

In Jesus, God brings deliverance but not in the way the disciples expected. We can learn a lesson from God's revelation in Jesus: We cannot predict the ways of God. The Jewish people expected God to come with military power; instead God chose to reveal God's self in a peasant named Jesus who lived and walked among the poor.

Looking back at the event as "armchair theologians," we can call Peter misguided and ignorant. A more useful application of this text encourages us to consider the ways we, like the disciples, try to fit God into our comfortable understandings of what we want God to be—understandings that often sound suspiciously like our own ideologies. As we look into a future as frightening as the one the disciples faced, we must look with the realization that God will continue to surprise us. We also rest assured that God's plans for the world are more wondrous than we can begin to imagine.

SUGGESTION FOR MEDITATION: **Reflect upon the title "Messiah." What does it mean for you to say that Jesus is "the Anointed One"?**

SUNDAY, AUGUST 29 • Read Matthew 16:24-28

This text shocks and provokes. It strongly suggests that we, as followers of Christ—the one who was tortured to death and nailed to a cross—might have to deny ourselves. Further, it suggests that we must deny ourselves to reveal God, as Jesus revealed God. Jesus implies that self-denial is woven into the very fabric of what it means to be God's people.

Our churches today often lack the call to self-denial. Language about self-denial still is preached in our pulpits and affirmed in our liturgies, but the church offers little help with regard to understanding how self-denial can guide the way the church goes about its business. Nor does the church provide a sense of accountability for the ways that clergy and laypersons can live a life of self-denial. Questions about how our clergy and laypersons spend their money and their time have become private issues, nobody else's business. In a market-driven society, the church has become another institution that provides programs and services for individual and familial fulfillment.

How can we avoid the temptations to live only to fulfill ourselves? Perhaps we need to remember why Jesus called us to deny ourselves in the first place: We are called to deny ourselves because in Jesus, God denies Godself for the world. Our calling requires that we imitate the One in whom we claim that God was revealed. Throughout the Bible, God's primary focus is being present in love and concern for what God has created. The paradox of self-denial is that it promotes a life not of drudgery but of joy. When we imitate the One who continually sacrifices for the sake of the world, we take our place as God's children, and we find salvation for our souls.

PRAYER: **God of the cross and God of the empty tomb, instill in me a willingness to sacrifice myself for your sake that I might imitate the One in whom you were revealed. Amen.**

New Beginnings

August 30–September 5, 1999 • Roland Rink*

MONDAY, AUGUST 30 • Read Psalm 149:1-4

As this new week begins, take stock of your own immediate situation. Can you, like the psalmist, praise the Lord? A new week begs new songs, new beginnings, new opportunities.

Sometimes we allow our little circles of pain and misery to blind us to our world. Look at nature, God's creation. Wonder at the mysterious interconnectedness and our reliance upon our Father's handiwork.

In this time of quiet at the beginning of this week, know with certainty: God will be with me in every single moment of it. God will be with me in the meetings and in the traffic, with me as I express my concern for my family, my friends, my enemies.

Allow the Lord to show you one new bit of creation on your way to work. Marvel at the color of the leaves on a tree you hadn't noticed before, the color of the clouds, the shine of raindrops on petals. Then give thanks to your Creator. What a privilege to be alive!

Consider yesterday's church service: Did I really praise God? Or was it just another Sunday service—slow, wooden, uninspiring? Decide now to step out of your familiar rut. Remind yourself, "I have a choice." I can choose to be happy or sad, angry or peace-filled, laughing or crying. The choice is mine to make for my life. Choose to be happy this day, this week, this month, this year.

PRAYER: Lord God, as I start this new week, give me the grace to sense your closeness. In traffic, during a meeting, wherever I may be, help me carry the joy of this psalm within me through the day and to share that joy with others. Amen.

---

*Husband, father of two, Christ follower, truth seeker, member of the Horizon Methodist Church, Gauteng, South Africa.

"**O**we no one anything, except to love one another." This new commandment makes me, a native South African, wonder how apartheid ever came about. South Africans are God-fearing people, yet they allowed the absolute antithesis of this commandment to become the law of the land. How can one love one another and reside in this segregated country?

Love crosses seas, moves over national borders, and is blind to the hue of another person. Why is it so hard for sophisticated, educated people to grasp the truth and understand the simplicity of loving our neighbors as we love ourselves?

In a world that has become increasingly violent—where is love for our neighbor? After nearly two thousand years what have we understood about loving our neighbor as ourselves?

As the scripture says, "The commandments...are summed up in this word: 'Love your neighbor as yourself.'" The *Oxford English Dictionary* offers the following options for the meaning of the word *commandment*: "command, order, bid. Soldiers follow the orders (command) of their "superior" officers to the letter. Let us, as soldiers of Christ, follow this order this day to the letter. Let us love one another as we love ourselves.

Today we must, with urgency, begin affecting the lives of those around us where we are. We must love one another unconditionally and without thought of "what's in it for me." If we follow the orders of the Lord, all obstacles to love will fall away. Today let us try to love all those whom God places in our orbit of life. We will do this with the empowering strength of the Holy Spirit.

And tomorrow?

PRAYER: Lord, help me. Empower me to love as you have commanded. I cannot do so without your help. Give me the grace this day to be open enough to love my neighbor as I love myself. Give me an understanding of your love for me, so that I may affect the situation of those you give me to love. Amen.

WEDNESDAY, SEPTEMBER 1 • **Read Matthew 18:18-20**

In South Africa the word *ubuntu* has risen to prominence. It has its root in the word *umuntu,* which means "a whole person." *Ubuntu* means "I am because we are." *Ubuntu* means that we are all related. *Ubuntu* means family, and so it is with the church.

Ubuntu means hospitality. I decided to break out of a rut: Over a seven-week period I visited the other Methodist churches on our circuit. What a diversity of worship, sanctuary, and color I experienced! The one fact that I discovered in my nomadic worshiping period was that we need to have a spiritual family, a home base, a community of faith to which we belong.

As the world and its peoples become more and more individualistic and isolationist, we need to claim the power of community. My wife received a diagnosis of malignant cancer in the throat. For a day or so we thrashed about, trying to come to terms with this devastating news. We told nobody about the problem. We prayed individually for healing. Eventually we spoke to our local church members, to folk in the USA (at the Upper Room), to people and family in Australia, and to folk in the UK. Soon we had a chain of prayer stretching around the world, strengthening us as a family for the days ahead and giving us courage to move forward.

My wife had no treatment for the cancer, no medication. Today, nearly thirty months later, I can tell you that the surgeons can find no trace of malignancy. The support of *ubuntu* and the grace of God brought healing. "For where two or three are gathered in my name, I am there among them".

Practice *ubuntu* in your life: "I am because we are."

PRAYER: Loving Lord Jesus, today I ask that you show me my family—at work, at school, at play—wherever I am. Forgive me for my feelings of self-centeredness and ego. Help me live in community where I am. Help me be you to the family you give me. Help me understand and acknowledge the gift that these people are to me. Amen.

This psalm is one of five closing hallelujah (or praise) psalms. Each begins and closes with praise. And the psalmist calls upon the people to bring something fresh to their music: a new song. Come and bring your understanding of your fresh experiences of God. And the psalmist calls for more than just song: Come dancing and playing musical instruments. Imagine being so happy and joyful that you sing songs of praise to God. When did you last shout aloud with joy in praise of our Lord? I cannot recall ever having done that!

Often we forget Jesus' promise to come again. For Christians, the second half of this psalm of praise (vv. 5-9) describes the rejoicing we believe will occur when Jesus triumphs over the evil darkness of this world. And the people of the nation help bring about this triumph. Their "two-edged swords" execute God's justice with double swiftness. With what two-edged swords do we face the world? How do we attempt to execute justice in the world? Sometimes the world seems to have blunted our swords. What action on our part might sharpen them again?

This psalm—though written in the time before Christ — gives expression to Jesus' return in victory. What an explosion of relief, joy, and happiness will accompany the ultimate victory of God, the triumph of good over evil, the knowledge that no amount of darkness can extinguish the light of a single flame.

Today, take heart. Reclaim your two-edged sword in order to triumph over evil. Look around you for fresh experiences of God's presence, and sing to the Lord a new song. Come singing, dancing, an playing. Shout aloud your praise to God!

PRAYER: **Loving God, make me aware of your presence and triumphant action in the world. Encourage to take up my two-edged sword with which I can execute justice. Make my life a hallelujah from beginning to end. Amen.**

FRIDAY, SEPTEMBER 3 • Read Romans 13:11-14

Is it possible to be awake yet asleep? Orgies, drunkenness, immorality, indecency, fighting, and jealousy: All these activities occur in the waking moments of humankind, yet one feels compelled to say that the participants in these activities must be asleep—asleep to the purpose for which God created them, asleep to the fact that our loving Creator made us in God's own image, asleep to the liberating truth that Jesus died for our sins.

Paul uses the imagery of sleeping and wakefulness, darkness and light to provide marked contrasts. Many of the activities and behavior identified above takes place under the cloak of darkness, a silent testimony to the fact that those involved would prefer not to be identified.

Paul reminds his audience that every day brings them one step closer to the kingdom. Seizing hold of this opportunity is not an action to delay: "It is *now* the moment for you to wake from sleep" (italics added). Wake up to the fact that we have been comfortably asleep. The night in this world is nearly over. The time has come to conduct ourselves as people who live in the light of day as awakened, aware individuals. Put on the Lord Jesus Christ and engage in actions and behaviors that can endure the brightness of daylight: compassion, kindness, humility, meekness, patience, forgiveness, and love (Col. 3:12–14).

Can you imagine how different this world could be if people woke up and adopted the model of Jesus for their own lives? As you begin your day remember that the darkness is almost over—so let it go. Awaken yourself to the wonderful possibilities of living in God's light *now*.

PRAYER: Lord, help me awaken to the fact that I have been sleeping. May I move into the light of this day clothed in compassion, kindness, humility, meekness, patience, forgiveness, and love. Amen.

SATURDAY, SEPTEMBER 4 • Read Matthew 18:15-17

As we speed relentlessly towards the twenty-first century, we have a unique opportunity to start with a clean slate in our relationships with others, a time of reconciliation. The words of the text speak clearly. We must go to our brother or sister and discuss privately and confidentially the problem that exists between us.

The church is much like other institutions. Disagreements arise because we are human. Differences of opinions are bound to occur. But Jesus tells us to go to that person and, in love, resolve those differences. If the results are not positive, we should take two persons with us and try again to reach some form of reconciliation. When all of the efforts come to naught, we as the church must make every effort to reintroduce the recalcitrant person to the ways of Jesus.

Jesus precedes these verses with the parable of the lost sheep (18:10-14). Like the shepherd who searches for the one lost sheep, the faith community is to make every effort and expend every resource to bring the one who has strayed back into the fold. The passage stresses the perseverance that successful living in community requires. Resolution of personal differences with those we love is seldom easy or comfortable. Preserving the fragile gift of life in community requires great care and sensitivity. Within the church, we commit ourselves to the well-being of others.

PRAYER: Lord, today I humbly ask for the gift of a reconciling spirit, which only you can give. I have been insensitive to others—forgive me, I pray. Lord, give me the strength to make right a relationship. Give me, Father, a spirit of tolerance and forgiveness. Make your body, the church, one again; unite us by your love for us. Amen.

SUNDAY, SEPTEMBER 5 • **Read Exodus 12:1-14**

Someone once said, "Faith means resting in the arms of the One who is faithful." The children of Israel find themselves in such a place as God instructs them in the intricate details of what becomes the first Passover. The people have to believe in these detailed instructions from God. They also need discipline to carry out the instructions, to follow the orders to the letter because the Lord is coming. They cannot be found wanting in obedience.

The details we read in these verses indicate that this ritual serves two purposes: one, to move into a new year, leaving the old one behind; two, to set out on the journey, leaving the old life in Egypt behind. All of the foods make no use of products of the culture or of the year being left behind. Roast the lamb on the fire—no pot or water. Bake the bread without leaven, a product of the previous year's harvest. New times, new lives, new hopes.

At the end of the twentieth century, the children of Israel can serve as our example. We believe the Lord is coming. Will we be ready? Have we been faithful to the One who gave us life? In our own lives, have we exercised discipline? Have we carried out the instructions of our Father to the best of our ability?

What in our culture or timebound existence shall we leave behind? What traveling clothes do we need? God holds out the promise of new times, new lives, new hopes. Are you ready for the journey?

PRAYER: Dear God, as this day begins help me see a sign of your promise. You know that I need to rest in your arms. Let me view this day as a gift from you. Give me the courage to say that I am available for you. Help me understand your will for my life. Amen.

God's Unconventionality

September 6–12, 1999 • Arvin Luchs*

MONDAY, SEPTEMBER 6 • Read Exodus 14:19-31

When I was a child, I loved the Saturday movie matinees. In addition to the cartoons and the feature, an action serial kept us on the edge of our seats. One week the hero would be tied in a baggage car as a runaway train careened toward a collapsed bridge over a canyon. At the fateful moment, the episode would end and we'd have to wait an excruciating week to learn that something unforeseen would intervene to save the day.

The Hebrew people stand at a fateful moment, trapped between the advancing armies of the Pharaoh and the watery abyss of the Red Sea. They have broken free from slavery in Egypt and have trudged mile after weary mile across the desert seeking the land of Yahweh's promise. But now there seems no way out. Fear, frustration, and confusion ensue. Some wonder if they have been led all this way to their graves.

They didn't count on God! The Book of Exodus reminds us that even though the people do not recognize it, God's power is leading and protecting them. There is a way out. Yahweh leads them through the sea.

When our journey seems to lead to a "Red Sea place," do we yield to anxiety, despair, and futility? Or do we realize God's power and count on God to get us through?

PRAYER: Gracious God, make me aware of your power surrounding me constantly, even in my darkest hour. Amen.

---

*Associate General Secretary of United Methodist Communications; clergy member of the Oregon-Idaho Annual Conference of The United Methodist Church; member of Belmont United Methodist Church, Nashville, Tennessee.

TUESDAY, SEPTEMBER 7 • Read Exodus 15:1*b*-11, 20-21

It isn't easy finding a place for God in our celebrations. A few years ago a colleague told me of his father's open-heart surgery. It was touch and go. The surgeon—a renowned specialist—emerged hours later to tell the family that all went well. "Thank God," my friend's mother exclaimed. The surgeon replied, "Why thank God? I'm the one who did the surgery." Our technological sophistication can easily lull us into a confidence in human power and competence.

More subtly, we suggest that God has given us talent, skill, or insight; and we have made a difference or changed things. In so doing, we keep the spotlight on ourselves and God's presence at arm's length.

The Hebrew people have no doubt who has brought them through the sea and delivered them from the Egyptians. They could have celebrated Moses' leadership, but no one hints of attributing celebrity to him. They could have rejoiced in their courage and determination, but the scripture gives no suggestion of self-congratulation.

The Hebrew people realize and acknowledge God's intervention to save them. They rejoice, sing, and dance in thanksgiving—not for their own perseverance but for Yahweh's victory.

God is just as much a part of our world, acting in power and love, bringing strength and salvation. Can we sing Miriam's song for God's victory in our hearts and lives?

PRAYER: Powerful God, give me grace to see you near and the song to sing praise for your victories. In Jesus' name. Amen.

WEDNESDAY, SEPTEMBER 8 • **Read Psalm 114**

My hobby is photography. The difficulty of capturing the majesty of a stirring landscape challenges me. Somehow the Rocky Mountains or the Smokies seem small and unimpressive in the small frame of a photograph. Classic landscape painters often include people and houses in their work in order to give the viewer a sense of perspective.

The psalmist tries to put his awe of God into words. The mere thought of attempting to give expression to the majesty of God so overwhelms the psalmist that human-size images do not adequately describe his perspective. His points of reference become mountains and hills and the sea. The psalmist writes that at Yahweh's presence the immense, seemingly immovable mountains "[skip] like rams," the hills gambol like frolicking lambs. Remembering the Red Sea deliverance, the psalmist proclaims that in God's presence even the seas run away.

We can easily lose our perspective on God. Our prayers, our worship, our teaching, even our casual conversation can easily slip into such comfort with the divine that we trivialize the Almighty. The psalmist reminds us that the God about whom we speak so easily is the source of all creation. God's power goes beyond any we have experienced or conceived. This powerful God chooses the people Israel and chooses to be incarnate in Jesus. This powerful God is with us today in the spirit and the power of the risen Christ.

PRAYER: Great and mighty God, help me recapture the wonder and majesty of your presence. Amen.

THURSDAY, SEPTEMBER 9 • Read Matthew 18:21-22

You almost can hear Jesus thinking, *He doesn't get it.* Peter has put the rabbi to the test. He wants to fix an exact number of times he must forgive a brother or sister in faith. Is seven enough? Jesus' response must have been startling: "Not seven times, but... seventy-seven" (in some versions, "seventy times seven"). Jesus does not offer a mathematical formula. He suggests that Peter forget about trying to count at all. Those who know God's grace should forgive one another without limit.

These words are hard ones for Peter to hear. They are difficult ones for us as well. The way of the world says, "once burned, twice careful." The world regards as foolishness our ongoing vulnerability to disappointment. But Jesus is not talking about how to get along in the conventional world; he's talking about a better world.

We haven't really forgiven if we keep track. To keep a count implies we harbor the memories of the past. Forgiveness means not only agreeing to overlook the trespasses but putting the matter out of our mind.

If we count, we retain some suspicion of the other person. To forgive involves reestablishing a new relationship of trust. It means being fully open to others and repeatedly vulnerable to those who have hurt us in the past.

That's what it means to live in grace, which is the way of God's reign. Peter didn't get it. Do we?

PRAYER: God of mercy, give me grace to forgive others as I have been forgiven. In Jesus' name. Amen.

FRIDAY, SEPTEMBER 10 • Read Matthew 18:23-35

Opinion polls in Palestine would not have agreed with Jesus. The conventional wisdom then—and now—supports the notion that we act in merciful and loving ways in order to earn God's favor and to assure ourselves of God's blessings and benefits.

The parable of the unmerciful servant reveals another idea. It's the story of a servant—probably a governor—who owes a great debt to the king. Jesus describes the amount as so huge that no one could imagine repaying it.

The servant pleads for mercy, and the king graciously forgives the debt. As soon as he leaves, the fortunate debtor encounters another who owes him a small debt, an amount trifling in comparison to the servant's former obligation. Yet the servant demands his due and offers no mercy. The fellow slaves report this behavior to the king, which stirs the king to anger, and he reimposes the obligation upon the hapless servant. Verse 33 clearly expresses Jesus' message (some scholars believe verses 34 and 35 were added later) when the king says, "Should you not have had mercy on your fellow slave, as I had mercy on you?"

That question turns the tables on us. Jesus proposes that we act mercifully and compassionately not because it will earn favor but as a small response to the abundant grace and mercy we have received. Showing compassion and mercy in gratitude is not the way this world works; it's the way of God's world.

PRAYER: Gracious God, as I have received so much from you, help me give to others. Amen.

SATURDAY, SEPTEMBER 11 • Read Romans 14:1-6

When I was learning to drive, my father shared some advice that has served me well. "Don't focus on the street just in front of the car," he said. "Look further down the road and see the bigger view." In today's scripture the apostle Paul suggests that the Christians in Rome extend the focus of their spiritual eyes to see the bigger picture.

The members of the church in Rome comprised a diverse and contentious group. People bickered about opinions, holy days, and diet. An inhospitable and judgmental climate prevailed. Paul likens them to insensitive guests at a banquet who criticize their host's servants. He suggests that they lift their eyes above and beyond their disagreements to realize that those differences are individual ways of honoring the same Lord and serving the same God. Instead of battling with one another, they can unite in thanks to God.

Paul could be writing to us. We also struggle with accepting diversity within the church. We too are quick to judge and slow to understand, accept, and appreciate one another. Our spiritual tunnel vision can corrode our spirits, blunt our witness, and undermine our mission. We would do well to heed the apostle's advice to take a bigger view—to be aware that even though we may not think or act alike, we all seek to worship and serve the same God through the same Jesus Christ.

PRAYER: **God of all people, as I relate to others both inside and outside my particular faith community, help me focus on the commonalities we share through you not on our differences. In Christ's name I pray. Amen.**

SUNDAY, SEPTEMBER 12 • Read Romans 14:7-12

Many scientists seek to find the primal elements of the physical world. Astronomers push observations deeper into space seeking information on the origins of the universe. Some physicists try to produce the coldest cold—absolute zero. Others delve into the atom to identify subatomic particles. Geneticists chart the gene code to describe the building blocks of life. In today's scripture, Paul probes the core ideas of the Christian's world.

The apostle knows the congregation in Rome has allowed differing ways of understanding and living out the faith to distract it. The members have splintered into contending camps over matters Paul considers peripheral to the faith. So he reminds them of the central reality of Christian living. We are rooted and grounded in God. Nothing in life, not even death itself, can shake us loose from our anchor in God. Christ's death and resurrection indisputably demonstrate this core reality.

Paul's point is that everything else pales in comparison to that one basic fact. As a result, the disputes among the Roman Christians that threaten to unravel their community are insignificant when compared with their common center in Jesus. That was true nearly two thousand years ago. It is true today.

PRAYER: God of all that is, was, and ever will be, give me grace to center my heart and mind on you—the true center of all. In Christ I pray. Amen.

Grace upon Grace

September 13–19, 1999 • *Joseph Iron Eye Dudley**

MONDAY, SEPTEMBER 13 • **Read Exodus 16:2-15**

If Moses were questioned about the meaning of his life in his care of Jethro's sheep and goats, he probably would say the work has little challenge or purpose to it. All he does is herd a group of hard-to-control creatures.

When I was about ten years old, a rancher asked me to watch his sheep. Early in the morning, my grandma packed a lunch and filled a jar full of water to take with me. I sat on the hillside watching the sheep in the hot sun. Those were the longest days of my life. Controlling the jittery sheep required far more work than I'd imagined.

Perhaps Moses feels the same way. Little does he know that God will use his sheep herding as preparation for leading a jittery and hard-to-control people out of slavery into the place where they can become God's people. When times get tough, they always wish that they had stayed in Egypt, saying things like, "There we could at least sit down and eat meat and as much other food as we wanted," (Exod. 16:3, TEV). In slavery they didn't have to depend on God's miracles and mercies; everything was predictable.

We stay in comfort zones of familiar things. We feel safe, secure, and in control; everything is predictable. We become slaves to predictability. Yet God calls us to move out of our comfort zones and to rely on God's miracles and mercies.

PRAYER: O God, thank you for your great faithfulness. Morning by morning new mercies I see. Amen.

---

*President of Cook College and Theological School; author; United Methodist minister; member of the Yankton Sioux tribe in South Dakota.

When Moses stands before the burning bush, God tells him to take off his shoes because he is standing on holy ground. Of course every time we stand before God we stand on holy ground. And because God is everywhere, all the time, wherever we stand is holy ground. God is always with us.

I propose another possible reason for God's asking Moses to remove his shoes. The shoes on his feet are humanmade. If Moses wants to be part of God's story, he has to be God-made. He has to do things God's way.

Perhaps that explains why the people have to remain in the wilderness so long. First God takes them out of slavery; then God has to take slavery out of them. Only in that way can God remake and reshape them.

Ah, this murmuring people! They move from viewing God as savior to losing faith in Yahweh, preferring death by natural causes in Egypt to the rigors of desert life. Taking their complaints to God, Moses and Aaron tell the people that they will see "the glory of the Lord." The manna will serve as a mark of God's presence with the people.

In this Exodus story, God's presence manifests itself in a tangible way, feeding the people both physically and spiritually. Catching enough quail every evening and gathering enough manna every morning to last for just one day enable the people's reliance on God daily—a fresh affirmation of God's presence each day. Soon the people naturally look for God's miracles and mercies every evening and every morning. Openness to this way of seeing requires daily conversation with God—an important part of our faith journey.

PRAYER: **Gracious God, help me count my blessings and name them one by one, every evening and every morning. Amen.**

WEDNESDAY, SEPTEMBER 15 • Read Psalm 105:1-6, 37-45

Wouldn't it be nice to know for sure that God is working in and through us in the present? We, like the people of Israel, often take years and sometimes generations before recognizing God's blessing in our lives. Only in Babylonian captivity do the people begin to write about the miracles and mercies of God in their history.

Until then, the Israelites had spent a lot of their time complaining about what they seemingly lacked. They had an unquenched desire to return to the "good ole days." Only as they journeyed on did they begin to see God's revelation to them through mighty deeds: leading them through a dry sea and a trackless wilderness. And in the journey, God's story and their story become one. While worshiping in a "strange land," they sing about God's power and rehearse their history in order to remember who they were.

We too are a people with a history full of God's miracles and mercies. Even while we busily complain about our lack of seemingly important things in life, God causes the sun to shine and the rain to fall. We have friends and family who stand beside us, and "while we were yet sinners, Christ died for us" (Rom. 5:8, KJV). God's power is something to sing about until it becomes an important part of who we are.

PRAYER: **O God, help me to sing of the wondrous story of the Christ who died for me. Amen.**

THURSDAY, SEPTEMBER 16 • Read Philippians 1:21-30

Isn't it nice to be in a win-win situation? That is how Paul describes his situation, to live for Christ or to be with Christ! An amazing assertion, especially when one considers that Paul writes this letter from prison. Paul's words in verse 12, "I want you to know…," indicate that he has moved into the body of his letter and is now relaying the purpose for his writing. He writes to tell the Christians at Philippi of his imprisonment.

Paul could have complained about not having enough food and water. He could have believed that God had put him in prison to die. But Paul accepts his situation as an opportunity to proclaim the good news of Christ in letter after letter to church after church. In addition, his being a prisoner gives him an opportunity to witness to persons he would not have seen otherwise—Roman soldiers.

With that kind of faith, Paul always found himself in a win-win situation. If he lived, he would live for Christ; and if he died, he would be with Christ. What gives an additional punch to Paul's situation is that while writing letters and witnessing, he is awaiting his trial. Execution is still a possibility. If killed, Paul wants everyone to know not only that he lived for Christ but that he also died for Christ.

That's the kind of faith I need: a faith that sees the miracles and mercies of God transforming what appears to be a losing situation into a win-win situation.

PRAYER: **Eternal and ever-present God, help me know that as I live for you, you always live in me and with me. Amen.**

FRIDAY, SEPTEMBER 17 • Read Philippians 1:21-30

It seems that Paul doesn't know if the time has come or not for him to die. If he lives, he wants to "add to [the Philippians'] progress and joy in the faith" (TEV).

In the fall of 1983, my mother's health was failing. During that time, regardless of our conversation, she would close by saying, "It won't be long, my son; I will go meet my Maker." The day came when we had to admit her to the hospital.

One morning my sister and I stopped to visit her. When we walked in, she smiled and said, "Mom and Dad came to visit me last night." Her mother and father had died about twenty years earlier. We all knew she wasn't going to get well. The Dakota Sioux support an old belief that when our time to die comes, our deceased loved ones come to visit. Until then we need to stand firm with "one common purpose...for the faith of the gospel" (TEV).

The apostle Paul asks the question, "For what is life?" (TEV). Life is a trust from God. God entrusts us with a life; someday we will give that life back to God. Meanwhile, because of the miracles and mercies of God, we experience progress and joy in our lives until we go to be with Christ and give back the life with which we have been entrusted.

PRAYER: O Creator and Giver of Life, teach me that it is by living for others that I live for you, prepare to meet you, and give back my life. Amen.

SATURDAY, SEPTEMBER 18 • Read Matthew 20:1-16

Everybody wants their fair share; and when we think we aren't getting it, we get upset. That's what happens in this parable. Those hired first think they aren't getting their fair share. The landowner answers, in effect, saying, "You have received what I promised you. These others are getting the same as you because I have chosen to give to them from what I have."

In the summer of 1996, my doctor told me I had cancer. During the first few weeks following the diagnosis, as a way of trying to accept the dreadful news, I got up early every morning and sat outside and watched the sun rise. Every morning the words of a hymn came to my mind, "Morning by morning new mercies I see" (Chisholm, 1923).

I considered it a miracle that regardless of how I was feeling, the sun always rose. God's mercy allowed me to live to see the beginning of another new day. The rising sun served to remind me that God indeed had provided all that I had ever needed. Near the end of the second week, I could affirm God's merciful provision for the first fifty-six years of my life and God's continuing provision for the rest of my life. Today, one year later, I am cancer free.

Just as God cares for me, God cares for you. You can believe that just as surely as the sun rises every morning.

PRAYER: O God, who causes the sun to rise every morning and paints the sunset every evening, help me see these as signs of your miracles and mercies for me. Amen.

SUNDAY, SEPTEMBER 19 • Read Matthew 20:1-16

What if the Hebrews had stayed in Egypt? They would have never seen the sea part. They would have never received the quail and manna or seen the water come from the rock. They would have never known of the Promised Land.

In the land of missed opportunities, this parable raises more questions than it answers: Why does the landowner himself go to hire the workers? Why does he go throughout the day to hire more? Why are some workers still without work at the eleventh hour? And perhaps the most troubling question of all is, Why do the people who worked hard all day long in the scorching sun get the same pay as those who came to work latest in the day?

This troubling parable addresses the resentment we may feel when others receive God's grace that we affirm in theory if not in practice—especially if it is practiced to someone else's advantage. Oddly enough, those who come to the fields last receive their pay first. And they get a full day's wages. What might those who came to the fields first expect? More, of course. If we get what we expect, is it still grace?

What if we never respond to the Master's call to work in the fields? We will never experience the miracles and mercies that happen every day, the grace upon grace. Because of God's mercies, we experience miracle after miracle as we make our way to our Promised Land. In God's fields of harvest, the quail chirps, manna sparkles, and water springs forth at unexpected times.

The miracle of miracles, however, is revealed in the coming of Christ in whom we see that God's majesty is in God's mercy. It's another paradox like "the last will be first, and the first will be last." May we remain open to God's joyous surprises that come to us as grace upon grace.

PRAYER: O God of miracles and mercies, teach me to believe that I am special to you because you made me that way. Amen.

2000

*Now is the time to order your copy of
The Upper Room Disciplines 2000*

Published for over 40 years, *Disciplines* is one of
the most popular daily devotional books available.
Year after year, *Disciplines* continues to appeal to
more and more Christians who, like yourself, desire
a more disciplined spiritual life based on scripture.
Be sure to order your copy today, while the 2000
edition is still available.

THE UPPER ROOM DISCIPLINES 2000
$8.95 each — 10 or more copies $7.61 each
Ask for product number UR863

Shipping Charges:
On prepaid orders,
we pay postage.
On "bill me later" orders,
the shipping charges will
be added to your invoice.

Please prepay if your
order is under $10.00.
*All payments in
U.S. funds, please.*

To Order Your Copies, Call:
1-800-972-0433.
Tell the customer service
representative your
source code is 2000D.

Or Write:
Customer Services
The Upper Room
P.O. Box 856
Nashville, TN 37202-0856

Sojourners to the Promised Land

September 20–26, 1999 • Trudy Corry Rankin*

I base this week's reflections on my work in a homeless shelter in my community. Each passage adds to my learning from those in exile from our society's Promised Land. Exodus 17:1 says that the Israelites "journeyed by stages" for forty years with new learning and leaning on God.

I watch and wait for each sojourner of the streets to journey "in stages" to that learning and leaning as well. The Promised Land eludes them. They desire stability and security, but street life has taken away any sense of control or hope in the future.

These sojourners have no sense of confidence in achievement. The Christian environment of the shelter encourages those who enter to make new choices, choices other than those that street life has demanded of them: addictive, illegal, or destructive behavior. Each is capable of moving to a new state of competence. As one explained to me, "I don't have to be stuck on stupid anymore!" In the process of this maturing, these sojourners of the streets begin to move to a stage of trusting God's provision for them, just as the sojourners of the desert finally did in Exodus.

In the quiet of this moment, I pray that we gain wisdom to recognize our stage in the sojourn to the Promised Land and that we learn to trust God's providence as well.

PRAYER: O Holy One, God of the desert and God of the streets, help me rid myself of pride, control, fear, and lack of trust that would keep me from leaning on you in the sojourn. Amen.

---

*United Methodist laywoman; member of The Academy for Spiritual Formation Forum; psychotherapist; counseling consultant for the Talbot House Homeless Ministry, Lakeland, Florida; member of Wesley United Methodist Church.

TUESDAY, SEPTEMBER 21 • Read Exodus 17:1-7

Is the Lord here or not?

The Israelites camp at Rephidim; they have no water. Moses, their supposed caregiver, makes no provision for their thirst. "Is the Lord among us or not?" In their desperation for water, they demand that Moses take care of it. Moses, fearing for his life, pleads to God for help. God gives him specific instructions. Taking with him someone he can trust, Moses will use the same staff he had used for an earlier miracle of provision. God will meet them in a specific location. And God provides water! This act answers the people's earlier question of whether God is in their midst or not.

Carolyn also wonders if God has deserted her as she seeks help for her addiction and street life. She has contacted countless agencies for help and even called her senator's office. No money. No help. While Carolyn has been sincere in her search, all the closed doors make her wonder if God no longer has concern for her.

In one final act of humility, she asked for help from a store owner who brought her to the shelter. Untrusting, she still didn't believe she would be allowed to stay. But she was, and she remains. Now three months clean, preparing to start school, she is proving her new intentions to her family. She has found God's provision for her in this place just as at the rock in Horeb. Now she can say, "God is here in this place for me."

PRAYER: **God of Moses, God of Carolyn, my God, through the sign of a miracle at a rock or at a shelter, you provide for us when we humble ourselves to ask. Help me to know that truth deep within me. Amen.**

WEDNESDAY, SEPTEMBER 22 • Read Psalm 78:1-8

Telling the stories

The writer of Psalm 78 feels compelled to tell the story of God's work with God's people to the next generation. By telling the story, the writer hopes the following generation will "not be like their ancestors." The repeating of the stories of history will strengthen the family and the community. I wonder about the stories here at the shelter.

The scripture speaks of repeating stories to the next generation. I find that the life experiences of just one week for these friends of mine are "generations" apart; one week brings amazing changes. They discover value in repeating their stories. I meet with them weekly to look back on goals and accomplishments. We proceed around the circle and hear the stories, the temptations, the regrets. I encourage; I challenge. I hear of the attempts to change, the difficulties of living in community, the unclear future.

The recent arrivals can't communicate their present experience. They are lost in self-pity, strung out on an addiction, or too afraid. But those who have stayed longer, those of the older "generation," begin to reveal their goals, their accomplishments of the week, and their emerging plans for their healing and salvation. The stories honor the journey. In the sharing, the storytellers begin to honor themselves. The time together solidifies the collective story of the community, drawing all generations together, slowly.

PRAYER: Help me, O God, to trust that the simple but profound act of telling our stories can lead to healing and salvation. Let me meditate in your Spirit on the vitality of our stories in Christ and the need to repeat them for the strengthening of the next generation. Amen.

THURSDAY, SEPTEMBER 23 • Read Psalm 78:12-16

Encouraging signs through improbabilities

In this portion of the psalm, the writer tells about God's provision for the people through blatant improbabilities of nature: God divides the sea. God makes a cloud by day and a fire by night to lead them. God gives water from a rock.

How odd—water from a rock and dividing the sea! God is trying to get the people's attention through unusual signs of encouragement. If they can understand the miracles of these improbabilities, they might soften their hearts and allow for God's leading.

I think of the blatant improbabilities of human nature that God uses with those of the shelter as well. Sam and John knew each other on the streets. Each had little time for the other unless it benefited himself. John, a recent arrival, fresh from the streets and out of the temptations of the drug world, had found a job. He realized at the end of his workday that he feared leaving work with his cash payment in his pocket. The temptation not to return to the shelter and to return to old habits was just too great.

Through the improbability of human nature, God's spirit of compassion caused Sam, one of the generation of a few more weeks, to go to John's place of work and walk him home. Sam parted the sea of temptation and brought him to the shelter safely. Sam offered John a fire through the darkness.

PRAYER: God, sometimes it seems to take a radical sign or improbability to remind me of your presence. I pray that you continue to be radical through your cloud by day and fire by night so that I can be assured of your presence. Amen.

FRIDAY, SEPTEMBER 24 • Read Philippians 2:1-11

The day-to-day living

Paul gives very specific ideas for the common life in Christ for everyday living together. He could be addressing the community today as it works out the chores, shares the bathroom and showers, and gets the meal on the table.

Paul encourages the community members to "be of the same mind, having the same love." Each is to look out for the interests of the others. By submitting their nature for transformation into Christ's nature, Christ's community can happen. Paul claims that sharing the Spirit of affection and compassion strengthens the whole community. With Paul's inspired guidelines of the common life in Christ, communities continue to struggle and develop.

How can the common life in a homeless shelter be transformed into the community Paul describes? How can the qualities of Christ's nature be encouraged in those who trust so little, in those who have been estranged? Is character always malleable to change and healing? Can the staff and volunteers trust in the growth of the divine nature?

Paul emphasizes that Christian community can happen. We, as Christians in the shelter, affirm this reality. We expect life in the Spirit to transform survival skills into compassion. Paul teaches us to be courageous enough to believe in this transformation.

PRAYER: Dear God, help me believe that any change is possible through you, with all hearts being made new in your Spirit. Help my unbelief. Amen.

SATURDAY, SEPTEMBER 25 • Read Philippians 2:12-13

Working out your own program

Paul goes on to describe our working out our own salvation, which affects our will and behavior. Our different life experiences and personalities affect the program of our salvation.

At the shelter we take Paul's advice and encourage residents to work out their own programs, setting goals that no one else can. AA and NA emphasize working out one's own program. But how does a person go about such an endeavor when one has spent the last few years with no direction, no goals, no encouragement, and no plans?

The beginning comes with the participants' tolerating order and exhibiting a willingness to obey the rules, with an openness to the community's authority. The common life expects goal-setting and follow-through. As participants' heads begin to clear of the street clutter, the belief that there could be salvation—even for me—slowly begins to emerge.

SUGGESTION FOR MEDITATION: Be silent in God's presence. Envision a handful of malleable, moist clay. See God's big hands holding the clay, beginning to shape it. Allow the Spirit to lead you in knowing more of the sculpting design God has for you in your own salvation. God may be finding lumps or gravel that need to be worked out. More moisture may be needed. Allow the silence to help you identify ways you can be more malleable to God's work in you and your program to remove the lumps and gravel.

By what authority?

By what authority do you come to sit with us and help us search for direction in our lives? You haven't lived on the streets. You haven't been addicted to drugs or alcohol. You have no idea how hard it is. By what authority are you here? Those of the shelter question me through their subtle resistance to my presence.

Their questions echo that of the chief priests and elders to Jesus about his authority. Jesus doesn't answer, but makes them think more deeply by asking them a question. I can only respond with a question as well: How can I not sit with you when I know of your need? I can only respond that I hope that God can offer compassion and accountability through me, one of God's people. I come to the shelter affirming my call to listen to your stories, trusting that you will experience God's presence through me

In verse 31 Jesus states, "Tax collectors and the prostitutes are going into the kingdom of God ahead of you." As I sit with my friends, I come to understand what that means. I learn more about that part of me that their lives have been—the Liar, the Trickster, the Conniver, the Manipulator, the Blamer, the Persecutor.

I meet up with myself in the presence of God and these friends, those who Jesus says may get into the kingdom ahead of me.

PRAYER: O God, I find it hard to admit to you those things about myself that disappoint me. Yet you already know them. The importance rests in my confession of them, and in that confession, my prayer for transformation by your Spirit. Thank you for your authority in my life, so that I can claim my authority in you. Amen.

A Covenant of Steadfast Love

September 27–October 3, 1999 • Billy Spangler*

MONDAY, SEPTEMBER 27 • Read Exodus 20:1-4

The Ten Commandments describe how God wants former slaves to behave as individuals, as a family, and as a community. Said another way, here's how to build a successful nation. Earlier God has extended the covenant with Abraham, Isaac, and Jacob to include the enslaved people of Israel (Exod. 6:2-8).

A covenant is a joint declaration to do a thing in good faith and generally specifies both tenure and benefits. The Declaration of Independence contains a covenantal relationship valued so highly by equals that they guaranteed its performance with their lives, fortune, and sacred honor.

Perhaps the most familiar covenants we enter into are matrimony and church membership. Marriage vows declare a covenant of faith before God and witnesses to live a selfless love in pursuit of mutual happiness. Church membership is a covenant of faith with God and witnesses to live and show God's love for others.

Today's reading exemplifies a superior/subordinate covenantal relationship: "I am the Lord your God, who brought you out...." Now, put me and my commandments first in your life. In return enjoy my love and all that it implies—a steadfastly boundless relationship, fulfilling, forgiving, and sustaining. Here's how I want you to live: Watch out for the lure of temporal things that may tempt you to create other gods; what they may offer is fleeting. Accept my covenant of steadfast love!

PRAYER: Lord, you show me your love in so many ways. Help me keep you first in my life, and in so doing may I uphold my part of the covenant. Amen.

---

*Moderator of an adult Bible study class, First United Methodist Church, Boerne, Texas.

TUESDAY, SEPTEMBER 28 • Read Exodus 20:7-9

As Genesis narrates the beginning of humankind, Exodus describes the birth of a nation. God's commandments of behavior are to become the articles of confederation.

Yesterday's scripture reveals the covenantal grace that God extends to the children of Israel—not because they sought it but because God offered it. God defines Israel's objective: to be a holy nation (Exod. 19:5-6). God's plan is national in scope, yet individual in implementation. A nation becomes holy when its people become holy. People become holy through a sanctifying relationship with God, forging a character that pleases God. Today's readings continue to tell us how.

"You shall not take the name of the Lord your God in vain" (RSV). Time was when people so revered God's name that none dared to say it aloud. Tragically, expletives from radio, television, at work, and at play punctuate the daily lives of adults and children. We cannot escape hearing the profaning of God's name. We implore God for favors, promising better behavior, only to concede to a habit of forgetfulness.

"Remember the sabbath day, to keep it holy" (RSV). If attending worship satisfies the requirement, are we then free to do whatever we wish? God commands us to keep the sabbath holy because God has blessed it. We are to set aside a day to honor God by showing we have no other gods. We demonstrate God's omnipotence in our lives by our behavior, and we offer praise for God's unmerited blessings. Jesus said, "If you keep my commandments, you will abide in my love, just as I have kept my Father's commandments and abide in his love" (John 15:10, RSV).

PRAYER: Gracious God, help me daily to keep your commandments and abide in your love. Amen.

WEDNESDAY, SEPTEMBER 29 • **Read Exodus 20:12**

Of the Ten Commandments, only the fifth offers a future benefit for compliance—"that your days may be long in the land which the Lord your God gives you" (RSV). While the biblical vow to the children of Israel refers to the land God covenanted with Abraham, Isaac, and Jacob, God has promised "steadfast love to…those who love me and keep my commandments" (20:6, RSV).

God's plan for Israel to become a holy nation requires implementation and execution at the family level. Said another way, we cannot order or legislate commendable behavior; we must teach by example, beginning in the home and passing it on.

How do we honor our parents? "By being good to them," answers a third-grade boy. "By telling them we love them," smiles a girl. Good answers but framed in the traditional mold of a primary Sunday school class.

Perhaps God's view of the fifth commandment goes further than just kind, obedient, respectful children. Parenthood, like life, comes as a gift from God. If we truly honor our heavenly Father, we concurrently honor our earthly parents and the nurturing they have given us. If we waste or abuse the talent and ability God has given us, have we not dishonored both God and our parents?

The fifth commandment whispers in our ear that parents also must live honorable lives before God and children if parents hope to receive honor in return. We learn honor from example. Honor reveals selfless love. The empty cross shouts Christ's love (honor) for us and honor for his Father too!

PRAYER: Heavenly Father, help me honor you by living an honorable life before the world's children, that they and others may seek and find your steadfast love. Amen.

THURSDAY, SEPTEMBER 30 • Read Exodus 20:13-20

The sixth through tenth commandments stress the importance of honorable interpersonal behavior in the creation of a holy nation. "You shall not kill,...commit adultery,...steal,...bear false witness,...[or] covet" (RSV) are rather clear. (Other Bible versions render *kill* as "murder" to account for mandated sacrifice of animals, death sentences, and war.)

We kill in other ways: Failure to encourage a child or an adult to venture forth in an unfamiliar role kills self-confidence. Silence instead of a smile or a hug can be an herbicide to sprouting hope. Failure to champion right over wrong murders decency with a sword of apathy.

Adultery pierces the very heart of a sacred covenant—betrayal of a holy communion. Blazing headlines suggest that fidelity is passé, the covenant of marriage obsolete. Other kinds of perfidy—deceit, hypocrisy, and bigotry—betray trust also.

Stealing takes the property of another without consent. Society often coins euphemisms for stealing by persons of prominence—*misappropriation* or *administrative oversight.* Stature does not mitigate God's laws. Slander is insidious theft. Failure to care for the poor constitutes theft by indifference.

The ninth commandment gives Israel the core of a judicial system—truth and the search for it. Truth represents the absence of falsity in word and deed, the essence of integrity.

Some suggest the tenth commandment explains the logic of six through nine, that coveting what belongs to another leads to murder, adultery, theft, and dishonesty. A consuming fantasy about that which belongs to another is an anathema to wholesome life.

Thunder and lightning punctuate God's covenant. The people tremble. God's grace is still overpowering today.

PRAYER: Help me, Lord, to honor you in word, thought, and deed. Amen.

FRIDAY, OCTOBER 1 • Read Psalm 19

God's steadfast love is the reason for our obedience to the Exodus covenant. The lyric poetry of Psalms celebrates this universal majesty with unrestrained praise and thankfulness.

Recreational travel affords the opportunity to worship in various churches along the way. Some mirror the little white clapboard, bell-tower steepled church of my youth; others offer an edifice of stone, stained glass, and seating for a thousand.

The intensity of enthusiasm expressed in congregational singing serves as my yardstick of a church's spirit. "O for a Thousand Tongues to Sing" offers opportunity to raise the rafters with the joy of a psalmist.

The author of Psalm 19 sees himself surrounded by evidence of God's ubiquitous, loving majesty, and he struggles with his poet's heart to express it. He tries example, illustration, and analogy to define his awe, only to stop abruptly with a silent confession— God's love is beyond words.

The psalmist tries eulogy: "The law of the Lord is perfect, / reviving the soul...sure,...right,...pure,...clean,...true" (RSV). The poet's rejoicing heart overflows with gratitude. Then his conscience whispers a warning—God's grace depends upon obedience. Keep God's commandments; there is great reward. One can visualize the psalmist falling to his knees, praying: "Clear thou me from hidden faults. / Keep back thy servant also from presumptuous sins; / let them not have dominion over me!"

Perhaps if we listen closely, we can join in the chorus with the heavenly choir, cloistered in the depth of the psalmist's soul, as it sings, "How Great Thou Art"!

PRAYER: God of love, let the words of my mouth and the meditation of my heart be acceptable in thy sight, O Lord, my rock and my redeemer. Amen.

SATURDAY, OCTOBER 2 • Read Matthew 21:33-46

A common thread weaves the Bible together—obedience to God. From the garden of Eden to the Resurrection and beyond, God challenges us to trust and obey.

In today's reading, a landowner has made a covenant with tenants he trusts. The covenant is broken with intentional malice when the covetous sharecroppers brutalize the landowner's inquiring representatives and subsequently murder his only son.

Jesus asks, "When therefore the owner of the vineyard comes, what will he do to those tenants?" (RSV). The chief priests and elders answer, "He will put those wretches to a miserable death, and let out the vineyard to other tenants who will give him the fruits in their seasons" (RSV). Their reply rings with righteous indignation; the tenants have betrayed the trust and obedience incumbent in the covenant. Only a gracious father would send his only son to give such miscreants another chance.

God has made us trusted tenants of a wonderful world and given us rules to live by. Like the biblical knaves, we have abused the responsibility of stewardship. We have ignored behavior prescribed by the Ten Commandments. The ranks of the homeless are rising. A lasting marriage has a fifty-fifty chance. Single-parent families increase daily. We build prisons as fast as schools. How convincing is our stewardship before God? Where would we be without God's steadfast love?

PRAYER: Lord, I am so like the vineyard tenants, ungrateful for the love and faith you offer. Forgive me. Help me live a life worthy of your boundless grace. Amen.

SUNDAY, OCTOBER 3 • **Read Philippians 3:4b-14**

A television journalist asked Billy Graham if he was a Christian. Dr. Graham answered softly, "I try to be." He went on to explain that being a Christian is an ongoing, endless quest—a process of becoming. The clergyman's answer captures the significance of today's reading. To be a Christian is not a goal one achieves like a college degree, conferred, possessed, and put away in a trunk. Like the goal of good health, we have to work at it continually.

Paul says if being a Christian is a goal rather than a destination, none has better credentials than he. None can match his piety in keeping the law. If keeping the law makes one righteous, Paul can claim it with impunity.

Idiomatically, Paul confesses that his life of righteousness pales when compared to Christ's life and his selfless sacrifice. If only I can have the faith to know him, to understand fully the power of his resurrection, to be like him—maybe then I might be worthy of resurrection. I haven't made it yet, Paul says, but I'm straining forward, pursuing the steadfast love of God by trying to live the faith of Jesus Christ.

Marriage vows grant legal relationships, not quality of relationships. That's a process of becoming. The birth of a child confers parenthood; it does not make a mother and father. Keeping God's law is a continuing process, not an end.

Nicodemus, another respected Pharisee, asked Jesus if the law was enough. Somewhere between Christ's reply and Christ's crucifixion, Nicodemus grasps the answer. Lovingly, publicly, Nicodemus helps Joseph care for the crucified body of Jesus. Nicodemus surrenders self-righteous esteem for the humble process of becoming.

PRAYER: Gracious God, by faith in your steadfast love help me witness for you. Make me a worthy recipient of your son's promise of eternal life. Amen.

Stand Fast in the Lord

*October 4–10, 1999 • L. Joey Faucette**

MONDAY, OCTOBER 4 • Read Philippians 4:1-4

"Stand fast in the Lord" (KJV). Easier said than done, right? Especially in a multitasking, multifunctioning, multicultural, postmodern society where life hurtles at such a fast pace you must run constantly just to stay close behind. This week we'll examine what Paul intends that we be and do as Christians who stand fast in the Lord.

This notion of "stand fast" may seem contradictory, for we associate "fast" with movement. When we consider the spiritual journey, we associate the journey with going somewhere, to a destination. However, Paul suggests that the journey *is* the destination, that the "how" of the journey is of primary importance, more so than the "where."

For instance, Paul encourages the Philippians to "rejoice in the Lord always." This encouragement is more "how" than "where." Regardless of where you find yourself in your spiritual journey, here's how to live it: Rejoice always. Ground your travel in rejoicing whether you walk through a darkened valley where the mist of life hangs low or sit atop a mountain where the wind blows pure and sweet. The Lord is in the valley and on the mountain.

"Stand fast in the Lord." Such a spiritual journey is only possible "in the Lord." When we try to stand fast in ourselves alone, we fail in sinful ways. But as Paul and the psalmist teach us, when we stand in the Lord, we receive peace and mercy for the journey. Where do you stand in your journey? In the Lord—or in yourself?

PRAYER: O Lord, may I stand fast in you this day and always, rejoicing in your presence. Amen.

---

*Pastor of First Baptist Church, Danville, Virginia; freelance writer and church consultant.

TUESDAY, OCTOBER 5 • **Read Philippians 4:5-9**

Regarding the journey as the destination, Paul teaches that to stand fast in the Lord, first pray about everything from the heart; and second, ponder about certain things from the head. The refreshment for the journey, Paul says, is peace.

Praying about everything from the heart sounds easy enough. You open yourself to God through Christ by claiming your life requests and, with thanksgiving in your heart, share those requests with God. But do you ever find yourself complaining to God about these requests [read "certain people"] without thanksgiving in your heart? It's an interesting balancing act, isn't it?

The purpose of making our requests known to God with thanksgiving is not that God needs informing, but that we need inspiring. We need to be reminded of our dependence on God and to be thankful for such an awesome God. We need to realize that by opening our hearts fully to God not only are those for whom we pray benefited, but we receive peace, a peace that keeps us standing fast in the Lord.

Paul teaches that the second way to stand fast in the Lord is to ponder certain things from the head. In this postmodern day when we can get information from every portable and potent way imaginable, our hunger isn't for knowledge but for wisdom. Wisdom is experience reflected and meditated upon critically. Wisdom anchors us in the Lord in a mercurial society. Paul offers the key to wisdom here by instructing us to ponder only certain things: honor and justice, purity and beauty, value and virtue, and the praise of Jesus Christ. Once we ponder these things, we learn and receive them in our minds. And once we set our heads straight on them, then we receive God's peace, which keeps us standing fast in the Lord.

PRAYER: **O Lord, grant me your peace as I pray about everything from the heart and ponder about certain things from the head. Amen.**

WEDNESDAY, OCTOBER 6 • Read Psalm 106:1-5

The psalmist believes that we stand fast in the Lord when we remember God's mercy. Mercy is such an interesting concept, isn't it? With mercy we receive an undeserved or unearned judgment. We get off the proverbial hook. We most often think of mercy when we want it, not when we should give it.

But for the psalmist, mercy is more than just an interesting concept. For him, the Lord's mercy to us elicits a response of thanksgiving for all the many ways and times the Lord has given us mercy. Such mercy isn't here today, gone tomorrow. The Lord's mercy endures eternally, throughout our lifetimes and life experiences.

For the psalmist, remembering the Lord's mercy with thanksgiving involves even more. Such remembering determines how we stand fast in the Lord, how we interact with the world in which we live. Specifically, the psalmist says, we "observe justice" and "do righteousness at all times" because we remember the Lord's mercy with thanksgiving. How do we do this?

We observe justice when we, in remembering the Lord's mercy, act in obedience to God's commandments. We live as a forgiven people who have been visited by God with salvation.

We do righteousness at all times when we, in remembering the Lord's mercy, see the good in people and treat them as God treats us—mercifully. Such goodness causes us to rejoice in the Lord and in the people of the Lord.

What will you do today to remember God's mercy to you and make it more than just an interesting concept? What will you do today to observe justice and do righteousness at all times? How will you claim as a part of your being the eternal mercy of the Lord this day?

PRAYER: O Lord, help me remember your mercy with thanksgiving today and act accordingly. Amen.

THURSDAY, OCTOBER 7 • Read Psalm 106:6, 19-23

Is it harder to stand fast in the Lord in this postmodern, technology-driven, change-littered culture? It sure seems that way, doesn't it?

The rapid pace of change confronts us everywhere. Go to the doctor's office for a visit; if you need a test, there's a new method of imaging your body. Go to buy a new vehicle, and it will probably have a computer-driven mapping system. Go to your child's school and watch the kindergartners surfing the Web. Go to the new grocery store, and you'll discover fully prepared meals that only require the microwave. Change is one of the few constants in this rapidly running society.

But change is nothing new to us. Not really. Ever since our creation, we've been confronted with change. And through the millennia, we've developed criteria for embracing and managing change—only some of our criteria aren't holy.

Take for instance our choosing to sin. Like the Hebrews in the wilderness, we can stand at the foot of a mountain on which God chooses to reveal the divine glory and change our glory (v. 20). Why do we change our glory? Because, again like the wilderness Hebrews, we forget God our savior.

Forgetting God our savior in this postmodern, technology-driven, change-littered culture is indeed easy. Standing fast in God's glory and not changing our glory requires more effort.

Standing fast in the Lord today requires personal criteria that remain firm in the midst of changing tides of social current. We anchor such criteria in remembering God's everlasting mercy and remembering God as savior.

PRAYER: O Lord, anchor me in remembering you as savior in the midst of all of today's changing tides. Amen.

FRIDAY, OCTOBER 8 • Read Exodus 32:1-6

It starts slowly at first, as it did for the Hebrews at the foot of the mountain, rising up out of the embers of your impatience. Some source of deliverance is delayed. The Lord isn't making good on a divine promise in a timely fashion. Never mind that God came through in high and holy fashion last time you found yourself enslaved in your own private Egypt. That was last time, and this is this time. You're not sure what has become of God, just as the Hebrews can't fathom what has become of Moses.

So, like the Hebrews in the wilderness, you make a new and improved God, fashioned from the broken-off things of your world—broken-off golden earrings. Something you can melt down and reshape into an image you like. A thing you like because you made it.

"This is the Lord which the day has made," you chant. "Let us rejoice and be glad, not in God, but in It." And you sit down to eat and drink, and then get up to play as if nothing has changed, as if all is right with your world. You feast on yourself and call yourself "Lord."

Nothing could be further from the truth.

This day, before the embers of impatience are fanned into a fire of faithlessness in your soul, stand fast in the Lord by asking yourself, "Why am I impatient with the Lord today? Do I really believe that I can deal with this wilderness situation on my own?" Promise yourself and the Lord that everything you break off today, even if it is golden, you will hand not to an Aaron whom you choose but to the Lord who has chosen you for remolding in the divine image.

PRAYER: **O Lord most holy, take my wilderness brokenness this day. Melt me, mold me, and shape me into your divine image and likeness. Amen.**

SATURDAY, OCTOBER 9 • Read Exodus 32:7-14

There it is. Unavoidable, concise, and clear, without a hint of confusion. There it is. Unambiguously stated and as plain as the nose on your face.

There it is: "And the Lord repented of the evil which he thought to do to his people" (RSV). Now we can dismiss this verse as an anthropomorphic projection from the author. Or we can debate the merits of process theology over neo-orthodox theology. Or we can exegete the words *repent* and *evil* and pursue a philosophical discourse about the problem of evil.

Or we can consider the overlooked, less glamorous portion of this passage:"which he thought to do to his people." Did the Lord think about wiping this "stiff-necked people" from the face of this earth? You bet. And wouldn't you? Look at how far the Lord has brought them—from slavery in Egypt to worshiping at a mountain with their leader, Moses, in the very presence of the Most Holy. If that's not transformational leadership, what is?

And what kind of grateful response do the Hebrews offer?—a golden calf that they call "Lord." Sure, the Lord considers pouring their hot-wax evil back on them.

But the Lord doesn't. Why? Because as Moses reminds God and as this verse notes, they are still God's people. No matter how many golden calves they mold, no matter how much jewelry they break off and melt, no matter how stiff-necked they are, they are still God's people. And as God's people, they receive grace and not evil from their Lord. Divine grace exceeds human sin again.

Whatever stiff-necked sin you commit this day, stand fast in the Lord as one of God's people. For while the Lord will think of various responses to your sin, grace accompanies your sin's natural consequences.

PRAYER: **O Lord, I praise your holy name for meeting my stiff-necked idolatry with grace this day. Amen.**

SUNDAY, OCTOBER 10 • Read Matthew 22:1-14

"For many are called, but few are chosen."

In our spiritual journey, this parable of Jesus calls us to pay close attention to the invitations we receive from our Lord to participate in the kingdom of heaven, for the kingdom of heaven is like a wedding feast. The best of the kingdom delicacies adorn the table. We simply need to come to the table dressed appropriately.

One of the greatest temptations we face in our spiritual journeys is taking God's invitations to partake of the kingdom lightly. What makes for fewer heart attacks in our physical diets—a light cuisine—does not make for healthier spiritual living. The spiritual nourishment the king invites us to enjoy enriches the Spirit. However, we decide whether to accept with blessing or reject with bane God's invitation to the table.

Interestingly enough, the king issues multiple invitations. When the first invitation fails to entice the wedding guests to come, the king sends a more detailed description of what's for dinner, hoping the menu will lure the guests. When that fails and the invitees slay his servants, the consequences of their sin drive them from the table with equal ferocity. The king offers the third invitation to all persons, "both good and bad," with the clear understanding that they are to come to a wedding. Some come inappropriately prepared for such an event.

Throughout our spiritual journeys, the King of kings extends invitation after invitation—each more enticing and alluring than the previous—in the hope that we will come to the kingdom wedding feast. As travelers along the way, we stand fast in the Lord when we look intently for the multiple invitations to the kingdom feast. As God invites and we accept and attend, God chooses us.

PRAYER: **O Lord, as I journey this day, may I perceive your invitations to the kingdom feast along my way and accept with a prepared heart. Amen.**

Faith-Filled and Thankful

October 11–17, 1999 • Helen P. Neinast*

MONDAY, OCTOBER 11 • Read Deuteronomy 8:7-18; Psalm 65

Who is the most thankful person you know? Who among your friends approaches life with a grateful attitude? Which of the people you know say "thank-you" m   often? How do you feel when you are around that person?

Who is the least thankful person you know? Who among your friends is least likely to approach life with a grateful attitude? How do you feel when you are around that person?

In the public television series based on the hymn "Amazing Grace," Bill Moyers interviews a very old man, a person so obviously in love with life that he carries joy in every crease of his face. Moyers asks this man what he has seen in his life of God's grace and what he has observed in the lives of others. The man's reply is interesting. He says, in effect, that it is more difficult to realize God's grace and to be grateful if you are either very rich or very poor.

I think this man is on to something. Today's passage from Deuteronomy takes special care to remind Israel to be thankful and to remember who brought them to safety and prosperity. In many ways, the entire Book of Deuteronomy serves as a careful reminder of God's powerful claim on us and our faith-filled response of heartfelt thanksgiving.

SUGGESTION FOR PRAYER: Read Psalm 65 aloud slowly as a prayer. Keep these words in your heart throughout the day: "Praise is due to you, O God, in Zion;…you make the gateways of the morning and the evening shout for joy."

---

*United Methodist campus minister at Emory University in Atlanta, Georgia; clergy member of the New Mexico Conference.

TUESDAY, OCTOBER 12 • Read Exodus 33:12-23

The stories in the Book of Exodus are so outrageous, so compelling, and so elegant that they can only be stories of faith. In this book, the people of Israel move from being slaves to Pharaoh to being enthralled with God. And through it all—from plagues to daring escapes, from courageous women to little babies adrift and in danger—through it all, God's voice is steady and sure.

In this passage, long after Israel's flight from Egypt, after the wilderness wanderings, after God's gift of the Ten Commandments, after the fiasco with the golden calf and God's forgiveness of Israel—after all that, Moses still asks whether God will be steadfast with these people that Moses leads. "Show me your ways, so that I may know you," Moses says.

God, in return, makes this promise, "My presence will go with you, and I will give you rest." But that is not enough for Moses. He persists, "Show me your glory, I pray." Moses asks for a sign that God will dwell with Israel without judgment and with grace.

God redirects the question. God answers Moses, and although the answer is straightforward, it is not clear-cut. The important thing, God says, is not glory but goodness: "I will make all my goodness pass before you....But you cannot see my face." The importance rests in knowing the kind of God who loves Israel, not in seeing this God's face.

This word from God—that I may know God's grace but not see God's face—has at times been the very word I needed to hear on my faith journey. Sometimes God's presence, God's face, is not all that obvious to me. Yet I can know that in the middle of faith's ambiguities and mysteries, God's presence is with me; and I will be given rest.

PRAYER: God, guide me this day, that I may know your presence and seek your will. Amen.

WEDNESDAY, OCTOBER 13 • Read Matthew 22:15-22

Jesus had a gift of wit that I often admire and sometimes envy. Time and again when approached by some shady, slippery, ill-intentioned group of detractors, he managed to cut through all their high-blown words and well-crafted traps to reveal the truth in its plainest form.

Matthew's story about the trap in the Temple is a clear case in point. Even though the disciples of the Pharisees enter the Temple and approach this new teacher with a question, education and enlightenment are the last things on their minds. They want to embarrass Jesus, to malign his credibility, to show him up as either a law-breaking revolutionary or as one willing to make concessions to a hated government. They carefully phrase the question in religious terms—though distinctly political ones. It is a genteel, well-heeled trap.

Jesus' answer, however, is anything but well-heeled. Asking whose image is on the government's coin and receiving the answer, "The emperor's," he says, "Give therefore to the emperor the things that are the emperor's, and to God the things that are God's."

On first hearing, Jesus' statement seems radical enough. But upon reflection, it becomes even more so. Jesus does not designate a secular realm and a religious realm, each equally respected. Instead, Jesus says that the religious realm practically preempts the secular realm. It is far more difficult—and far more rewarding—to give ourselves to God.

PRAYER: **Give me a keen mind and a discerning heart that I may hear your words, O God. Move through me this day, and let me be for others a sign of your presence in this world. Amen.**

THURSDAY, OCTOBER 14 • Read 2 Corinthians 9:6-15

"To recite the marvels of God in the liturgy is necessary. But to care for the orphan and the widow and to give hospitality to the sojourner and the stranger are concrete ways of remembering God....To do one without the other is to misunderstand the nature of God's creatures."

These words of Don Saliers in *Worship and Spirituality* reflect the sense and sentiment of Paul's words in Second Corinthians. To be sure, Paul wanders a bit in this passage before he gets to the heart of his message; many of Paul's writings meander. He talks about sowing sparingly and reaping sparingly, of sowing and reaping bountifully, of not giving compulsively or reluctantly. He even appears to approach the idea that giving benefits the giver in some way, material or spiritual. But then he returns to the heart of his message: When we give generously and cheerfully to others' needs, we worship God.

To give oneself generously to the needs of the world is also at the heart of our faith. As Kat Duff, author of *The Alchemy of Illness*, reminds us: "Faith is not something you must have or cannot lose, but something you practice because the world depends on it." The words of great religious leaders like Mahatma Gandhi, Martin Luther King. Jr., Mother Teresa, Nelson Mandela, and Desmond Tutu all speak to this great truth: Our duty, our privilege, is to give ourselves generously to the world in big ways and in small ways, noticed or hidden, every single day or once in a lifetime. It matters. What we do—out of our faith—matters.

In advocacy for change in our society, in giving direct help of our time and money, in this kind of wholehearted worship of God—in these ways we remember the world to God. By the same token, in these ways we remember and honor Christ.

PRAYER: **God, I know of no limits to your love for me. Help me live without limits in my love for your world. Amen.**

FRIDAY, OCTOBER 15 • **Read 1 Thessalonians 1:1-10**

There is, I think, no finer or more amazing gift than the gift of friendship. For centuries poets, songwriters, novelists, philosophers, and theologians have tried to capture the essence of friendship between two human beings. "Blessed is the influence of one true, loving human soul on another" (George Eliot). "Whoever finds a faithful friend has found a treasure" (Sirach 6:14). "Friendship is a sheltering tree" (Samuel Taylor Coleridge).

Paul's first letter to the Thessalonians is in many ways a tribute to friendship. The letter is warm, full of fond and kind words. It is spontaneous and full of emotion. Paul and others have left the new community at Thessalonica unwillingly, and they anxiously await news about the welfare of their friends in faith. Heartened by word of the community's strength, they thank God for the witness of these converts to the "faith and labor of love and steadfastness of hope in our Lord Jesus Christ." They pledge to remember these new friends in their prayers, and they offer eloquent thanks to God for these people.

We too must honor and cherish our friends. We must pray for them, be present for them, give thanks for them. We must befriend others, as we have been befriended. Sometimes that is not easy. Sometimes it requires more than we think we have to give. Yet we do it. We befriend someone. We befriend someone; another befriends us. And we are grateful to know and be known to one another.

In the same way, Christ gives us his friendship, a friendship not just for the easy days but through the tough ones. Thus we find ourselves forever grateful for the friendship we have with Jesus Christ, whose incarnation boldly stated how much God wanted to be with us. This friendship holds much promise. Thanks be to God!

PRAYER: Deepen my friendships, God. Deepen my friendship with my family and with those around me. Deepen my friendship with your creation. Deepen my friendship with you. Amen.

SATURDAY, OCTOBER 16 • Read Psalm 99

When Dag Hammarskjöld, former Secretary General of the United Nations, died in a plane crash in 1961, three items were recovered from the briefcase he had with him: a copy of the New Testament, a copy of the Psalms, and a copy of the charter of the United Nations. Hammarskjöld perceived that his work moved beyond the political realm; it was a religious calling.

So it seems appropriate that Hammarskjöld, as a world leader, carried with him a collection of psalms that time and time again remind us of God's claim on the whole world, on all of creation, and on all of our lives. Psalm 99 expresses with power and certainty the central message of the psalms: God reigns!

It is not we who are in control; our efforts will not secure justice or safety in this world. Rather, it is God who reigns, God who works justice in the world. We belong not to ourselves but to God: God reigns.

This psalm goes on to tell us who God is, this God who is "great in Zion" and "exalted over all the peoples." This God is both a lover of justice and a forgiving God. How, we ask, is this possible? How can God be both a forgiving God and an avenger of wrongdoings? To call God both forgiving and avenging makes a radical claim about God. We understand God's holiness not as absolute transcendence and freedom but as involved, committed, and forgiving love.

God reigns! The people tremble. We tremble at the power of God's love of justice, and we tremble at the power of God's love of forgiveness. This is the power of the message of the psalms.

PRAYER: **O God, reign in my heart and in my world this day and forevermore. Amen.**

SUNDAY, OCTOBER 17 • Read Luke 17:11-19

We can easily turn the story of the ten lepers into a prim, smug lesson about gratitude and ingratitude. In my elementary years of Sunday school, the story made me feel guilty about my ingratitude for my cousins' hand-me-down clothes. When I got older, the story got swept up in the observance of social niceties and made me wonder if I had been properly thankful for someone's kindness toward me. When I finished graduate school and started preaching, I didn't know what else to do with the story. So sometimes I simply skirted it, gave it short shrift, and focused the sermon elsewhere.

But a couple of years ago, I read a short commentary on the story that gave the story back to me. The commentary writer indicated that this story really has two parts. The first part is a simple healing story: the lepers cry for help; Jesus responds; and the healing occurs as they go to the priest for their official declaration of health. The second part of the story centers on the Samaritan's salvation. The Samaritan returns, praises God, and expresses his gratitude to Jesus. Jesus says, "Your faith has made you well," but the word he uses to say "made well" is the same word often translated "to be saved." For this commentator, the story of the ten lepers is not a story about ingratitude but a story of ten being healed and one being saved.

That simple shift of perspective dramatically changes the focus of the story. Now instead of focusing on gratitude and ingratitude, I must consider why the Samaritan—the only foreigner in the group —comes back to receive the full blessing of Jesus' life and ministry. Perhaps familiarity breeds complacency; only through the eyes of the stranger does Jesus reveal faith in new ways. Perhaps from the stranger we will learn new attentiveness, new excitement, new hopefulness.

PRAYER: Open my eyes, my mind, and my heart, O God, that I may know you in new and unfamiliar ways. Amen.

Looking toward the Promised Land

October 18–24, 1999 • *Bruce C. Birch**

MONDAY, OCTOBER 18 • **Read Deuteronomy 34:1-8**

It has always seemed a tragedy that Moses dies without entering the Promised Land. After forty years of leading Israel through the trials of the wilderness, God allows him to see the whole extent of the Promised Land, but Moses dies on Mount Nebo in Moab. Earlier tradition attributes this event to Moses' lack of faith when God brought forth water out of the rock for Israel (Num. 20:12). Yet here at the time of Moses' death, we hear no word of this judgment. God shows him all of the land that will become Israel's home and simply states that Moses will not enter there. Moses dies in honor and respect, and Israel grieves.

How often in our lives do we fail to reach the Promised Land of our hopes? It is actually a common human experience. We journey through life's struggles and often wind up short of the full measure of our hopes and plans. We, like Moses, often end up looking toward the Promised Land but not entering there. But the story of Moses' death suggests that this experience is not a tragedy but a natural part of human existence. We never achieve all of our dreams. We often leave the completion of our hopes and dreams to those who come after us—our children, our friends, our community of faith. Yet our journey enriches us as hopefully we envision our goals and dreams. Meaning does not lie in achieving everything we had planned for our lives. This week's readings suggest ways in which we can find meaning even when we can only look toward the Promised Land of our fullest hopes.

PRAYER: O Lord, we give thanks for visions and hopes that enrich us on the journey, even when we do not fully realize them. Amen.

---

*Professor of Old Testament at Wesley Theological Seminary, Washington, D.C.

TUESDAY, OCTOBER 19 • Read Psalm 90:1-6

This psalm is the only one associated with the name of Moses. Its opening superscription calls it "A Prayer of Moses, the man of God." In our reading for today, the psalmist meditates on the frailty of human life, particularly when compared to the eternal character of God. Measured against the scale of divine things our human lives are but a passing moment. The reality of God surpasses the age of the earth's mountains.

This realization of our human frailty can discourage us. Most of us have had times when we have felt insignificant and unnoticed in the world around us. Most of us have had moments when we imagine that the God who created the universe surely has little time or regard for us or our problems. Maybe Moses, whose life and leadership we associate with forty years of struggle in the wilderness, is the most appropriate name to associate with this psalm.

Yet the key to this psalm lies in its opening verse. Perhaps this verse speaks Moses' message to us as he shares from the experience of his struggles. Perhaps we can think of this verse as Moses' word to us from Mount Nebo where he only glimpses the Promised Land. Moses tells us that he has been at home all along the way. The Lord is our dwelling place. To acknowledge this fact is to be at home whatever our life circumstances, the struggles of our journeys, the failure of our dreams. When God becomes our constant home, then the enduring, eternal nature of God does not challenge our human frailty. When God becomes our constant home then the moments of our lives become part of God's eternity. We participate in the drama of creation through our participation in God with whom we dwell. God is not the prize at the end of our life's journey but our constant companion, enriching the journey along the way.

PRAYER: O God, my dwelling place, make me mindful of your constant presence in the midst of my journey. In joy, in struggle, in fulfillment, in disappointment, give me the assurance that I always dwell with you. Amen.

WEDNESDAY, OCTOBER 20 • Read Psalm 90:13-17

This portion of the psalm reading begins with an intercession asking God to turn from anger to compassion. Perhaps this psalm is attributed to Moses because of Moses' intercession for Israel with God.

If we begin with verse 13, we have no motivation for this intercession. In verses 7-12 the psalmist speaks of experiencing life's troubles as the anger of God. Certainly most can identify with that feeling. When difficulties and troubles arise, we all tend to ask, "Why has God done this to me?" When life's troubles and our own human limitations deny us the fulfillment of cherished hopes or committed goals, we often bitterly blame God and allow disappointment to cloud our entire lives.

But this psalm of Moses suggests another response. "Satisfy us in the morning with your steadfast love, so that we may rejoice and be glad all our days." We do not experience God's love only as the goal we reach when all our hopes and plans reach fulfillment. God's steadfast love is available to us every morning. Thus, we can rejoice and be glad every step of life's journey, not just when we reach some promised land of our fondest hopes.

When my three-year-old daughter died of leukemia, I was bitter at the loss of the life we could have had together, but a wise friend helped me see that even her short life carried more importance than her death. I could not allow the loss of her unlived years to dim the joy and gladness she had brought for the three years of her life. God's blessings did not lie only in the hopes I had lost; God had blessed me through her life every morning of her days.

PRAYER: O God of all my days, in my times of struggle, pain, or disappointment, help me remember with joy and gladness the many mornings when I have known your steadfast love. Amen.

THURSDAY, OCTOBER 21 • Read 1 Thessalonians 2:1-8

Paul writes to the church in Thessalonica, remembering the circumstances when he first came to them and founded the church in that place. Things had not gone as well as expected. His ministry met with great opposition from the Jewish community in Thessalonica. The uproar became so great that it forced Paul and his companions to leave before they had finished their work there (Acts 17:1-10). Now Timothy brings word to Paul that the small community in Thessalonica is continuing its ministry but longs to see Paul face to face (3:6-10). Paul writes to encourage them and suggests that he and they are united in faith and love even when he cannot be present with them physically.

Most of us have beloved family members or friends from whom life's circumstances have separated us. I live hundreds of miles from my mother, my brothers and sisters; my son has moved to a distant city to take advantage of a job opportunity. In such times of separation, memory, a uniquely human capacity, enables what is no longer physically present to be present within us. Photo albums, mementos, and letters help nourish that memory and keep it alive within us.

Paul cannot be in Thessalonica, and he wishes to encourage the church there. But first he must call the Thessalonians to share memories with him—memories of the rich time they had together when he first came, despite the opposition to his ministry. Memory becomes the basis of shared identity and renewed commitment.

Sometimes in our churches we become so busy that we forget to share the stories that make us who we are. The nurture and sharing of our biblical heritage, our historical roots, our local histories, our personal journeys encourage the work of the church, providing the foundation for our action as the people of God.

SUGGESTION FOR MEDITATION: **Recall an important memory from your faith journey that you might tell to encourage others.**

FRIDAY, OCTOBER 22 • Read Matthew 22:34-40

In response to a challenge by opponents among the Pharisees, Jesus sums up the whole of the Law and the Prophets by pointing to two great commandments: the commandment to love God without reservation and the commandment to love one's neighbor as fully as oneself. The challenger, learned in the law, had hoped to trap Jesus in the tangled details of the law. Jesus has found in the law not entanglements but principles of faithful living.

Jesus quotes from Deuteronomy 6:5 and Leviticus 19:18. Both of these verses are part of Moses' legacy—not only to Israel but through Jesus to the church. They comprise part of the Torah, the five books of Moses, the stories and commandments that define God's covenant people. In a strange way, although God did not allow Moses to enter the Promised Land, through his giving God's law to God's people, Moses' legacy continues long after his physical life. Through his faithful work, Moses is more fully present with Israel through many generations in the Promised Land than his physical body could ever have been. Once again Jesus draws on the law of Moses to give identity to God's people and Jesus' own followers.

How often we fail to reach a goal and conclude that our work has been in vain. We fail to achieve an office, a program goal, a relationship, a personal standard—and we think we have failed. But if we have labored faithfully and invested our lives with integrity, then our contributions will endure in unexpected ways. Our contributions will enrich and give identity to the communities in which we have played a part.

PRAYER: **O Lord, teach me that by loving God and neighbor, I most truly become myself. Amen.**

SATURDAY, OCTOBER 23 • Read Matthew 22:41-46

This is not an easy passage to follow. Jesus' opponents have been trying to embarrass and discredit him by catching him in tangled arguments about the law. In these verses Jesus finally becomes impatient with this game. He can play the game as well as they. The point of this passage is not in following Jesus' argument about how the Messiah can be the son of David, who calls the Messiah Lord. Jesus silences his opponents by being as deft at word games in the Torah as they are. This is the game of the legal hairsplitters. And when Jesus has silenced them, we are left to ask of his argument, "So what?"

The contrast between this hairsplitting game (which Jesus can play) and Jesus' own straightforward penetration to the heart of the law in the preceding verses (34-40) provides the point of this passage in Matthew's Gospel. When Jesus directs our attention to the heart of the law through love of God and neighbor, we need not ask, "So what?" We know we are at the center of what makes for faithful living—living that will make a difference in the world—living that will define God's people in the world.

Sometimes our own goals—the Promised Lands we seek—get caught up in the games people play. When we look at what we value and seek, does a closer examination cause us to say, "So what?" Or can we look beyond these goals—some more worthy and some less—and ask whether in pursuing them we have furthered the love of God and neighbor. If we live in love of God and neighbor, then it will matter less whether we achieve all that people expect of us in the games they play than that we live faithfully toward our vision as God's faithful people.

SUGGESTION FOR MEDITATION: Examine your life in the past week. How have your actions furthered love of God and neighbor?

SUNDAY, OCTOBER 24 • Read Deuteronomy 34:9-12

We return to Mount Nebo. Moses has died short of entering the Promised Land. But the tone of this passage is not disappointment or tragedy. Verses 10-12 celebrate Moses' life as one of the great witnesses in all biblical story. God worked wondrous things through Moses.

No doubt Moses had hoped to lead Israel personally into the land God has promised. This was not to be. Instead, before he died, Moses laid hands on Joshua; now Joshua will lead Israel into the Promised Land.

We appropriately set our sights on hopeful goals for ourselves and for the sake of God's kingdom. But we should not imagine that worthy goals depend solely on ourselves. We are a part of families, communities, and congregations. We are inheritors of the visions of those who went before us, and we will pass our unfinished visions on to those who come after us. We do not live toward our dreams in isolation but as part of a great cloud of witnesses. If we fail to reach the Promised Land of some cherished goal, surely a Joshua nearby will pick up where we left off—especially if we can willingly pass the "spirit of wisdom" on in gratitude to those who can and will continue our labors.

Most of us will end our lives with a long list of things we had hoped to do left undone. As we gaze into the Promised Lands we may not reach, we must not give in to disappointment. We must count the many mornings we have known God's steadfast love and pass the vision on to those who come after us in gratitude that God's promises never depend on us alone for fulfillment.

PRAYER: O Lord, I give thanks for the promises you have given and toward which I live. Pass the spirit of wisdom through me to those who take up the vision where I must leave off. Amen.

God's Sheer Goodness

October 25–31, 1999 • Debra* and Gary** Ball-Kilbourne

MONDAY, OCTOBER 25 • Read 1 Thessalonians 2:9-13

A news story broke last week in our area about a retired colleague in ministry who allegedly has been less than "pure, upright, and blameless" in his recent conduct toward a believer. Although secular and ecclesiastical judicial processes will determine his guilt and consequences, the scandal has created one more barrier to presenting the gospel to a cynical world.

This—and too many incidents like it—remind us of two truths about the gospel of Jesus Christ:

1. The world at large judges the gospel as lived out by its ministers—lay and clergy.

2. The gospel is ultimately the word of God and therefore does not depend on its human bearers for its truth.

Unfortunately, people do judge the gospel of Christ by the lives of those who claim to profess it. Skeptics outside the church readily point fingers at the hypocrites within. Who wants to associate with persons whose lives lack congruity with their claimed beliefs?

Fortunately, the gospel of Christ does not depend upon human beings—even Christians—for its truth. Even someone as blameless in his conduct as the apostle Paul gives thanks that those who hear the gospel from his lips move their attention to focus on what God has to say them. Do people hear God's word spoken to them through your conduct?

SUGGESTION FOR PRAYER: Pray that the conduct of all believers might be "pure, upright, and blameless" for the sake of proclaiming the gospel to the world.

---

*Pastor of Flame of Faith United Methodist Church in West Fargo, North Dakota.

**One of the pastors of First United Methodist Church, Fargo, North Dakota.

TUESDAY, OCTOBER 26 • Read Joshua 3:7-13

In recent years, many congregations have experienced the transition of leadership from an older generation to a younger one. Whether the older generation intentionally trains its younger replacements or simply dies off and leaves the next generation to fend for itself, such transition inevitably comes.

Perhaps the greatest fear of each new generation of church leaders is that no one will follow. Even though times and circumstances change, the ways of the older leadership have become comfortable. To enter into an unknown future seems frightening. Even though we may rightly and necessarily discard new paths, the new generation of leaders worries, "Why should anyone follow my lead?"

Some years ago, we followed as pastors of a congregation two gifted pastors who retired that year. I remember looking around the filled sanctuary on my first Sunday and thinking, "This is Cecil's and Janet's church. What do I think I am doing here?"

Imagine Joshua standing on the east bank of the Jordan River. Joshua's mentor Moses has died. Indeed, no one remains alive from the generation of Hebrew leaders and people who fled Egypt into the desert wilderness decades earlier. Moses' mantle of leadership now falls onto Joshua's younger shoulders.

However, the Lord speaks to Joshua: "Beginning today I will show the people that you are their leader, and they will know that I am helping you as I helped Moses" (Josh. 3:7, CEV).

Faithful and competent leadership by each successive generation will come by the Lord's hand upon those leaders.

SUGGESTION FOR MEDITATION: Think about the lay and clergy leaders of your congregation. Pray that God be with them as they lead.

WEDNESDAY, OCTOBER 27 • Read Joshua 3:14-17

You might want to compare this telling of the Israelites' crossing of the Jordan River with that of their crossing of the Red Sea decades earlier, as told in Exodus 14:21-31. What differences do you find?

In my mind's eye, I can visualize significant differences between these two similar stories. When the Israelites crossed the Red Sea fleeing from Egypt, imagine how the people must have hurried across the seabed with the enemy's chariots hot on their heels! Despite the marvel of water standing up in walls on either side and Moses' promise of God's leading them toward a better life, how great their fear and panic must have been!

I imagine the crossing of the Jordan River to be far more stately. No enemy chases them now. Egypt and slavery have been left miles and years behind. The priests carrying the ark of the covenant cross first, leading an orderly procession of the people. Armed with God's covenant, they march forward to meet new challenges, rather than rushing across to flee past oppression.

Life provides times for either type of crossing. Sometimes we flee headlong from some fearful foe, hoping against hope that God is protecting us, leading us, preserving us. Sometimes we march determinedly toward a new future, bravely following where God leads.

In which manner are you crossing your rivers at the moment? Neither is wrong; but it helps to know what river you are crossing, why you are crossing it, and Who is helping you to cross.

PRAYER: **Powerful, gracious God, part whatever rivers I face today, so that I can flee the evils of the past and face the challenges of the future. Amen.**

THURSDAY, OCTOBER 28 • Read Psalm 107:1-7

Now thank we all our God,
with heart and hands and voices,
who wondrous things has done,
in whom this world rejoices.

Each Thanksgiving congregations throughout the United States sing Martin Rinkart's moving hymn, "Now Thank We All Our God." He composed the hymn at a time of great distress, when hundreds—including several of Rinkart's own family—had died of sickness. The hymn captures much of the spirit of Psalm 107—itself a hymn in praise of God's mercy and steadfastness during times of adversity.

We may break down today's reading in this way: Verse 1 offers an introduction to the psalmist's intent in praising God. Verses 2 and 3 identify the audience—those who have been redeemed from specific troubles as well as those who know themselves to be helpless without the goodness of God. Verses 4-7 speak of persons who have known physical or emotional hunger and thirst.

As you read these verses, think of your own specific troubles. How have God's steadfast love and goodness enabled you to stand in the face of trials and adversities? As you look to the future, for what do you need God's support?

Whether we read only these verses or, as a result of reading them, find ourselves drawn further into the passage, we will discover that the psalmist is praising God for God's *hesed*—God's sheer goodness.

Because of God's innate goodness and steadfast love—God's *hesed*—Martin Rinkart and an unnamed psalmist before him could praise God, even in the midst of deepest despair.

SUGGESTION FOR MEDITATION: Thank God for God's goodness—*hesed*—for you today.

FRIDAY, OCTOBER 29 • Read Psalm 107:33-37

Consider the adversities the psalmist recalls throughout Psalm 107: hunger and thirst, darkness and gloom, sin and affliction, storm and sea. Each affliction gives opportunity to experience God's goodness.

Must we have experienced a storm at sea to be properly mindful of the goodness of God's deliverance? No! These categories merely serve as examples of human difficulty. For example, who among us—though we may never have set foot in a boat—has not been lost and "at sea" regarding decisions? When we have reached decisions, especially under God's guidance, who among us has not known relief? Whether a day is filled with joy or difficulty, we can depend on a God who continually strives to bring forth goodness.

The apostle Paul, who suffered many of the things the psalmist wrote about centuries after this psalm's first singing, celebrated the steadfast love of God when he wrote Romans 8:31-39. Nothing "in all creation, will be able to separate us from the love of God in Christ Jesus our Lord" (Rom. 8:39).

We live in a truly dangerous world. Violence seems rampant and random around us. Natural calamities can strike without warning. We have no absolute guarantee of personal safety in this life. However, in spite of injury and tragedy, we can remain confident of one thing: Our God is good and will love us eternally no matter what else happens!

SUGGESTION FOR MEDITATION: Consider when you have rejoiced in God's steadfast goodness, particularly in the midst of life's difficulties.

We might entitle this text and that of tomorrow's, "Caution! Reader Beware!" Surely Matthew 23–25, sometimes called the "chapters of woe," are filled with judgment. Reading chapter 23, Christians may easily misinterpret Jesus' words about Jewish leaders of his day. What does he mean?

Jesus found fault with some scribes and Pharisees of his day. Specifically, their lives did not outwardly reflect their words and teachings; they enforced hundreds of difficult-to-keep rules upon the Jews in an attempt to keep the Law; and they were overly concerned with their own position in the community. To borrow a current phrase, these religious leaders were "talking the talk without walking the walk."

Might we have similar concerns about ourselves? A few years ago a new Christian echoed Jesus' concern by commenting that some Christians exercised an overzealous concern with "appearance management." Perhaps he's right!

For the next twenty-four hours, try to practice the three things Jesus found lacking in the scribes and Pharisees:

1. Match your words with your conduct. (And don't be surprised if you discover some hypocrisy lurking within you! Many of us have discovered that our words and conduct don't always match.)

2. Do not demand of others a Christian lifestyle that you are unwilling to follow yourself.

3. Practice acts of practical piety—such as prayer and service—because of the resulting spiritual benefit rather than because others might think well of you.

After twenty-four hours, review your experience. What did you discover?

PRAYER: God, I want to be a Christian—a better Christian. Help me be your humble servant this day. In Jesus' name. Amen.

SUNDAY, OCTOBER 31 • Read Matthew 23:8-12

When I was growing up, a woman in my community regularly visited the sick. She stocked her freezer with soup stock and casseroles, awaiting the time when someone would need nourishment during illness. Many times her kindness included caring for children whose parents were stressed, ill, or lacking childcare. This she did in addition to being a mother herself, a wife, a counselor, and a Sunday school teacher. In later years—after her "first" retirement—she counseled inmates at a prison, putting into use several counseling degrees and years of honed skill in a voluntary task. Still later, she became a caregiver for the dying through the hospice movement.

Throughout each of these roles and others, persons knew the woman as "Leona," "sister," "friend," or even "that nice lady." I knew her as "Mother." Rarely, if ever, did I hear her called by her titles—though she had credentials galore.

My mother had little concern about roles and titles. When I asked her why she did the things she did, she sometimes became pensive. It never occurred to her that she should lead her life differently! The things she did for others were all part of being a Christian. Jesus modeled a kind of "servant leadership" that emphasized acts of loving kindness rather than titles and roles.

Christians have no room for pride! Brothers and sisters all, we are each a part of God's family where titles and distinctions created by those titles are of little importance.

When people reflect on your life, how would you like to be known? What title might best reflect the fact that you are a Christian?

SUGGESTION FOR MEDITATION: Record all the different titles—or roles—by which you are known. Circle the ones you value most. Consider what those titles say about you. Pray that God will use you effectively in each of your many roles and tasks.

The Eternal Now

November 1–7, 1999 • Hoyt L. Hickman*

MONDAY, NOVEMBER 1 • Read Matthew 5:1-12
ALL SAINTS DAY

When the New Testament speaks of the saints, it refers to Christians collectively, not just to a few persons of outstanding spiritual attainments. We have been made holy—saints—by God's free gift. We celebrate all the saints on this All Saints Day.

But this understanding does not entitle us to be content with our present way of life. We are called to become what we are—to attain the character that befits our sainthood. That is why on this day we may look especially at Christians past and present who provide good role models for us. That is why, when we look at particular saints, we reflect on their most admirable qualities.

What are these saintly character traits? The Beatitudes summarize these character traits, and that is why we traditionally reflect on them on All Saints Day. The familiarity of the Beatitudes often makes it hard for us to realize how radically they challenge the values of our society and call us to a whole new way of life.

SUGGESTION FOR MEDITATION: **Read the Beatitudes again as if for the first time. Experience the shock of what they say. What are they saying to you about your life?**

---

*Retired United Methodist minister; served as Director of Worship Resource Development for the denomination from 1972–93; teaches at Drew University from time to time.

TUESDAY, NOVEMBER 2 • Read 1 John 3:1-3

Many Christians observe the day after All Saints as All Souls Day, or Day of the Dead—often with spooky customs that speak openly of death and may even make fun of it. Protestants have ignored this day because of its historic association with praying people out of Purgatory and because of our broad interpretation of All Saints Day. Yet on Hallowe'en—All Saints Eve—we have similar customs.

And this day after All Saints raises some serious issues. This day challenges us to expand our view beyond the Christian community to *all souls*.

This day challenges our deeply held taboo against facing the reality of death. It reminds us that, since God takes away the sting of death, we may freely talk and express our feelings about death to one another. Sharing multiplies our joys and divides our sorrows.

This day challenges us to face our sins and failures and those of all souls from the worst sinner to the greatest saint in the confidence that God is not finished working on any of us. "Beloved, we are God's children now; what we will be has not yet been revealed. What we do know is this: when he is revealed, we will be like him, for we will see him as he is. And all who have this hope in him purify themselves, just as he is pure."

SUGGESTION FOR MEDITATION: **Reflect on one or more of the above challenges. Are there people (souls) for whom God is giving you a concern? What are your innermost feelings about death, and where do you need to grow in your ability to face death? Where do you need to let God work on you?**

WEDNESDAY, NOVEMBER 3 • Read Matthew 25:1-13

"Keep awake..., for you know neither the day nor the hour." Already advertisements and store displays serve to remind us that Christmas will be here before we know it. The Christian calendar has a reminder for us too.

The Advent season doesn't begin until the fourth Sunday before Christmas, but all through November the lectionary readings reflect a pre-Advent mode, reminding us to be awake and ready for Christ's coming again. The word *Advent* means coming, and the season celebrates the comings of Christ—Christ's coming two thousand years ago, Christ's comings today in Word and Spirit, and Christ's coming in final victory. Some Christmas carols such as "O Little Town of Bethlehem" move us from the long ago to the here and now: "O holy Child of Bethlehem, descend to us, we pray."

Are you ready, not just for Advent and Christmas but for the comings of Christ that they celebrate? Christ can suddenly and unexpectedly appear—not only in that day of ultimate victory, not only in the moment of our own death but in moments of truth and of personal testing that bring Christ before us in the most astonishing disguises.

SUGGESTION FOR MEDITATION: **Where in your life are you least ready for Christ to show up? Is Christ already there, and have you failed to recognize him? What are some of the disguises in which you may encounter Christ? What can you do to be prepared?**

THURSDAY, NOVEMBER 4 • **Read 1 Thessalonians 4:13-18**

Paul is looking forward to the Lord's coming in final victory. He assures his readers that in that day the dead in Christ will be reunited with the living in an eternal communion with the Lord.

Christians have engaged in much fruitless debate over the timing and other details of Christ's coming in final victory, especially in these last days before the calendar turns to a new millennium. Let's concentrate on the basics.

Christ came two thousand years ago and comes today but has not yet come in final victory. Swords have not yet been beaten into plowshares, and the peace and justice promised by the prophets are not yet ours. The coming of Christ has both "already" and "not yet" dimensions.

Are we in the last days before that final victory? Paul and the Thessalonians thought so. Many think so today. If by last days we mean days when Christians are to be prepared at all times for the final coming of the Lord, then we have been in the last days for two thousand years, and none of us knows how long the last days will continue.

God will bring about the final victory of good over evil. All who have trusted in God will share eternally in the glory of that victory. In that glory we will recognize the Christ who came in humility long ago. That is enough.

SUGGESTION FOR MEDITATION: What does Christ's coming in final victory mean to you? Have you been insensitive to the evil in the world that testifies to the ways in which Christ is yet to come? What in your life does Christ need to overcome on the way to final victory?

FRIDAY, NOVEMBER 5 • Read Joshua 24:1-3a, 14-25

The tribes of Israel have been in the Promised Land for a while. They are growing accustomed to a new way of life. They find themselves among people of other cultures whose ways contradict what they have been taught. They have started adapting to their new surroundings and conforming to the ways of the people around them.

Their leader Joshua calls the people of Israel to a definite decision and leads them in deciding for the Lord: "Choose this day whom you will serve,…but as for me and my household, we will serve the Lord." He doesn't pretend that this decision is easy or let them get away with something halfway; he makes a covenant with the people and gives them specific laws and ordinances.

Sometimes our moving into a new situation—possibly the Promised Land of realized ambitions—strongly tempts us to conform to our new culture by adopting ways that we cannot reconcile with God's ways. We may tell ourselves that someday—but not today!—we'll return to God's ways.

The voice of Joshua comes to us over the centuries loud and clear: "Choose this day whom you will serve." And we can follow his example in serving the Lord.

SUGGESTION FOR MEDITATION: Where in your life have you wandered from your resolve to serve God? Where are you trying to serve two masters? What things in your life do you need to put away because they interfere with your fulfillment of God's calling for your life?

SATURDAY, NOVEMBER 6 • Read Psalm 78:1-7

The psalmist teaches us that we are bound together in a covenant community that persists through the generations. All these generations—past, present, and future—are in the covenant community together. We become the beneficiaries of the heritage our ancestors in faith passed on to us, and we have a solemn obligation to pass that heritage on to generations yet unborn.

There is an old saying that the Christian church is always one generation away from extinction. In other words, the community of faith will survive the death of those now living only as we pass the faith on to the next generation. If we remember and teach what God has given the covenant community, we benefit not only ourselves but our posterity; if we forget, we hurt them as well as ourselves. And we can teach not only our biological children but others who become our children in faith.

If we celebrate All Saints Sunday tomorrow, we can renew our solidarity with the saints from whom we have received our heritage and with those to whom we are called to pass it on. Then on some future All Saints celebration our children in faith can remember us as among the saints from whom they too will have received a goodly inheritance.

SUGGESTION FOR MEDITATION: **Think of one or more specific persons who passed on the Christian message and teachings to you. What did they do or say that was most helpful? How, specifically, can you do for someone else what those persons did for you?**

SUNDAY, NOVEMBER 7 • **Read Revelation 7:9-17**

John, exiled on the island of Patmos in a time of persecution, saw "a great multitude that no one could count, from every nation, from all tribes and peoples and languages," praising God. He was not alone, not even alone with God. He was part of a great community of faith that embraced the living and the dead.

In the Apostles' Creed we say, "I believe in...the communion of saints." Today All Saints Sunday celebrations may heighten many congregations' awareness of this communion. In one congregation, as the name of each of the honored dead is read, the people respond with a loud and clear "Present!" and a deep bell is solemnly rung.

When on this or any day we celebrate Holy Communion, the liturgy reminds us that we are joining our praise with that of all God's people on earth and all the company of heaven. At that table, we commune with the church in all times and all places. Yes, even generations yet unborn join with us in a living presence that transcends time and space.

Humanly speaking, you may be alone at this moment in your daily worship. But spiritually speaking you are not only in the presence of God but also joined in your worship by the whole communion—the whole community—of saints.

SUGGESTION FOR MEDITATION: **Reflect on one or more saints. How can the saints' spiritual presence uphold you? What benefit might you derive from their qualities?**

Encouragement

November 8–14, 1999 • Gregory S. Clapper

MONDAY, NOVEMBER 8 • Read Judges 4:1-7

A friend of mine once described his worship habits so powerfully and succinctly that I have never forgotten his words. He said simply, "I worship every week because I forget."

We might not have thought of putting it just that way, but I think what he said is true for most of us. We need constant reminders of God's place in our life because we forget so quickly. Simple distraction is probably the greatest deterrent to spiritual formation. We sometimes find it easier to fight off the larger temptations of life (because of their obvious nature) than to remember God in our everyday busy-ness.

The scripture for today does not explain precisely what caused the Israelites to slip again into doing "what was evil in the sight of the Lord," but one thing is clear: They have forgotten about God and have gone off to "do their own thing."

We need encouragement—hourly, daily, weekly—to remember who God is and what God has done. Our weekly ritual of "going to church" then should not just be about learning the great story of God's action in the world, but should also be about being reminded of what we had once learned—and have forgotten.

PRAYER: Lord God, the stories of the repeated failures of your people, as seen in the judges, the kings, and the prophets of Israel, show me how pitifully short our human attention span is. Forgive me this day for forgetting you, and pour out your grace so that today I can remember you and serve you in humble joy. Amen.

---

*United Methodist minister currently serving in the Chapman-Benson Chair of Christian Faith and Philosophy at Huntingdon College, Montgomery, Alabama.

In the face of the people's forgetting God and falling into evil, the Lord calls out Deborah to be a judge, a temporary ruler. Thus Deborah finds herself in the august company of Gideon and Samson as a leader of her people in this time of judges before the institution of kingship. Yet was she a great warrior like Gideon or Samson? No, but God's people could not have defeated their oppressor King Jabin without her. Just what did she do?

Deborah says to Barak, "God commands you to lead our troops; go and do it." Deborah's example can inspire those of us not called to dramatic action for God, such as literally fight battles in wartime or preach to thousands or otherwise be doers of so-called "great deeds." Deborah is the archetype for those who stand behind the "doers" and say, "This is your calling; go and fulfill it."

Perhaps we will never call and encourage a general to lead an army, but every day brings opportunities to call and encourage all we encounter to follow God's leadings. We may not know what every other person is supposed to *do*—not all of us are prophets in that way. But we do know what God calls all believers to *be*, and that is living reminders of God, trees in God's garden who grow the "fruit of the Spirit" (Gal. 5:22-23).

If you cannot find anyone to encourage on the Christian walk today, then look in the mirror and encourage yourself. God is calling you to it.

PRAYER: Holy One, let me be like Deborah and make clear your calling in at least one person's life today. Amen.

WEDNESDAY, NOVEMBER 10 • Read Psalm 123

If we usually read the Bible to find how we *should* feel and act, the Psalms will disappoint us. Psalms say who we *are*, not "this is how we *should* be." They are cries from the heart, and for that reason they help us. We can never receive God's grace, healing, and encouragement until we speak the truth about who we are— whatever that truth looks like.

In this psalm, the people lift up their eyes to the Lord in heaven and ask for God's mercy. Why? Because they have had enough of scorn and contempt. What seems especially galling to the author is that this scorn and contempt come from "those who are at ease" and "the proud."

Lifting up our eyes—looking Godward—is, of course, something to be commended on all occasions. But this psalm presses us to ask, "Just *why* are we calling for God's mercy?"

Here the opinion of *the proud,* not *God's* opinion of us, drives us to ask God for mercy. The psalmist cannot bear the scorn and contempt coming from such people . Please help us, God!

When we cry out in moments of injured pride, will it surprise us if God responds to such prayers with a call to humility? In humility we can confess that such prayers come to our lips when we look to the world for affirmation and encouragement instead of to God.

PRAYER: **Lord Jesus, speaking my heart frees me, but I do not always like what I hear. Thank you for hearing my unvarnished prayers that all too often squeal and scrape on your ears. Most of all, help me seek your approval and not the world's. Amen.**

THURSDAY, NOVEMBER 11 • 1 Thessalonians 5:1-11

In this reading we see that end-time predictions are not just something ushered in by the coming of the year 2000. Even in Paul's day the "times and seasons" of the coming end generated lively concern. Paul says that regarding the end, "You do not need to have anything written to you." Yet he *does* write the Christians at Thessalonica anyway. They don't need new revelations or even new teachings; what they need is something simple yet profound—encouragement. Paul tells them to "encourage one another and build up each other, as indeed you are doing."

En–courage–ment: the word itself means to give courage to someone; to offer the resources to face trials, temptations, anxiety, and—in this case—uncertainty. Paul reminds the Thessalonians that the day of the Lord will come like a thief in the night, but this uncertainty should not concern them or us. We can live with uncertainty if we remember who we are and what "armor" we are called to wear.

Reminiscent of Ephesians 6:10-17, Paul here tells the people to "put on the breastplate of faith and love, and for a helmet the hope of salvation." This kind of encouragement is worthy of the name— not a call to pull ourselves up by our own bootstraps but to use the resources that God alone can provide, the three foundational virtues of faith, hope, and love. With these resources we can rest easy with the truth that "whether we are awake or asleep we may live with him."

PRAYER: God, my strength, ready me this day by filling me with faith, hope, and love. This is the encouragement I need. Thank you. Amen.

FRIDAY, NOVEMBER 12 • 1 THESSALONIANS 5:1-11

In verses 9-10 of this passage, Paul says, "For God has destined us not for wrath but for obtaining salvation through our Lord Jesus Christ, who died for us, so that whether we are awake or asleep we may live with him." How easy it is, when we read this passage, to skip over the little subordinate, relative clause set off by commas, a seemingly unimportant little phrase—"who died for us." Yet those four words convey the most dramatic and inspiring reason to be encouraged that one could imagine.

If the only part of the Bible that we read was Jesus' "Sermon on the Mount," we could easily categorize Jesus as a great spiritual teacher who said powerful and inspiring things about how to live. When we read the *whole* New Testament, though, we come to a different, more radical, conclusion: The writers of the New Testament regarded Jesus as a *savior*, not just a teacher. His self-giving death made all the difference for us. Jesus "died for us."

If we can remember that our God is one who loves so extravagantly as to experience death for us, then we can persevere through anything, including death. The reality of this saving death should so permeate our lives that our speech evidences it (as Paul's did), not just in grand sermons on Calvary but also in our everyday words of encouragement that help us persevere toward the goal of faithful living.

PRAYER: Savior Jesus, help me hold within my heart this day the simple yet mysterious and powerful truth that you died for me. Let this truth enliven me to go out and do the work that you have given me this day. Amen.

SATURDAY, NOVEMBER 13 • Read Matthew 25:14-30

The parable of the talents stands in the Bible just after the parable of the ten bridesmaids which ends, "Keep awake therefore, for you know neither the day nor the hour" (Matt. 25:13). Immediately after the parable of the talents, Jesus goes on to speak about the Son of Man coming in his glory (v. 31). The setting for today's parable, then, is Jesus' talking about the end times.

What could come between an admonition to "keep awake" and a description of the end times? Just what we have in the parable of the talents: a call to work. This world will end, and God will give a final reckoning. But through this parable Jesus tells us not to fixate on that unknown time in the future but to use our talents in the here and now. Let's not wait around for the last judgment; let's get busy!

While "work" can carry negative connotations as something onerous and distasteful, work is in fact what we were made for. Work is not punishment. Work, as the physicists define it, is simply energy expended. Before the Fall, God made man to till and keep the garden (Gen. 2:15). God gave us energy so we could spend it.

Should we look over our shoulder and be envious of the work we see others doing or get discouraged because others around us seem to have more talents than we do? No. God asks only that we do the best we can—"each according to his [or her] ability."

PRAYER: Creator God, thank you for breathing life into me this day. Help me express my gratitude for this life by spending my energy today as you would have me spend it. May your will be done on earth as it is in heaven. Amen.

SUNDAY, NOVEMBER 14 • Read Matthew 25:14-30

In the parable of the talents, each of the three slaves receives temporary use of different amounts of money, each according to his ability. The first two invest and double their money. The text refers to the third, who does nothing useful with his talent, as "wicked and lazy" and "worthless." The third slave winds up being thrown into the outer darkness where there is weeping and gnashing of teeth.

On first hearing, this parable and the fate of the third slave might shock us. If we are shocked, then so be it; for this parable is meant to carry a strong message: Being timid is not the same as being humble.

Some people go through life equating boldness with being proud. Some think that acknowledging that God has given us gifts, abilities, and "talents" to use is the same as bragging. Some think that speaking the truth as we know it is presumptuous.

Jesus in this parable says, "Stop being obsessed with yourself and get out into God's good world and do God's good work!" Humility is acknowledging that what we have, we have as a gift. Not using what we have is not humility; it is a waste!

Sometimes our encouragement comes not as a quiet word of understanding but as a bucket of cold water poured on our heads. It may not be pleasant, but it might be just what we need.

PRAYER: Thank you, God, for seeing me as I am and meeting me in my need. I trust your wisdom and compassion to whisper gentle reassurances when I need them and to shake me awake when I need that. Thank you for shaping your love to the different contours of each day of my life. In Jesus' name. Amen.

The Shepherd King

*November 15–21, 1999 • Carolyn Brown**

MONDAY, NOVEMBER 15 • Read Ephesians 1:20-23

Sunday is Christ the King Sunday. Today's verses use unequivocal language to describe Christ the King. The New Revised Standard Version speaks of Christ as seated at the right hand of God, "far above all rule and authority and power and dominion, and above every name." All things are under his feet and he is "head over all things." This is the situation "not only in this age but also in the age to come." The Good News Bible insists that "Christ rules...above all heavenly rulers, authorities, powers and lords; he has a title superior to all titles of authority in this world and in the next." It claims that God has made Christ "supreme Lord over all things." The New Jerusalem Bible uses the words *enthroning, principality,* and *sovereignty* and ascribes to Christ a name, "above...any other name that can be named."

This is strong language for people who struggle with competing loyalties and who work hard at juggling diverse commitments. The good news is that because Christ is King, none of the powers that seem to be tearing us and our world apart can finally overwhelm us. Therefore, we need not fear or allow any power or any person to intimidate us. Because Christ is King, the good news is that we know who we are and have the focus we need to cope with all the other powers competing for our attention. We respond to them within the framework of Christ's kingship. There is no bad news.

SUGGESTION FOR MEDITATION: **Make a mental list of the powers that are trying to take over your life and the life of your community, nation, and world. In the presence of Christ the King, assign them their proper place.**

---

*Director of Children's Ministries, Trinity Presbyterian Church, Atlanta, Georgia.

TUESDAY, NOVEMBER 16 • Read Ezekiel 34:11-16

Three of the four texts for Christ the King Sunday feature Christ the King acting not as a grand potentate but as a good shepherd who cares for the sheep. Texts that mesh the king and shepherd images fill the Bible.

Ezekiel's message about the shepherd's gathering the scattered sheep reflects a common Middle Eastern shepherding practice. All the shepherds of a village would merge their flocks into one larger flock, which they would then tend as a team. When the time came to separate the flocks, the shepherds depended on their ability to recognize their own sheep and the sheep's ability to distinguish and respond to its shepherd's unique whistle.

Ezekiel addresses the Jews in exile, those feeling lost in the foreign crowds. Ezekiel promises them that one day God will call them out of the crowd and take them home.

Many people today share the exiles' feeling of being lost in the crowd. We feel we are "just a number." We work at repetitive assembly-line, fast-food, or cubicled jobs that have little meaning. We feel overlooked, undervalued, unnoticed, lost. Ezekiel's message to us is twofold.

First, Christ the King will not lose us in the crowd. Like a good shepherd, Christ knows us, watches over us in the crowd, and will come for us.

Second, we are to watch for scattered sheep lost in the crowd around us and to tend them in Christ's name.

PRAYER: God, watch over the crowd and watch over each person in the crowd. Keep me alert to hear your whistle in the din, and keep me responsive to that whistle so I stay close to you. Help me see others lost in the crowd around me. Teach me to recognize them, to reach out to them, and to love them. Amen.

Not all sheep are created equal. Some are bigger and stronger than others. They tend to use their bulk to claim the best grass and the clearest, coolest water. Some shepherds might permit this power struggle, chalking it up to the survival of the fittest. Ezekiel's shepherd, however, asserts his power and position on behalf of the weak, the strayed, and the injured. Like other prophets before him, Ezekiel places the poor and downtrodden under the special protection of God. The most powerful and the least are one flock and have one shepherd. There are no separate spaces or separate rules for the stronger and the weaker. The shepherd sees to it that all are fed with justice.

Not all people are equally strong or have equal access to the resources of life. Ezekiel insists that the strongest and the weakest, the richest and the poorest, the most developed and the least developed all have a place in the flock. Urban ghettoes and walled private communities, crumbling public schools and private schools that promise excellence are not the plan of God's shepherd.

The shepherd insists that we all belong together and affirms our oneness as a flock rather than our disunity as a collection of individuals free to go our own way and grab whatever we're able to grab. The shepherd stands in our midst working for justice, keeping the appetites of the strong in check, and making sure that the weak get their fair share. A shepherd's work is not easy. Shepherds find themselves in the middle of sheep-butting contests and mired to their knees in foul water. The Shepherd King found himself on a cross. Hard work—but it keeps the flock together.

SUGGESTION FOR PRAYER: Make a mental list of stronger and weaker people—both individuals and groups. Lay before God your concerns for each of them and his or her place in the larger community.

THURSDAY, NOVEMBER 18 • Read Matthew 25:31-46

In today's litigious society, it is important not to be responsible. Before working on house construction for Habitat for Humanity, volunteers must sign waivers promising not to hold the organization responsible if they are hurt on the job. A sign on the back of a large dump truck reads, "I am not responsible for damage caused by road debris kicked up by this truck."

A young man stands trial for the murder of his three teenage friends to whom he served alcohol before they accidentally ran their jeep into a tree killing themselves. The defense lawyer insists to the jury, "He is not his brothers' keeper. That is too much to ask of a twenty-year-old."

When something goes wrong, everyone seems to run from responsibility. Disclaimers abound. Disclaimers present a problem (witness insurance claims settled out of court in order to avoid finding out the truth) and an embarrassment (witness politicians proclaiming lack of involvement in any political plan gone awry). These days we do not even wait for a problem before clearing ourselves of responsibility. We avoid responsibility by avoiding any involvement at all. We circle our wagons to take care of ourselves and those we love and leave the rest of the world to fend for itself.

On the other hand, we have Marian Wright Edelman of the Children's Defense Fund calling on every American to take responsibility in some way for a child not in his or her own biological family. And we have King Jesus separating those who respond to the needs around them and those who, for whatever good or bad reason, do not respond.

Taking responsibility may be one of the most challenging and critical disciplines facing God's people today.

PRAYER: I see those who are hungry, thirsty, lonely, without clothes, sick, and in prison every day, O God. Help me be willing to respond to them. Amen.

FRIDAY, NOVEMBER 19 • Read Matthew 25:31-46

When we read Ezekiel 34:17-19 beside Matthew's account of the separation of the sheep and goats, an interesting point is made. The goats of Matthew's account have failed to notice Jesus among them. The fat sheep in Ezekiel's text are so busy getting the best grass and the coolest water, that they unintentionally ruin the grass and water they do not want. What the goats and the fat sheep share is preoccupation with their own needs and lives. They are not paying attention.

Preoccupation with ourselves is an easy trap to fall into. Life is busy: keeping up with a job; maintaining a home; getting the shopping, laundry, and cooking done; raising children. It can wear you out. Days can pass without time to read the newspaper or do more than simply get the next task done or the next need met.

People get sick and die in our neighborhood. We buy products produced in factories that do irreparable harm to the environment. Critical laws are passed. Whole nations rise and fall. And we never notice. Or, if we do notice, we are too overwhelmed to respond with more than horror. What could we do anyway?

Together these texts suggest that preoccupation with our own lives may be one of the most sinful traps we face at the end of the twentieth century. We can no longer protest, "When was it that we saw you...?" The media makes sure we know. That leaves us, like goats or fat sheep, with "we did not notice" or "we did not care."

PRAYER: Lord, keep my eyes open enough to see those around me in need. Keep my heart open enough to care about them. Keep my life open enough so that I can devote time, energy, and resources to meeting those needs. Amen.

SATURDAY, NOVEMBER 20 • Read Ephesians 1:15-23

The letter to the Ephesians opens with a greeting and a prayer for the readers. The prayer is rather like three wishes. The wishes are not for relief or safety nor are they related to any particular crisis or event. They are prayers for understanding and growth. The writer prays that God will give the readers an ever fuller grasp of the hope on which Christians live, an appreciation for the riches to be found in the Christian community, and an understanding of the immensity of God's power at work in the world—big wishes, all.

SUGGESTION FOR MEDITATION: Often our prayers for others focus on specific situations and needs in which God's presence and power seem critical. In our prayers we tend to leave people on their own between crises and big events. Today, follow the example of the letter writer and make three prayer wishes each for individuals and groups you love or have concern about. What kind of understanding, growth, and appreciation do you wish before God for your friends and relatives? What wishes might you have for groups to which you belong or for groups of people in the larger community? Lay all these people before God and make prayerful wishes for them, wishes worthy of the people God created them to be.

SUNDAY, NOVEMBER 21 • Read Psalm 100

This familiar psalm needs no explanation, but perhaps it needs an invitation to pray it freshly. So today, read and meditate on the psalm in two sections: verses 1-3 and verses 4-5. Each section combines a call to worship with a specific reason for worshiping.

Begin by reading the psalm thoughtfully.

FIRST MEDITATION: The pronoun in verse 3 that refers to humanity gives us something to work through. For starters we must cope with the fact that the pronouns related to people are first person plural rather than singular. God has created not "me"—and you too, by the way. Instead God has created "us." God has created a people, a community, a group. This psalm is not one to sing in private; the community is to sing it. The question is, "Which community? Who is "us"? Is it my own group of godly friends? my church or the people of my church whose faith is like mine? my denomination? the Christian church? the Judeo-Christian family? all the people of the world? Read verse 3 interpreting "us" in each of these ways—and others of your own. How do the different understandings of the pronoun change your understanding and use of the whole psalm? Which one does God call you toward? Why?

SECOND MEDITATION: After reading verses 4-5, read Psalm 136. If possible, read it responsively with a partner. Add more verses to tell about Jesus and about your own experiences with God. Then reread the whole of Psalm 100 as your prayer.

The God Whose Face We Long For
November 22–28, 1999 • Peter J. Storey*

MONDAY, NOVEMBER 22 • Read Psalm 80:1-7, 17-19

The people of Israel had a wonderfully frank relationship with their God. They had no hesitation in telling God exactly how they felt. In a time of deep suffering, when sorrow is their daily bread and they feel that they drink nothing but tears, the psalmist boldly calls on God to wake from slumber and come to Israel's rescue. He knows that *if only God's face can shine upon them again, they will be saved.* The psalmist repeats this litany of longing with remarkable confidence: "How long wilt thou resist thy people's prayer?" (NEB).

In the frighteningly dark years of apartheid's oppression in South Africa, we came to know that psalmist's feelings—a mixture of anguished despair and mysterious hope. Our minds told us that the regime was all-powerful and could defy all opposition for years to come. Our faith told us that God would not—could not—allow this horror to go on unchallenged and that we must continue to struggle in God's strength. During Advent we drew great encouragement from the promise that God, whose face seemed shadowed and turned away from us, would come among us again.

God kept that promise and intervened in our plight, defeating the source of our suffering and oppression. God's promise still stands for those of us who struggle right now.

PRAYER: When I pass through times of despair, lift my soul, O God, with the promise that your face will once more shine upon me to save me. Amen.

---

*Bishop and pastor in the Methodist Church of Southern Africa; past president of the South African Council of Churches.

TUESDAY, NOVEMBER 23 • Read Isaiah 64:1-9

People often ask why God doesn't act more obviously and power-fully in history to right the wrongs and put evil to flight. Paradoxically the God of the Bible is an intervening God who rescues the people of Israel from their oppressors, yet often seems absent.

Even as he raises this paradox, the prophet knows part of the answer. If the people who have experienced God's power and love fall into wrongdoing and unbelief themselves, if no one invokes God's name and clings in faith to God, then the face of God will be turned away—not so much in anger, as in sorrow and hurt. Clearly recognize that the Santa Claus image of God offered by the purveyors of cheap grace in this indulgent era is not the God of the Bible. A judgment has to be faced, especially by those who claim to know God best and fail to trust their lives to God.

Yet, in the midst of this lament, the writer reminds God that God is still the people's father, the potter whose hands shape them. The genius of the prophets rests in their ability to proclaim the disciplining judgment of God, necessary for our growth and homecoming, while never losing their certainty that they are deal-ing with a loving parent.

And the sign of restoration is the face of God: "Do not remember iniquity for ever; look on us all, look on thy people" (NEB).

PRAYER: Thank you, God, that when I do wrong and cease to look to you, even your judgment is a way of parenting me. You can restore the relationship between us with your grace, and I can know the warmth of your face again. Amen.

WEDNESDAY, NOVEMBER 24 • Read Mark 13:24-27

This passage, as well as the entire chapter, evokes images of struggle and conflict incomprehensible to those Christians who have domesticated Jesus into a personal savior with no cosmic mission. But Jesus came not only to offer us individual salvation; he came to do battle with evil's power and return a rebel world to its rightful owner—God. This struggle has a climax in the restoration of the reign of God and the acknowledgment of the one who was crucified and rejected. The imagery of the Son of Man "coming in the clouds with great power and glory" (NEB) reminds us that God will have the last word in the story of planet Earth. Evil is not the most powerful force in the cosmos.

Until that time, we can expect struggle, and we can better endure that struggle because we know that the ultimate victory has already been won. When we look back on World War II, we know now that although that terrible conflict seemed to go on forever, certain moments—some quite early in the war—determined its outcome. In the heat of battle, the Royal Air Force pilots of 1940; the soldiers at El Alamein, Stalingrad, Normandy, and Iwo Jima; and the sailors in the Battles of the Atlantic and Midway did not know that those battles were turning points in the gigantic struggle.

When we wonder about the presence and power of evil in this world, we can know that, no matter how long we must endure, Christ has already fought the decisive battle—and won—on Calvary.

PRAYER: O God, help me see that my witness is part of your struggle for the whole world. Give me courage through knowing that ultimate victory is yours. Amen.

THURSDAY, NOVEMBER 25 • Read Deuteronomy 8:7-18

THANKSGIVING DAY

Coming from Africa, where the topsoil is most times only a couple of inches thick, I am constantly amazed by the richness of the soil in most of the United States of America. Even without the added wealth of its commerce and industry, the land alone, like the lavish description of Canaan we have just read, is an incomparable treasure-house. Unlike so many places in the world, the United States has sufficient resources for all.

Today is Thanksgiving Day for citizens of the United States. Thoughtful people will pause in wonder and gratitude that they live in such a land, where, as in Canaan, no one needs to live in poverty or to want for anything.

Why then, even in the most generously endowed continent on earth, are there still poor and hungry people, who today will not give thanks at laden tables but will wonder why they are on the outside, looking in? Could it be that, having received so much, many in this land have forgotten from whence their bounty came and think they created it themselves? Often those who boast that their land is "God's own country" are slow to give God credit for an absolutely undeserved generosity and continue to think their prosperity is their own work.

Such people like to call themselves "self-made" men or women. The Bible simply calls this boast forgetting the Lord our God. The writer of Deuteronomy goes on to warn the people of destruction if they forget to acknowledge their debt to a bountiful Creator.

PRAYER: Bountiful God, I deserved nothing, and you gave everything. Teach me to be humble and grateful. Remind me constantly that I can best express my gratitude by sharing your gifts with those who have least. Amen.

FRIDAY, NOVEMBER 26 • Read Mark 13:28-37

Part of the meaning of Advent is to remind us of the "end-times"—the final and triumphant coming of Christ that will close history as we know it. Some people make a living out of predicting when all this will happen, which is somewhat remarkable, seeing that not even Jesus or the angels of heaven know—only the Father.

The common factor in Jesus' references to his second coming relates not to dates and times but to readiness. It is precisely because nothing like this can be predicted that we are called to live lives consistently open to Christ in an ongoing way.

Someone has said, "*Live* as if Christ were coming today, and *work* as if he were not coming for a thousand years." I should strive to live a life that is always open to the scrutiny of Jesus, while at the same time getting on with the job of spreading God's kingdom. If I do this, I can smile with a word attributed to Mr. Wesley. When asked what he would do if Jesus returned on the morrow, the great evangelist looked into his diary and said, "I shall rise at four as usual, mount my horse and leave for Bristol, where I am to preach and order the affairs of our societies. If the Lord should come, he will find me in the saddle, going about his business."

Something tells me Jesus takes more pleasure in down-to-earth, practical preparedness of this kind than with pie-in-the-sky predictions.

PRAYER: **Lord, hold me secure in the knowledge that history rests in your hands as well as in this small moment called the present. Give me the grace to live and work in the fullness of life that Jesus promised. Amen.**

SATURDAY, NOVEMBER 27 • Read 1 Corinthians 1:3

As a pastor, I have always felt deeply privileged to give the blessing, or benediction, to the people of God. At that moment I know I am sharing in a ritual as old as the Christian faith, words that, in one way or another, have been part of Christian worship since the birth of the church. Long ago, I decided to share that privilege: I encouraged the members of my congregation to say the benediction together. With our people holding hands, making eye contact, and speaking the words strongly to one another, the time of benediction has become a powerful spiritual moment.

This is the way community should be. The benediction is our prayer for one another, a time when we wish for one another the most precious gift life can bestow—the gift of God.

We always run the risk of our faith's becoming simply another self-improvement course or a system of belief or a way of making the world a better place. All of these may be *part* of faith; but at its heart, faith is about receiving God. Jesus came to offer us a relationship with the living God, who comes to us as Father/Creator, as Son/Savior/Lord, and as Holy Spirit/Encourager. The gifts of grace and peace about which Paul speaks flow from this relationship into our lives, making us different.

The world has its own greetings. People say, "Have a good day" —a kindly wish. Christians say, "Have the grace and peace of God" —a saving gift. We offer this supernatural, transcendent gift to one another in the benediction. None can give the grace and peace but God. None can mediate it but Jesus. None can sustain it but the Holy Spirit.

SUGGESTION FOR MEDITATION: **Use Paul's benediction as your prayer for all you meet today.**

SUNDAY, NOVEMBER 28 • **Read 1 Corinthians 1:4-9**

FIRST SUNDAY OF ADVENT

Advent is the time of expectancy—of faithful waiting. It is the time of making our hearts ready for Jesus. Soon we will relive the Christmas story and recall how this Jesus came from glory to be humbly born in Bethlehem.

Just as we can never plumb the ocean's mighty depths but can at least wade into the surf and feel its texture, taste its salt, and know its cleansing vigor, so I like to think of Jesus as the "shoreline" of God, where I can touch the edge of the eternal. In the life, death, and resurrection of Jesus of Nazareth, God comes in a way we can relate to. The God whose face we long to see comes with a human face in Jesus.

In this passage, Paul talks of waiting "expectantly for our Lord Jesus Christ to reveal himself" (NEB). Jesus comes in different ways: He has come already in his Bethlehem birth; he reveals himself to us in the Holy Spirit, his invisible presence; and he will come in glory when it is time to close human history. We need to be open to what each of these ways of knowing Jesus tells us.

But there is another kind of waiting. In Romans 8:19, Paul says, "The created universe waits with eager expectation *for God's [children] to be revealed*" (NEB, italics added). Is it possible that this tired, old world, so long alienated from God, is yearning for something new—a new kind of humanity, liberated from the things that chain our souls?

Paul reminds the Corinthians that God has called them to share in Jesus' life. This Advent the best proof of Jesus' coming will be the life of Jesus lived out in our lives.

PRAYER: Let your face, O Christ, be seen in mine, your love be known in my loving, your peace in the peace I share. Amen.

Proclamation and Promise

November 29–December 5, 1999 • Trudy Archambeau*

Proclaim comfort!

The God of covenant issues the call: "Comfort my people!" Encourage and strengthen them. Repeated for emphasis and urgency, the imperative verb *comfort* strikes an obvious note of contrast with the people's current situation, which is one of discomfort, discouragement, and discontent. Now into their hopelessness comes the prophetic word of hope.

To lift the fearful mood of the struggling and doubt-filled people, Isaiah combines prophecy and poetry in this opening chapter of his Book of Consolation (Isa. 40–55). Familiar with the custom of removing barriers and obstacles from the road of approaching conquerors or kings, he calls upon the people to participate in preparing the way for the Lord's arrival. Make the way smooth and even. Make level the hills and valleys. God is coming!

Isaiah then paints a powerfully inclusive word picture, declaring that all people shall see the revelation of the Lord's glory and stand amazed at the wonder of God. The scene reminds me of the opening ceremonies of the 1998 Winter Olympics in Japan. Technology made it possible to coordinate a choral production so that choirs on five different continents could sing together. All voices sang in unison, regardless of location and time zone. A glorious moment, but one that pales in comparison to the anticipated splendor and majesty when all people experience God's glory together.

PRAYER: God of comfort and glory, help me sense in the vision of Isaiah a prelude of what you have in mind for all people. Amen.

---

*Writer of worship liturgy; certified lay speaker; adult church and Bible study leader at Aldersgate United Methodist Church, Redford, Michigan.

TUESDAY, NOVEMBER 30 • Read Isaiah 40:6-11

The promise of provision

The divine call continues, "Cry out!" Proclaim a message from God. In response to the prophet's questioning of what the message would be comes the sobering answer about withering grass and wilting flowers. Using vivid images, Isaiah likens human life and conditions to fading grass and wildflowers that grow for only a moment before passing away beneath the scorching heat of the desert wind. The hearers of the prophetic message see themselves portrayed as temporary beings. But they also recognize the hope-filled truth reminding them that their pain and suffering will not last forever. World systems and structures are transitory. The bonds of captivity are being broken. Only the word of God stands unwaveringly, firm and steady through all eternity.

God has been at work in the wilderness places of the people's hearts, preparing them for the divine advent. Now the prophet of good news becomes a herald for the coming theophany. Shout the good news from the mountaintops, "Here is your God!" The messenger describes the coming of God in terms of triumph and power.

Suddenly the image shifts to a portrayal of gentle shepherd. God is envisioned as feeding the flock, gathering the young ones in loving arms, caring tenderly for the weak and powerless. God, both strong and gentle, provides for all the needs of the flock, carefully leading them to restful places.

When my mother lay dying in the hospital, unable to communicate with me, all I could pray was, "O God, shepherd her home." I knew that the One we both trusted was there beside her, guiding her to a new life.

PRAYER: **Eternal God of provision and protection, help me see you coming into my life this day to care for me and to travel with me step by step. Amen.**

WEDNESDAY, DECEMBER 1 • Read Psalm 85:1-2, 8-13

The promise of peace

This psalm promises peace to discouraged strugglers and stragglers. The communal prayer moves from recalling God's past mercy, forgiveness, and pardon (vv. 1-2), to the listening mode (v. 8). To those who do not return to foolish ways but who turn to God in their hearts, God's message promises peace. Saving help is close at hand.

With its emphasis on peace and salvation, this psalm becomes a natural part of the Advent-Christmas season. The psalmist employs exuberant images, personifying the attributes of God, to help clarify the description of God's coming realm. Word pictures seem to explode from the writer's imagination and dance in free and joyous abandon across the stage. God's steadfast love and faithfulness meet in warm enthusiasm. Righteousness and peace kiss and embrace each other in glad reunion. Right relationships are reestablished.

A sense of restoration and rightness will characterize the reign of God. What has been torn apart will be mended. Broken pieces of human life will be reunited by the glue of God's constant love. Shattered fragments will find healing. God's shalom will reintegrate the wounded and scattered, restoring wholeness.

Whether looking for immediate deliverance and relief from pressing current problems or looking ahead to the arena of eschatology, the psalm concludes with a scene of preparation for God's arrival. Here righteousness goes before, clearing the way and making a path for God. God takes the initiative. God's own righteousness and faithfulness perform the duties of guide. God's dealings with humanity mark the course for us to follow.

PRAYER: **Just and holy God, still today I need a Savior. I need to be saved from all that separates me from you. Set things right in Christ, I pray. Amen.**

THURSDAY, DECEMBER 2 • Read Mark 1:1-5

Proclaim and prepare

Mark starts his story at the beginning, which, for him, is nothing less and nothing more than the good news of Jesus Christ. Writing to encourage and strengthen early Christians facing trials of suffering and persecution, Mark reminds readers that all is not hopeless. God has provided a way. For Mark, the good news proclaimed is that salvation comes in the life, death, and resurrection of Jesus Christ.

Combining the prophetic words from Malachi and Isaiah, Mark sets the stage for the appearance of John the Baptizer. Without the prologue of a birth narrative, Mark pictures John baptizing in the desert, preparing the way for the One who will come later. Mark portrays John as a road-maker, literally fulfilling the words of prophecy and paving the way for the Coming One. Declaring the urgent need for repentance, John uses the waters of the River Jordan to make clear his message. People from all around the Judean countryside flock to hear John preach and to be baptized by him. The Jews, familiar with ritual cleansing, also practiced cleansing by baptism for proselytes into Judaism. But here on the banks of the Jordan, their own need for confession and forgiveness clearly confronts them. Recognizing their need, large numbers leave the shoreline and wade into the river to confess their sins and be washed clean.

Today the church serves as God's servant of the prophetic word. How do we proclaim God's message? How do we tell and interpret the story? How are believers living their identity as Christians and preparing the way for the Christ who still comes, seeking entry into people's hearts? What kind of roads are we building?

PRAYER: This Advent season, O God, prepare me for your coming. Help me, like John the Baptist, to make ready your way in others' lives. In Christ I pray. Amen.

FRIDAY, DECEMBER 3 • Read Mark 1:6-8

The promise of power

Reminiscent of the prophet Elijah, John the Baptizer dresses himself in camel hair and a leather belt. Eating locusts and wild honey in the wilderness, he ignores conventional habits and lifestyles. He proclaims by his appearance and his simplicity that he has a statement to share and a difference to make.

For long centuries the prophetic word from God has been silent. Now, in John, the word is heard once again. John sees himself as unworthy of being the forerunner of Christ, knowing he has not merited the right even to bend over and loosen the sandals on the feet of the Coming One. John is well aware that his own ministry in the desert is a mark of God's grace.

The declaration of the coming baptism with the Holy Spirit is a promise of power. Like the people listening intently to John's words on the banks of the Jordan River, people today need power. Our world sometimes seems to be fragile and crumbling, full of moral deterioration and decay. Injustice and poverty, violence and abuse imprison the human spirit. Dark and heavy clouds of possible biological and chemical warfare and destruction loom on the horizon. Environmental dangers threaten to harm all God's creation.

Even the future of the church seems precarious. Some experts tell us that before the midpoint of the new century, a large percentage of churches will close their doors. Facing bleak and uncertain times, we must not forget who we are and whose we are. We are people of God, recipients of God's promises. Relying on the power of the Holy Spirit is the only way to deal effectively with personal difficulties or the conditions of a wounded world and a struggling church. Christ's power is still available to accomplish what God has in mind.

PRAYER: Never-failing God, fill your people and your church with the power of your Spirit. In Jesus' name I pray. Amen.

SATURDAY, DECEMBER 4 • Read 2 Peter 3:8-10

Proclaim patience

People are growing impatient. Why is God so slow in acting? When will the Second Coming of Christ become reality? They even question God's intention of keeping God's promises. Or have they possibly misunderstood God's revelation?

Distorters of the truth and false teachers of the Christian message fed on these natural, normal questions and sought to undermine the reliability and persuasiveness of the gospel. They tried to shake the believers' faith with confusion and doubt. Into the mood of uncertainty and skepticism, the writer of Second Peter declares that God is not slow. God is merciful and patient.

Quoting Psalm 90:4, the writer states that God does not measure time as humans do. God measures time in terms of heart-response to the word. God measures time in terms of changed hearts. God measures time in heartbeats of repentance.

Echoing words of Old Testament prophets and Jesus himself, Peter reminds readers that the day of the Lord will come as suddenly as a thief in the night, totally unpredictable and unexpected. In contrast to the perceived notion of slowness and delay, earth and heavens will disappear with a sudden rushing roar. But God wants no one to perish. God does not want even the least of the lost to stay lost.

God is being patient with believers to get the word out until it reaches the shoreline of every life. God is waiting for the good news to be published in every heart, changing each heart and turning it toward Christ and light. God is waiting till everyone can hear the music and sing the song of joy. God is waiting until everyone has opportunity to accept the invitation, "Come to the party!"

PRAYER: **Ever-patient God, what can I do this day to make real your love and grace and mercy in someone's life? Amen.**

SUNDAY, DECEMBER 5 • Read 2 Peter 3:11-15*a*
SECOND SUNDAY OF ADVENT

Preparing for the promise

Recognizing the reality of living in the meantime, between the already and the not yet, the author of Second Peter poses a question to his readers: Since everything as we know it will one day be destroyed, what kind of people should we be now? Rather than being fearful of the end, the writer encourages all of us to be people waiting for and working for the coming day of God and the promised creation of new heavens and a new earth.

Such a new order will find righteousness at home. Living within that promise means striving to be at peace with God and living holy lives of integrity and spiritual stability, embodying the name and nature of Christ. Second Peter's advice takes on increased relevance as we approach a new decade, a new century, and a new millennium.

I like the story told and sung about runners in a Special Olympics race. One runner stumbles and falls. The other contestants come back to gather around him and help him up. Then all join hands to walk across the finish line together. The story helps define God's reason for patience. We can help others celebrate the victory of salvation today. We can help others live in a way that does not just look forward to an eschatological celebration but is an everyday celebration of Christ's presence. We can help others join us, not just in the promise of one day seeing Jesus face-to-face, but in the seeing of Christ by faith today. Preparing for God's promise means being willing to walk forward hand in hand into a new millennium, or a new day.

PRAYER: Ever-present, ever-coming God, help me live faithfully this Advent season. As I think about your coming—past, present, and future—remind me anew that your intention is not a postlude at the end but a prelude for a glorious new beginning. Amen.

The One We Do Not Know

December 6–12, 1999 • Mark Galli*

MONDAY, DECEMBER 6 • Read Isaiah 61:1-4

Isaiah brings us the good news that we can own up to our bad news. He presents the bad news in stark terms that honestly depict the tragedy of the human situation: They speak of lives in devastation and ruin and ashes—like people today who are oppressed by the incessant demands of work and family and culture, those brokenhearted by a long string of disappointments, those captive to others' opinions and their own degrading habits.

We do not use words like *devastation* or *ruin* to talk about our lives. We speak of "not quite meeting our goals" or "doing better next time." We speak not of tragedy but of bad luck. If we just hang tough and stay positive, things will get better.

But the prophet reveals that trying a little harder for a bit longer does not ultimately change our situation: We are wanderers in hot deserts, lonely captives in solitary confinement, beggars wandering cold-hearted cities. We need something more than euphemism, something more than even optimism. We need a miracle.

Which is just what the prophet promises. His words are not motivational mantras but truth. He notes that the Lord will comfort, provide, bestow, plant, rebuild, and renew—not positive thoughts, not hanging tough, not human effort.

Because of the promise of a miracle, we don't have to live in the dreamy world of euphemism, masking from ourselves the tragedy of our lives. We can face our tragedy—and rejoice at the promise on the other side.

PRAYER: Lord, thank you for the prophets who have told us frankly who we are and what you promise to do about it. Amen.

---

*Editor of *Christian History* magazine; member of St. Mark's Episcopal Church, Glen Ellyn, Illinois.

TUESDAY, DECEMBER 7 • Read Isaiah 61:8-11

The Lord does not love justice, as this passage claims.

In the normal course of this world and in the normal course of language, the phrase "I, the Lord, love justice" does point to some elementary truth. In the normal course of life, there are robberies—the unjust taking of goods. There is lying—the unjust expression of truth. God and the people of God indeed despise these petty injustices.

But then there is the Great Injustice, the Great Injustice we delight in. The Great Injustice comes as a gift of God, our "reward" for sin.

While we were sinners, Christ died for us, Paul tells us. God in righteousness and justice rewards us with an everlasting promise: In spite of our manifest and ongoing iniquities, our injustices against God and neighbor, God loves us.

A God who loves justice punishes injustice. A God who loves justice does not reward injustice, let alone reward it eternally.

Yes, Christ died on the cross for us, a complete sacrifice for our sin. But his death only counts as such because our heavenly minded God decided that it counts. God answers to no higher moral order, but is the rule maker. And in the cosmic equation, in no way does the death of Christ actually make up for our sin—any more than punishing my daughter for my son's negligence in doing his chores. Still my son would be grateful if I counted her punishment as atonement for his negligence.

And so does God count the death of Christ in our favor. It's not right; it's not just. But thank God for faithfulness that transcends justice. God rewards us and makes promises to us that last more than a lifetime of sin.

PRAYER: Lord, thank you for not treating me justly but with great mercy. Amen.

WEDNESDAY, DECEMBER 8 • Read Psalm 126:1-6

To live as Christians is to live in a dream state.

The best dreams are those from which we do not want to awaken. In them we enjoy unabandoned play, or everything suddenly makes sense, or we relish the embrace of a lover. And when the alarm buzzes in the darkness of a cold winter morning, and another day of duties begins to make demands on us, we shut our eyes and try to extend the dream, the wonderful dream.

But duties press upon us, and we put our feet on the cold floor and hobble down to the bathroom. In minutes the dream is forgotten, and reality envelopes us with its demands, worries, and responsibilities.

To live as Christians, however, is to continue to live the best of the best dreams: the dream of unending Sabbath rest, when we can cease from our labors; the dream of a life that makes sense, and where it doesn't make sense, the peace and trust to live in the mystery; the dream of a life lived in the constant embrace of Love.

So important is this "dream" that we must strive weekly—in worship, in prayer, in scripture reading—to remember it. That's what all the means of grace are about: exercises to help us remember that the "reality" of burdensome responsibility is not as real as the dream.

And then, like the psalmist, we can laugh—partly because the dream is such a joy, partly at ourselves for our silliness in so quickly forgetting the dream. And mostly because we are reminded once more how when God gets hold of us, everything gets turned upside down and inside out.

PRAYER: Lord, fix in my mind the dream, and fix in my heart the joy of knowing its reality. Amen.

THURSDAY, DECEMBER 9 • Read Luke 1:46-55

The church has used this passage for generations to help give expression to its praise. Mary announces good news here: The Lord performs mighty deeds, lifting the humble, filling the hungry with good things.

But when we look at the passage more carefully, we see this is also one of the most sobering of passages. With the good news comes some hard news: God will scatter those who are inwardly proud, bring low the exalted, and send the rich away empty.

This shouldn't surprise us. The gospel has been a two-edged sword from the beginning: "Repent and believe," says Jesus at the beginning of his ministry. But today, unfortunately, only one edge of the sword is sharpened: God is good. God is love. God will forgive. God will help. It's not that this message is untrue, but when left by itself, the good news becomes trite and simplistic; God sounds like a doting grandfather who just pats us on the head no matter what we do.

Nor does this message, by itself, address the full reality of the human situation. In fact there are those (like the Pharisees and ourselves at times!) who live with a self-righteous spirit or who oppress the poor. To such is offered forgiveness—thank God—but a forgiveness preceded by repentance. Without repentance, all we can expect is a stern discipline. As Mary notes in this passage: The proud will be brought low.

The judgment of God is, of course, just another expression of divine love: "The Lord disciplines those whom he loves" (Heb. 12:6). God's love, it turns out, is not something just to praise but also something that makes us kneel in reverent, sobering awe.

PRAYER: Lord, help me better understand the fullness of your love and the seriousness with which you love us. Amen.

FRIDAY, DECEMBER 10 • Read 1 Thessalonians 5:16-24

Little did Paul realize that in this little passage he would confront head-on one of the great lies of the twentieth century: that emotions just happen to us, that we can do nothing about them except "work through them," that emotions are neither good nor bad.

Apparently Paul affirms some emotions like joy as good. He also seems to think that some emotions are not feelings that happen to us, but feelings we can produce: "Be joyful always" (TEV), he commands his readers. If we're feeling something other than joy, it seems we're to put ourselves into a state of joy.

For some Christians, Paul's instruction amounts to putting on a facade of joy: the smiling face and the lilting voice that are a social requirement in certain pious circles. This hypocrisy is not what Paul would have us aspire toward.

But neither would Paul have us wallow in existential despair or pine away as we mouth hopeless blather about the suffering of the world. Instead, the joy we can know and can will for ourselves is a joy that lives this life as if it is a disaster—which it is, and as if hope is the final word—which it is. We can live in disaster in hope because the hope is grounded in a promise that will simply not go away: The one called Faithful will do it; the Alpha and Omega will bring history to its glorious end.

This is the joy Paul commands us to produce at will, which, when you think of it in this light, is not all that hard to produce. During those times when life threatens to sabotage our joy, we simply have to remember the reality that in the end will sabotage despair.

PRAYER: Lord, thank you for hope, which is always mine. Amen.

SATURDAY, DECEMBER 11 • Read John 1:6-8

It is 4 A.M. in the course of our life, and we've been up since 1 A.M. We can't get back to sleep because we're worried about getting fired or about whether our oldest will graduate from high school or about what happened to the love that bound us to our spouse for so many years. And we sit with our glass of warm milk, trying to relax enough to go back to bed to wait for the dawn, which always so effectively masks the darkness that envelopes our hearts; and we sit and rock and look out the window; and the night remains dark and cold; and we look again at the clock, which in the last hour hasn't seemed to move.

And it's been 4 A.M. for so long in the course of our life that when someone comes along and says, "Don't be so glum. It's already 4 A.M., and dawn is coming. Sun and new life are on their way!" it's hard to believe. This word of a parabolic John announces the coming of light into our eyes. We should know better than to doubt the word of hope, because we know the hope is real. But it's been 4 A.M. in our lives for so long that it seems like the dawn will never come and that we will be condemned to living at 4 A.M. forever, never being able to sleep in peace.

It is indeed understandable if we no longer believed in the dawn and in the men and women, like John, who announce the dawn. It would be understandable if we called them idealists, optimists, religious fanatics, pie-in-the-sky dreamers. It would be understandable but wrong.

PRAYER: Lord, help me always believe with hope in the coming of the Light into my life. Amen.

SUNDAY, DECEMBER 12 • Read John 1:19-28

John reminds us of the counterintuitive message we must proclaim: "Among you stands the one whom you do not know." It is not the usual gospel message, which is a series of similes: God is like a mother who comforts her children; God is like a father who watches over us; God is like a fortress, strong to defend. We bend over backward striving to make people see that God is like, well, us and the world we know.

But John reminds the religious of his day that God is not like anything we know or experience. The Jews expected a political messiah, but the Christ came wrapped in mystery. He stood among them, and they did not recognize the one for whom they longed.

This little scene reminds us that God categorically differs from us, differs so much that even the word *God* trivializes the One to whom we're trying to refer. The most that can be said about God categorically is that God is incomprehensible: Among us stands one whom we do *not* know and will never know.

This paradox is perhaps the most attractive part of the gospel. A god who is so very much like us and this present world order is not a god worth dying for. A god who in a crowd breezily waves to be easily spotted, like a beauty queen in a parade car, is not worthy of worship.

The God of the gospel stands among us incognito, seldom recognized—which is why God continues to intrigue and attract us. It is the mystery of God—the mystery of love, the wonder of grace, the incomprehensible dynamic of the Trinity—that amazes us and causes us to follow and worship for an eternity of mystery.

PRAYER: Lord, help me understand you as the incomprehensible One and to praise you for this mystery. Amen.

Called into Covenant with God

December 13–19, 1999 • Nathan D. Baxter*

Even when we have well-intended purposes for God's work, it is good to keep in mind that God's will must always prevail. Faithfulness does not simply mean offering our best for God but, rather, listening to discern what God may wish us to do.

King David has a sincere desire to do something great for God. Inspired by his own sense of pleasure, David notes that he himself lives in a house of cedar. If this pleases him, surely an even greater house for the ark will please God. This makes sense, doesn't it? But God desired to build a spiritual lineage (or "house") of David. From this heritage God would choose both the time and descendant who would build a temple. More importantly, from the spiritual lineage would come the messiah.

How often in our lives do we assume what will please God, based upon our human experiences of pleasure rather than the spiritual knowledge we gain from our spiritual life? We gain spiritual knowledge by intentional openness to God, by listening for and sensing the presence of God. Spiritual knowledge comes with the openness and expectation that God does have a will and a purpose, a purpose that we can know through prayerful living.

However, the word of God comes to David through the prophet Nathan, and David is able to hear. Persons of faith live to please God through their being and their actions, knowing God's pleasure comes through prayerful listening.

PRAYER: Grant, O God, that the rhythm of each day may include time to be present with you, to know you more clearly, and to love you more dearly. Amen.

---

*Dean of the Washington National Cathedral, Washington D.C.

TUESDAY, DECEMBER 14 • Read 2 Samuel 7:16

So often we humans need reminding about God's understanding of "kingdom." Today's passage connects with the story of King David's misguided desire to build a temple when God actually wanted David to establish a dynasty. Thousands of years later, we too associate kingdoms with power over land and physical assets. Each of us, in our personal realm, seeks control over physical things, while our nations and states vie for land, oil, and political power. In contrast, God's kingdom involves giving up and letting go. Acknowledging the dynasty of God is the saving of souls. The kingdom of God is the community of Christians of every generation.

As a result, those of us who minister and worship in big, beautiful buildings face a special challenge—remaining focused on God's kingdom as we grapple with the realities of heating bills and the ongoing stewardship of structures made by human hands. Ironically, those same buildings offer us unique opportunities for witness. People drawn to our impressive facilities become pilgrims, seeking and finding God in new ways. The question is, Do we offer opportunities for seekers to turn over their lives and their wills to God in new ways?

Like David, we find that the challenge comes not only in knowing God's will but in laying aside our priorities and preferences to say yes to those of God. Great edifices have their place, but the priority of God's kingdom in any age is the redeeming of souls.

PRAYER: Use me, O God, to guide someone to know your love and discover your kingdom. Amen.

WEDNESDAY, DECEMBER 15 • Psalm 89:1-4, 19-29

Some say yes to the call and will of God. How wonderfully secure is God's faithfulness to King David and the people of Israel. Certainly the psalmist understands the importance of David's right relationship to God. Israel's very existence depends upon God's faithfulness to them through the divine guidance of David.

No one questioned David's rule of Israel as God's anointed person. Chosen from among his people, David would know the glorious promise from God of protection, faithfulness, and love forever.

God has fulfilled the oath between God and David to establish his line forever in the "Son of David," Jesus the Christ. God has made a new covenant with the people of the earth in the giving of the only begotten Son, whose kingdom will have no end.

Through Jesus, God covenants to be present to all, faithful to the end of time. That promise comes to each of us in the midst of our sorrows as well as our joys. Accepting God's grace and unconditional love is to know that God has anointed each person to share in this precious gift.

God has come to us, the Word made flesh, incarnate in the Christ child. We have the opportunity to say yes to God in our own generation. Today God invites us into the holy fellowship with those of other generations and those yet to come. God invites us into partnership with God through Jesus Christ. Today we can become vessels for God's love, mercy, forgiveness, and faithfulness.

PRAYER: Almighty God, who has promised to be with all who come to you, open my heart that I may hear your call. May my actions be led by your promise of faithfulness and may my confidence be in your unfailing love, made known in Jesus our Savior. Amen.

Thursday, December 16 • Read Psalm 89:1-4, 19-26

One of life's hardest lessons is learning to expect the unexpected. Sometimes the unexpected comes as a gift, a wonderful surprise, an unimagined opportunity, a serendipitous blessing for which we find ourselves totally unprepared. Sometimes the unexpected comes as a terrible blow, perhaps a natural disaster or the death of a loved one or a disabling injury or illness or a shattered relationship or a war or the collapse of an institution that has provided our security or the sudden lapse of our own self-control.

A vital religious faith has the spiritual power to cope with the unexpected. What kind of God invites such faith?

The psalmist sings again and again of the Lord's "steadfast love" that is "established forever." Saint Paul's long list of the vicissitudes that cannot "separate us from the love of God in Christ Jesus our Lord"—"neither death, nor life, nor angels, nor rulers, nor things present, nor things to come, nor powers, nor height, nor depth, nor anything else in all creation" (Romans 8:38-39)—echoes that music. Such steadfast love is covenant-love, the basic article of faith that unites Jews and Christians.

Recent biblical scholarship has heightened our awareness of God's steadfast love—and of our commission to embody such love in all our relationships. The majestic psalmody of the King James Bible renders the Hebrew word *hesed* as "mercies," surely among the characteristics of a loving God. The New Revised Standard Version translates *hesed* as "steadfast love" or "loyalty"—an even more embracing characteristic: "I will sing of your steadfast love, O Lord, forever."

Steadfast love transcends idolatries of nation, party, possessions, or even church. It is a love that empowers us to meet the unexpected and still sing of the glory of the Lord.

Prayer: Dear God, I do not know what this day will hold. But I ask that you hold my hand and grant me a quiet trust in your faithfulness. Amen.

FRIDAY, DECEMBER 17 • Read Romans 16:25-27

As an antagonist of the Christians, Paul had heard about this Jesus, but he did not know him. That began to change for Paul in an encounter with the risen Christ on the road to Damascus. We can imagine Jesus asking Paul, "But who do you say that I am?" Paul replies, "Lord," without realizing how true that is. Blind to the possibilities at first, and then, beginning to see again, both physically and spiritually, Paul spent several years pondering, reflecting, learning, praying. Aware of his new transformed life in Christ, he emerged as an apostle and missionary.

Our understanding of the concluding verses of Paul's letter to the Christians in Rome depends on how we answer Jesus' question, "Who do you say that I am?" With these closing verses, Paul hopes to elicit a response of faith in Jesus Christ. Jesus makes God known in a unique way. Kept secret through many ages, God's plan is revealed at the time of God's own choosing, a plan for all the peoples of the world, not simply the possession of a few people or tribes.

Paul responds in faithful obedience to the steadfastness of God. God invites each of us to this obedience of faith. God does not coerce us. God allows us to take the time we need. But God continues to work on us and in us and through us to the end that we might enjoy the fullness of God's abundant life. Once we acknowledge God's presence, which Jesus shows us in the most personal and convincing way, we discover transformation and strength. Our greatest joy comes in proclaiming through word and deed the gospel of Jesus Christ.

PRAYER: God, truly wise and truly loving, thank you for your gift of Jesus. Help me know him and enjoy the new life he offers, today and always. Amen.

SATURDAY, DECEMBER 18 • Read Luke 1:26-38

We often voice the question, "How did Mary know that this was an angel, and an angel of God?" As Christians we know that the one who offers us salvation is the fulfillment of the angel's promise. Mary has every reason to doubt, yet something in the gentleness, the caring reassurance of the angel suggests something good and true. The angel's words to Mary requite her fear and affirm her special-ness before God. The angel offers sensitive and clear responses to her questions, saying in effect, "The Holy Spirit will make this miracle happen in ways as gentle and complete as a shadow."

No, we are not Mary, but we are potential bearers of God's grace to the world. We all have had moments of visitation in our lives, whether we have said yes or no—perhaps an urge to give to some purpose, to volunteer service in some effort, to visit with someone who may be in sickness or need, to speak a word of prayer or hope to some person. And in that moment, perhaps we had a sense of being overshadowed by the Spirit of God with surety and caring, a sense of purpose that went beyond our own reasoning and confidence.

Like Mary, when we say yes to the visitation of God's invitation to us, we become recipients of God's grace. The results are often far beyond what we know or imagine.

Perhaps the most needed gift in our world today is Christians open to the visitation of God in their everyday life, Christians with faith enough to say yes to the gentle lure of God, the overwhelming shadowing of divine grace that enables us to be God's servants in a world desperately in need of grace.

PRAYER: Use me today, O God, to be a bearer of your love, your peace, your hope to someone. Amen.

SUNDAY, DECEMBER 19 • Read Luke 1:26-39

"Hail, O favored one, the Lord is with you!" (RSV). Did you say "favored"? An out-of-wedlock pregnancy that defies explanation in her own day and ours disrupts Mary's betrothal plans. She gives birth to a son in a barn after a long trip. She raises a son who lives a turbulent life. She watches him alienate people of power and antagonize the nation's religious leadership.

Mary evidences confusion about the nature of Jesus' ministry from time to time. Then after the three brief years of Jesus' public ministry, she watches him die on a cross and buries him in a borrowed grave, a man abandoned by the few followers he had been able to muster. Did you say "favored"?

Today many writers promise success, well-being, and prosperity in exchange for faithfulness. In fact, all this and more have become the measure of God's presence in our lives. In part, this success-measured understanding of the gospel arises from a dangerous misreading of the Bible, but it also arises from a general, cultural climate unique to our country and our place in its history.

By contrast the angel refers to Mary as "favored" because she will play a role that is closely connected with God's work. Her connection with that work does not necessarily spell success, wealth, or position. It is, first, last, and foremost, a matter of placing herself at God's disposal.

PRAYER: Dear God, it is hard not to expect rewards of material or social success for my faithfulness. Yet I know that serving you is a response of love. Help me grow in my love for you and your purpose that I might find peace in whatever you will. Amen.

The True Light

December 20–26, 1999 • *Russell Montfort**

MONDAY, DECEMBER 20 • **Read Psalm 98**

Getting rid of categories

Do you know, I believe it! I still believe it. God in holiness and righteousness will bring order to this world one day. Psalm 98 says, "He will judge the world with righteousness, and the peoples with equity."

Our waiting during Advent is not simply waiting for the party to begin; we spend this time rejoicing in the sweet possibility of the peaceable kingdom. *Light one candle.* He will not always wait. *Light two candles.* He is coming with a love so pure that it will break our hearts. *Light three candles.* His love will purify our hearts and burn away our desire. *Light four candles.* He is here, just beyond the shadows there. Are you certain that you want him here?

God comes "to judge the world with righteousness, and the peoples with equity." It is pleasant to consider Jesus as "mine" or "ours," but he taught us to think beyond those narrow categories and to break the bonds of race, religion, political structures, gender, age, and culture.

Jesus. Born in a nowhere place, illegitimately, among a captive people. Jesus. Who has refocused the way we see one another and the way we speak of one another and the way we treat one another.

PRAYER: God, take all of the categories away so that we may fully love one another. Amen.

---

*Retired United Methodist pastor and teacher who now thinks about things while living in Charlotte, North Carolina.

TUESDAY, DECEMBER 21 • Read Isaiah 52:7-10

How beautiful are your feet

Many of us spiritualize the scripture to the point that we decide that it has little or nothing to do with us. When Isaiah writes a song about the messiah who will come to announce peace and salvation and who calls the people to sing for joy, we prosy people think he is speaking only of a time long past involving people long dead.

But now we live in a time after the fact; Messiah has come, and we are called to pass along the comforting good news of peace and salvation. We have a song to sing, not necessarily before throngs of people; it can be a simple exchange between two friends. Christmas ought to put us in touch with one another. Maybe not everyone every time—but a note, a phone call. And the connection doesn't have to come on Christmas Day. Any time will do.

My wife and I have these friends—a family with an enormous amount of children—who on Christmas Day called and sang "We Wish You a Merry Christmas!" And in the background, we could hear shouts and shoves and what sounded like life. Their song came as a message of love and peace.

Christmas is not like that for everyone. For many it is a cold, isolated, hurting, hungry time. The message of Isaiah is that Christ came into life, both the upbeat and the downbeat parts of it. He is present. He doesn't give the pleasant parts to some and the painful parts to others. Life just is. And through his presence, he comforts, inspires, and redeems it.

You can make him present to others, no matter what the circumstances in which they find themselves. Simply speak to them. Call them. By name. In the name of Christ. How beautiful are your feet and how pleasant your voice when you share with someone the message of peace and salvation.

PRAYER: O God, help me understand that I am called to proclaim the good news of your presence with us in Jesus. Amen.

WEDNESDAY, DECEMBER 22 • Read Luke 2:22-40

A disturbing thing

Many of us have had a hard time accepting the idea of God's being present in a baby. We like our gods to have power and authority. We want to know that our gods can get us out of tight places as the result of quick, little laser prayers aimed directly at the god—the whatever-you-want-I-will-do-for-you god.

We see the baby, the one born in Bethlehem, the one of whom Simeon said, "This child is destined for the falling and the rising of many in Israel."

I see the baby. I think about how easily he could have been eliminated. Just put a hand over his mouth. Or drop him on his head or fail to feed him. He would have died.

And he was called God-with-us—Emmanuel!

He disturbs our ideas about God—about the god who exists mainly to do nice things for us and to get us out of tight places.

But every year that baby Jesus stuff comes back at us, which requires us to think differently of God. Our world is dominated by the fastest, the strongest, and the smartest. Those are the ones rewarded and acclaimed. It is no wonder then that to some the birth of Jesus—the baby—is troubling, or at best, something only of sentimental seasonal value.

The baby requires a shuffling of values, a reordering of hierarchy. It maybe means that the first will be last and the last first. We see our lives differently. We acknowledge our vulnerability, and our infirmities become our gifts.

It is a disturbing thing—looking at The Baby.

PRAYER: Great Holy God, it is a wondrous thing that I see in the birth of this child; our humanity and our weakness are accepted. Amen.

THURSDAY, DECEMBER 23 • Read Isaiah 9:2-7

Too many lights

After living in another part of the world for several years my family arrived back in our American hometown for a visit. As we circled the city to land at the airport, I could see the city lights sparkling below. Actually, the city more than sparkled. Floodlights illuminated buildings, shopping malls, parking lots, streets, and playing fields.

Later someone asked me what I was feeling about my return. While very glad to be there, I said something that surprised even me. I said, "There are too many lights!"

Later I tried to understand my feelings, and I think I did at last. Too many lights confuse us to the point of thinking that reality is only that which is illuminated by artificial light. Banks, malls, and playing fields were the only reality in the otherwise darkened night. The lights say, "Here are the important things," but they illuminate a world cut off from stars and wonder and mystery.

Isaiah says that the people who walked in darkness would see a great light, because among them would be born a child whose names would fall all over one another—names like Wonderful and Counselor and Mighty God and Everlasting Father, and, here is a noteworthy one—the Prince of Peace.

Having to deal with so many brightly and artificially lighted entities confuses us. Where is the True Light?

The child came and grew up and started preaching, admonishing us to let our light shine in such a way that those who see us would find it easy to praise God. The light that shines in us, he is saying, is not our own light but God's shining through us. We turn out all the lights that confuse us and dampen the fires that consume us and see things as they really are. We cease our self-absorption and start to see the lights sparkling beyond us.

PRAYER: God, I allow myself to be blinded by artificial light, not *the* Light that lights the way into your presence. Amen.

FRIDAY, DECEMBER 24 • Read Luke 2:1-7

CHRISTMAS EVE

Don't be afraid

Near the end of our Christmas Eve worship, following the Holy Communion and with the service coming to a close, the pastor moved toward the Advent wreath. All four of the purple candles burned vigorously, at different heights, according to when they had been lighted during the Advent worship services. The tall, thick, white Christ candle stood in the middle of the wreath, unlighted.

Now it was time to light the Christ candle, and the pastor moved quietly toward it. The worshipers strained to see in the dimly lit room. They leaned forward or looked around those seated in front of them. It was a moment of great expectation and power.

The pastor touched the light to the unburned wick, and a flame leapt upward, which drew an audible sigh from the hundreds of worshipers tightly fitted in the pews on this most auspicious of nights. It was as if when the flame suddenly sprang up, Christ had come. The pastor said afterward that he hesitated just before he lighted the candle, thinking to himself, *What if when I light this candle, he comes? What if I light this flame and Jesus comes into this place—here, now? What if what we have longed for, planned for, made preparation for, happens and he comes into our presence?*

And the pastor stood there in the presence of the light with a frightened look on his face—as if he might have set into motion something so powerful, so wonderful, so mighty and everlasting that the world could not go back to what it had been.

PRAYER: **On this holy night, God, I long without fear for the holy presence of Jesus among us. Amen.**

SATURDAY, DECEMBER 25 • Read Hebrews 1:1-5; John 1:1-14

CHRISTMAS DAY

That's the way I would have done it

If I were God, and I wanted to be known by humans of whom it was said they were made in God's image; if I were God and my nature was Love, then I would come among those humans as one of them—"the reflection of God's glory and the exact imprint of God's very being." I would come among them as Jesus. That's the way I would have done it.

Then people would not only know what God is like, they would also know the possibilities for their own lives. And their knowledge of God would no longer be abstract and theoretical; it would be based in the reality of a single human life.

On this day of days, we celebrate Jesus' coming among us, born among us as one of us. Here was *The Word, The Absolute Truth of God, The Great I Am Which Was before Creation* now born to a teenaged peasant girl in a barn in an obscure corner of the world.

It was no longer necessary to practice mysterious rituals— burning incense and prayers recited by vested priests in garments of gold and silver—in order to invoke the presence of the Holy God. The Holy God was here. Is here. There in a stable. Here at my table.

Thank you, great God of the universe! Thank you, Father of our Lord Jesus Christ. Thank you, Lord, who "founded the earth" and whose hands created the heavens. You who in the beginning created the world out of nothingness are the same God who said of Jesus, "You are my Son; today I have begotten you."

If I were God, and I wanted people to know how much I loved them, that is exactly the way I would have done it.

PRAYER: Holy God, through Jesus you have revealed to us your nature. It is love. And as love requires an object, you have made us in your loving image. And what love requires of us, you give us the power to do. To be. Through Jesus. Amen.

SUNDAY, DECEMBER 26 • Read Psalm 148; Luke 2:8-14

Praise him, all his angels

It could hardly have been any more unnoticed, the birth of that boy. Mary and Joseph had walked down to Bethlehem from Nazareth probably grumbling the entire way, the way we do about being inconvenienced by government edicts. Joseph had to go register in his home district and that registration no doubt meant taxes. And when they got to Bethlehem, there was no room in any inn.

And the boy was born that night.

The stories that we tell now about that night are glorious with a lighted sky and choruses of angels proclaiming a new thing: God has come among us. And who attended the birth? A few shepherds. For the most part, rough young men with dung on their sandals, but men who nonetheless were in touch with the natural world: They knew the stars by name and they knew when a wind came up in the west and whether or not there was a storm brewing. They were unsophisticated but they knew there was music in the air and there was an unusual brightness and that something of cosmic importance was happening.

If they had a song to sing that night, it would have been something like Psalm 148: "Praise the Lord! Praise the Lord from the heavens; praise him in the heights! Praise him, all his angels; praise him, all his host!"

It was the kind of night when everything in and on the earth praised God—"fire and hail, snow and frost, stormy wind fulfilling his command . . . Kings of earth and all peoples, princes and all rulers of the earth! Young men and women alike, old and young together!" But most people were in their homes, in their comfortable homes, sorting out the busyness of their lives; and they missed it. When it happened, they missed it.

PRAYER: Help us to stay alert to your voice, God; we know that you still speak, and we want to hear. Amen.

God's Word Runs Swiftly

December 27–31, 1999 • Michael E. Williams*

MONDAY, DECEMBER 27 • **Read Jeremiah 31:7-14**

I had gone to visit Hubert at the hospital where he was awaiting the amputation of a second leg. His first amputation had taken place several years earlier. Having been a severe diabetic for some years he knew that his life might come to this tragic occasion someday. Removing his other leg would extend his life while at the same time transforming it irrevocably.

I was Hubert's pastor and friend, but there seemed to be nothing I could say that would even begin to comfort him. He knew that this surgery was just one more step toward his body's giving out entirely. We talked about his feelings, and he seemed very philosophical about the operation. Yet I still sensed a deep sadness, and as we talked and prayed I wished from the depths of my heart that I could do more. I knew that what I had to offer Hubert was limited

As I was about to leave, feeling that my visit had brought very little comfort to my friend, there was a knock at his hospital room door. In walked a man on two prostheses having already lived through two leg amputations. This visitor had a greater authority to speak a word of comfort because of his previous suffering. God had turned his tragedy into a gift, a gift he shared with Hubert.

PRAYER: Generous God, thank you that our tragedies can be turned into blessings for others. Amen.

---

*Pastor of Blakemore United Methodist Church, Nashville, Tennessee; General Editor of The Storyteller's Companion to the Bible.

TUESDAY, DECEMBER 28 • Read John 1:10-18

The church calendar refers to this day as the Feast Day of Holy Innocents. It commemorates the children who died because of Herod's fear of the birth of another king, a king who would take his throne away. I had known both the story and the name of the feast day for a number of years.

But ten years ago, on December 28, 1989, that date changed for me forever. At 12:35 P.M. on that day, my wife gave birth to our first child, Sarah. When I looked at Sarah I thought she was the most beautiful baby ever to enter this world. Her mother agreed with me wholeheartedly. Now Margaret and I laugh at ourselves, because Sarah's photos from that time picture a red and wrinkled little baby who looks very much like every other newborn. You see, we were looking at her through the eyes of first-time parents, through the lens of a mother's and a father's love.

Since the day of Sarah's birth, the children in the cruel story of Herod's fear have had a face—the face of my daughter. No longer are they faceless, nameless characters. I feel for every parent who has ever lost a child to death, abduction, or poverty. I hear their stories, and the fear wells up inside of me. *What if one of my children suddenly disappeared?*

The holy innocents still die in this country and around the world. God sees each of them with the eye of a mother's and father's love. To God each is the most beautiful precious child that was ever born. Neither the circumstances of their birth, the color of their skin, nor the language and culture they will one day learn matter.

In each child I see the face of my own child. In each child I see the face of the child Jesus who escaped Herod's wrath but could not escape the cruelty of the world entirely.

PRAYER: **Gracious God, help me view all your children through the eyes of parental love. May I see Jesus in the face of every child. Amen.**

WEDNESDAY, DECEMBER 29 • Read Ephesians 1:3-6

Several years ago another pastor in my annual conference invited me to baptize her child. This young woman had been a youth in one of the churches I had served years earlier. She had gone on to college and seminary and was now one of my colleagues in ministry. She scheduled the baptism for Sunday evening so both of the small, rural congregations she served, along with her family and many friends, could attend.

She had adopted Daniel from Peru, and the process had been long and difficult. This history of struggle just seemed to make the delight of Daniel's baptism even more joyous. That same day Bishop Peter Storey from South Africa had come into town to teach for a continuing education event I was directing. I invited him to come with me that evening.

I had received directions to the church, but I must have taken a wrong turn somewhere. I drove around on unfamiliar backroads for what seemed to be an eternity. Neither Bishop Storey nor my wife, Margaret, seemed overly concerned. I was getting frantic.

The church was so far out in the country, and I had driven around lost for so long that we arrived just in time for the baptism. As I led the service, looking out on the sea of faces in that little country church, it struck me that this is what the community of faith is all about.

We are all God's children by adoption, as the writer of Ephesians puts it. Our country of origin, our skin color, our native language, and the place on earth we call home make no difference. Baptism makes sisters and brothers of us all.

PRAYER: **Loving God, I thank you that you have brought me and all your beloved children into your adopted family. Amen.**

THURSDAY, DECEMBER 30 • Read Psalm 147:12-20

There was a time in my younger days when I used to run ten-kilometer races. Never being a fast runner, I always wound up at the back of the race. In one race, a runner passed me wearing a t-shirt that bore the words: *When the going gets rough, sprinters quit.*

Psalm 147 affirms that God's word doesn't quit. God's word runs swiftly, says the psalm. For the Christian, two questions are basic to our religious quest: "Who is God?" and "Who are we?" To love God and our neighbor we have to be clear about our answers to these questions.

Psalm 147 emphasizes that God's very nature is to give gifts. Finest wheat, snow like wool, frost like ashes, hail like crumbs, the winds that blow, and the waters that flow—all are gifts from God's generous hand.

God's statutes and ordinances represent the most profound of these gifts, though. The commandments God gave to Israel, which Jesus summarizes as love of God and neighbor, are special gifts. They make us partners with God in making the world into the place God wants it to be.

Also we cannot contain God's word in any of the boxes we try to put it in. God's word is a living, breathing reality—not ours to possess but one that runs ahead of us. What an image! We have to run even to try to keep up with God's living word. This reality makes sense, though, since after two thousand years we've been unable to contain or even keep up with Jesus, God's living Word.

PRAYER: Thank you, God, for your many gifts, especially for your word that precedes me wherever I go. Amen.

FRIDAY, DECEMBER 31 • Read Psalm 8

A fellow who lived in the rural part of Middle Tennessee where my mother grew up responded in this fashion when people asked him what kind of Christian he was: "Well, I reckon I'm the regular kind. I cuss when I get mad and pray when I get scared." This kind of assessment of human virtue might lead one to cry out, as the psalmist did, saying in effect, "Who are we mortals that you pay any attention to us?"

Who are we, after all, here at the end of the twentieth century, two thousand years after the life of Jesus? We are certainly more technologically advanced than ever before, but is the world a more peaceful and loving place for having experienced two millennia of Christian witness and influence? Most people would say that it is not. Sadly, many of the conflicts around the world today involve Christians fighting other people or allowing other religious traditions to encourage fighting among ourselves.

Has the cussing or the praying of regular Christians had more impact? We have received blessing, but have we been a blessing to all nations?

Psalm 8 makes the radical assertion that God creates humans as little less than their maker. Apparently the image that God holds of us is far greater than the image we have of ourselves. Now at this time, when we stand at the threshold of a new century and millennium, let us pray that we will grow into the image that God holds of us.

PRAYER: **Creating God, you made me in your image. Now help me grow into the person you have created me to be. Amen.**

The Revised Common Lectionary* for 1999
Year A – Advent / Christmas Year B
(Disciplines Edition)

January 1–3
Isaiah 63:7-9
Psalm 148
Hebrews 2:10-18
Matthew 2:13-23

EPIPHANY, January 6
*(These readings may
be used for Sunday, January
3.)*
Isaiah 60:1-6
Psalm 72:1-7, 10-14
Ephesians 3:1-12
Matthew 2:1-12

January 4–10
BAPTISM OF THE LORD
Isaiah 42:1-9
Psalm 29
Acts 10:34-43
Matthew 3:13-17

January 11–17
Isaiah 49:1-7
Psalm 40:1-11
1 Corinthians 1:1-9
John 1:29-42

January 18–24
Isaiah 9:1-4
Psalm 27:1, 4-9
1 Corinthians 1:10-18
Matthew 4:12-23

January 25–31
Micah 6:1-8
Psalm 15
1 Corinthians 1:18-31
Matthew 5:1-12

February 1–7
Isaiah 58:1-12
Psalm 112:1-10
1 Corinthians 2:1-16
Matthew 5:13-20

February 8–14
THE TRANSFIGURATION
Exodus 24:12-18
Psalm 2 (*or* Psalm 99)
2 Peter 1:16-21
Matthew 17:1-9

February 17
ASH WEDNESDAY
Joel 2:1-2, 12-17 (*or*
  Isaiah 58:1-12)
Psalm 51:1-17
2 Corinthians 5:20*b*–6:10
Matthew 6:1-6, 16-21

February 15–21
FIRST SUNDAY IN LENT
Genesis 2:15-17; 3:1-7
Psalm 32
Romans 5:12-19
Matthew 4:1-11

February 22–28
SECOND SUNDAY IN LENT
Genesis 12:1-4*a*
Psalm 121
Romans 4:1-5, 13-17
John 3:1-17 (*or* Matthew
  17:1-9)

March 1–7
THIRD SUNDAY IN LENT
Exodus 17:1-7
Psalm 95
Romans 5:1-11
John 4:5-42

March 8–14
FOURTH SUNDAY IN LENT
1 Samuel 16:1-13
Psalm 23
Ephesians 5:8-14
John 9:1-41

March 15–21
FIFTH SUNDAY IN LENT
Ezekiel 37:1-14
Psalm 130
Romans 8:6-11
John 11:1-45

March 22–28
PASSION/PALM SUNDAY

  Liturgy of the Palms
  Matthew 21:1-11
  Psalm 118:1-2, 19-29

  Liturgy of the Passion
  Isaiah 50:4-9a
  Psalm 31:9-16
  Philippians 2:5-11
  Matthew 26:14–27:66
  (*or* Matthew 27:11-54)

Week of March 29—April 4
HOLY WEEK
(selected lections)

Monday, March 29
Isaiah 42:1-9
John 12:1-11

Tuesday, March 30
Isaiah 49:1-7
John 12:20-36

Wednesday, March 31
Isaiah 50:4-9a
Hebrews 12:1-3
John 13:21-32

Maundy Thursday, April 1
Exodus 12:1-14
Psalm 116:1-2, 12-19
1 Corinthians 11:23-26
John 13:1-17, 31b-35

Good Friday, April 2
Isaiah 52:13–53:12
Psalm 22
Hebrews 4:14-16; 5:7-9
John 18:1–19:42

Holy Saturday, April 3
Job 14:1-14
Psalm 31:1-4, 15-16
1 Peter 4:1-8
Matthew 27:57-66

April 4
EASTER SUNDAY
Jeremiah 31:1-6
Psalm 118:1-2, 14-24
Acts 10:34-43
John 20:1-18

April 5–11
Acts 2:14*a*, 22-32
Psalm 16
1 Peter 1:3-9
John 20:19-31

April 12–18
Acts 2:14*a*, 36-41
Psalm 116:1-4, 12-19
1 Peter 1:17-23
Luke 24:13-35

April 19–25
Acts 2:42-47
Psalm 23
1 Peter 2:19-25
John 10:1-10

April 26–May 2
Acts 7:55-60
Psalm 31:1-5, 15-16
1 Peter 2:2-10
John 14:1-14

May 3–9
Acts 17:22-31
Psalm 66:8-20
1 Peter 3:13-22
John 14:15-21

May 10–16
Acts 1:6-14
Psalm 68:1-10, 32-35
1 Peter 4:12-14; 5:6-11
John 17:1-11

ASCENSION DAY, May 13
*(These readings may be used
for Sunday, May 16.)*
Acts 1:1-11
Psalm 47 (*or* Psalm 93)
Ephesians 1:15-23
Luke 24:44-53

May 17–23
PENTECOST
Numbers 11:24-30
Psalm 104:24-34, 35*b*
Acts 2:1-21
John 20:19-23 (*or* John
7:37–39)

May 24–30
TRINITY SUNDAY
Genesis 1:1–2:4*a*
Psalm 8
2 Corinthians 13:11-13
Matthew 28:16-20

May 31–June 6
Genesis 12:1-9
Psalm 33:1-12
Romans 4:13-25
Matthew 9:9-13, 18-26

June 7–13
Genesis 18:1-15
Psalm 116:1-2, 12-19
Romans 5:1-8
Matthew 9:35–10:8, (9-23)

June 14–20
Genesis 21:8-21
Psalm 69:7-18
Romans 6:1b-11
Matthew 10:24-39

June 21–27
Genesis 22:1-14
Psalm 13
Romans 6:12-23
Matthew 10:40-42

June 28–July 4
Genesis 24:34-38, 42-49,
58-67
Psalm 45:10-17
Romans 7:15-25*a*
Matthew 11:16-19, 25-30

July 5–11
Genesis 25:19-34
Psalm 119:105-112
Romans 8:1-11
Matthew 13:1-9, 18-23

July 12–18
Genesis 28:10-19*a*
Psalm 139:1-12, 23-24
Romans 8:12-25
Matthew 13:24-30, 36-43

July 19–25
Genesis 29:15-28
Psalm 105:1-11, 45*b*
Romans 8:26-39
Matthew 13:31-33, 44-52

July 26–August 1
Genesis 32:22-31
Psalm 17:1-7, 15
Romans 9:1-5
Matthew 14:13-21

August 2–8
Genesis 37:1-4, 12-28
Psalm 105:1-6, 16-22, 45*b*
Romans 10:5-15
Matthew 14:22-33

August 9–15
Genesis 45:1-15
Psalm 133
Romans 11:1-2*a*, 29-32
Matthew 15:10-28

August 16–22
Exodus 1:8–2:10
Psalm 124
Romans 12:1-8
Matthew 16:13-20

August 23–29
Exodus 3:1-15
Psalm 105:1-6, 23-26, 45*c*
Romans 12:9-21
Matthew 16:21-28

August 30–September 5
Exodus 12:1-14
Psalm 149
Romans 13:8-14
Matthew 18:15-20

September 6–12
Exodus 14:19-31
Psalm 114 (*or* Exodus
    15:1*b*-11, 20-21)
Romans 14:1-12
Matthew 18:21-35

September 13–19
Exodus 16:2-15
Psalm 105:1-6, 37-45
Philippians 1:21-30
Matthew 20:1-16

September 20–26
Exodus 17:1-7
Psalm 78:1-4, 12-16
Philippians 2:1-13
Matthew 21:23-32

September 27–October 3
Exodus 20:1-4, 7-9, 12-20
Psalm 19
Philippians 3:4*b*-14
Matthew 21:33-46

October 4–10
Exodus 32:1-14
Psalm 106:1-6, 19-23
Philippians 4:1-9
Matthew 22:1-14

> **THANKSGIVING DAY
> (Canada), October 11**
> Deuteronomy 8:7-18
> Psalm 65
> 2 Corinthians 9:6-15
> Luke 17:11-19

October 11–17
Exodus 33:12-23
Psalm 99
1 Thessalonians 1:1-10
Matthew 22:15-22

October 18–24
Deuteronomy 34:1-12
Psalm 90:1-6, 13-17
1 Thessalonians 2:1-8
Matthew 22:34-46

October 25–31
Joshua 3:7-17
Psalm 107:1-7, 33-37
1 Thessalonians 2:9-13
Matthew 23:1-12

> **ALL SAINTS DAY
> November 1**
> *(May be used for Sunday,
> November 7.)*
> Revelation 7:9-17
> Psalm 34:1-10, 22
> 1 John 3:1-3
> Matthew 5:1-12

November 1–7
Joshua 24:1-3a, 14-25
Psalm 78:1-7
1 Thessalonians 4:13-18
Matthew 25:1-13

November 8–14
Judges 4:1-7
Psalm 123
1 Thessalonians 5:1-11
Matthew 25:14-30

November 15–21
CHRIST THE KING SUNDAY
Ezekiel 34:11-16, 20-24
Psalm 100
Ephesians 1:15-23
Matthew 25:31-46

November 22–28
FIRST SUNDAY OF ADVENT
Isaiah 64:1-9
Psalm 80:1-7, 17-19
1 Corinthians 1:3-9
Mark 13:24-37

> THANKSGIVING DAY
> (USA), November 25
> Deuteronomy 8:7-18
> Psalm 65
> 2 Corinthians 9:6-15
> Luke 17:11-19

November 29–December 5
SECOND SUNDAY OF ADVENT
Isaiah 40:1-11
Psalm 85:1-2, 8-13
2 Peter 3:8-15*a*
Mark 1:1-8

December 6–12
THIRD SUNDAY OF ADVENT
Isaiah 61:1-4, 8-11
Psalm 126 (*or* Luke 1:47-55)
1 Thessalonians 5:16-24
John 1:6-8, 19-28

December 13–19
FOURTH SUNDAY OF ADVENT
2 Samuel 7:1-11, 16
Psalm 89:1-4, 19-26
Romans 16:25-27
Luke 1:26-38

December 20–26
FIRST SUNDAY AFTER
CHRISTMAS DAY
Isaiah 61:10–62:3
Psalm 148
Galatians 4:4-7
Luke 2:22-40

> CHRISTMAS EVE
> **December 24**
> Isaiah 9:2-7
> Psalm 96
> Titus 2:11-14
> Luke 2:1-20

> CHRISTMAS DAY
> **December 25**
> Isaiah 52:7-10
> Psalm 98
> Hebrews 1:1-12
> John 1:1-14

December 27–31
Jeremiah 31:7-14
Psalm 147:12 20
Ephesians 1:3-14
John 1:10-18

1999

JANUARY

S	M	T	W	T	F	S
					1	2
3	4	5	6	7	8	9
10	11	12	13	14	15	16
17	18	19	20	21	22	23
24	25	26	27	28	29	30
31						

FEBRUARY

S	M	T	W	T	F	S
	1	2	3	4	5	6
7	8	9	10	11	12	13
14	15	16	17	18	19	20
21	22	23	24	25	26	27
28						

MARCH

S	M	T	W	T	F	S
	1	2	3	4	5	6
7	8	9	10	11	12	13
14	15	16	17	18	19	20
21	22	23	24	25	26	27
28	29	30	31			

APRIL

S	M	T	W	T	F	S
				1	2	3
4	5	6	7	8	9	10
11	12	13	14	15	16	17
18	19	20	21	22	23	24
25	26	27	28	29	30	

MAY

S	M	T	W	T	F	S
						1
2	3	4	5	6	7	8
9	10	11	12	13	14	15
16	17	18	19	20	21	22
23	24	25	26	27	28	29
30	31					

JUNE

S	M	T	W	T	F	S
		1	2	3	4	5
6	7	8	9	10	11	12
13	14	15	16	17	18	19
20	21	22	23	24	25	26
27	28	29	30			

JULY

S	M	T	W	T	F	S
				1	2	3
4	5	6	7	8	9	10
11	12	13	14	15	16	17
18	19	20	21	22	23	24
25	26	27	28	29	30	31

AUGUST

S	M	T	W	T	F	S
1	2	3	4	5	6	7
8	9	10	11	12	13	14
15	16	17	18	19	20	21
22	23	24	25	26	27	28
29	30	31				

SEPTEMBER

S	M	T	W	T	F	S
			1	2	3	4
5	6	7	8	9	10	11
12	13	14	15	16	17	18
19	20	21	22	23	24	25
26	27	28	29	30		

OCTOBER

S	M	T	W	T	F	S
					1	2
3	4	5	6	7	8	9
10	11	12	13	14	15	16
17	18	19	20	21	22	23
24	25	26	27	28	29	30
31						

NOVEMBER

S	M	T	W	T	F	S
	1	2	3	4	5	6
7	8	9	10	11	12	13
14	15	16	17	18	19	20
21	22	23	24	25	26	27
28	29	30				

DECEMBER

S	M	T	W	T	F	S
			1	2	3	4
5	6	7	8	9	10	11
12	13	14	15	16	17	18
19	20	21	22	23	24	25
26	27	28	29	30	31